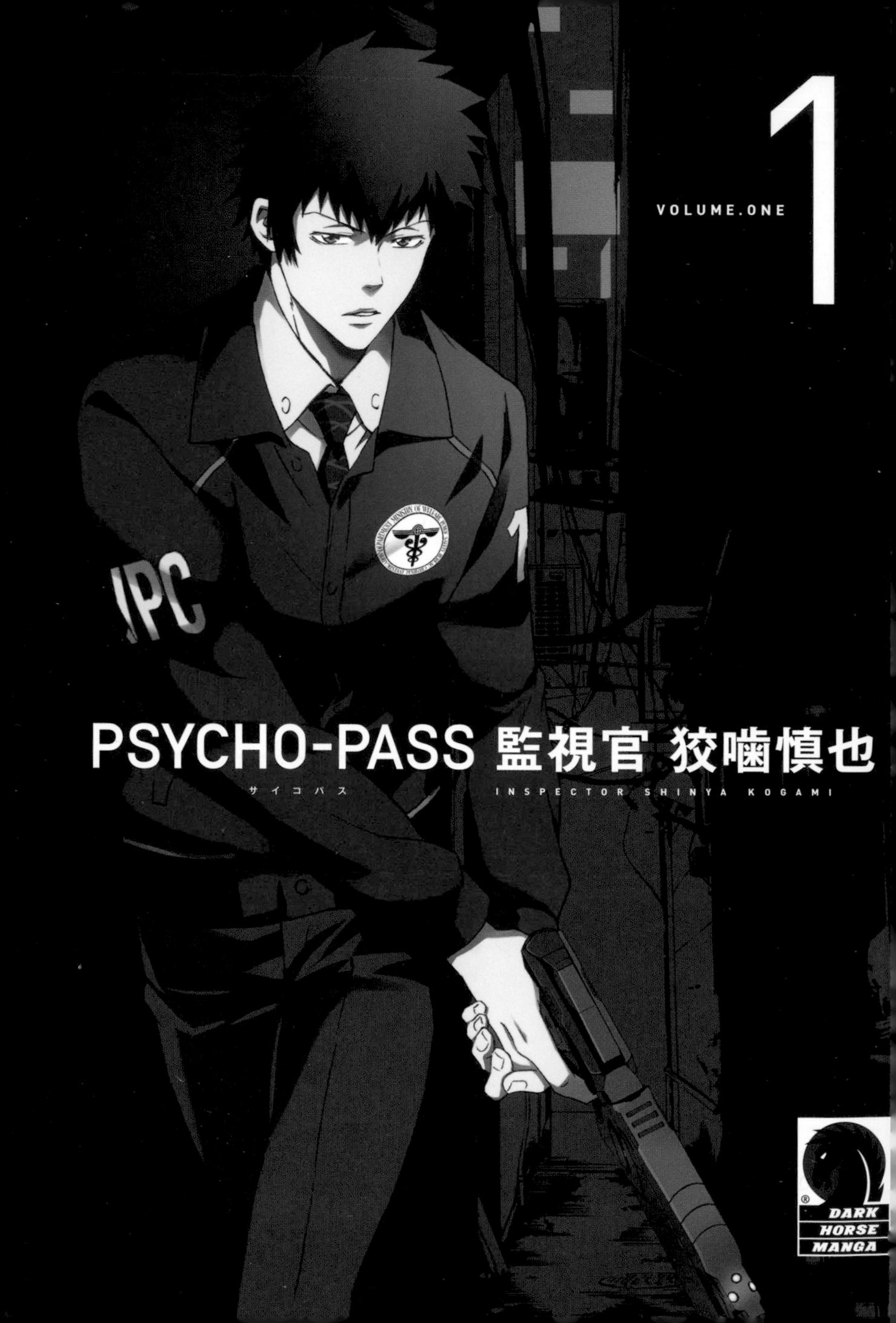
1
VOLUME.ONE
IPC
1
PSYCHO-PASS 監視官 狡噛慎也
サイコパス
INSPECTOR SHINYA KOGAMI
DARK HORSE MANGA

PSYCHO-PASS 監視官 狩噛慎也

サイコパス

INSPECTOR SHINYA KOGAMI

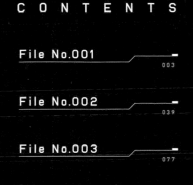

1

VOLUME.ONE

CONTENTS

File No.001 — 003

File No.002 — 039

File No.003 — 077

File No.004 — 107

ART
NATSUO SAI
SCRIPT
MIDORI GOTOU
SOURCE
**PSYCHO-PASS
PRODUCTION COMMITTEE**
ORIGINAL STORY
GEN UROBUCHI

TRANSLATION BY:
KUMAR SIVASUBRAMANIAN
LETTERING AND TOUCHUP BY:
STEVE DUTRO
EDITED BY:
CARL GUSTAV HORN

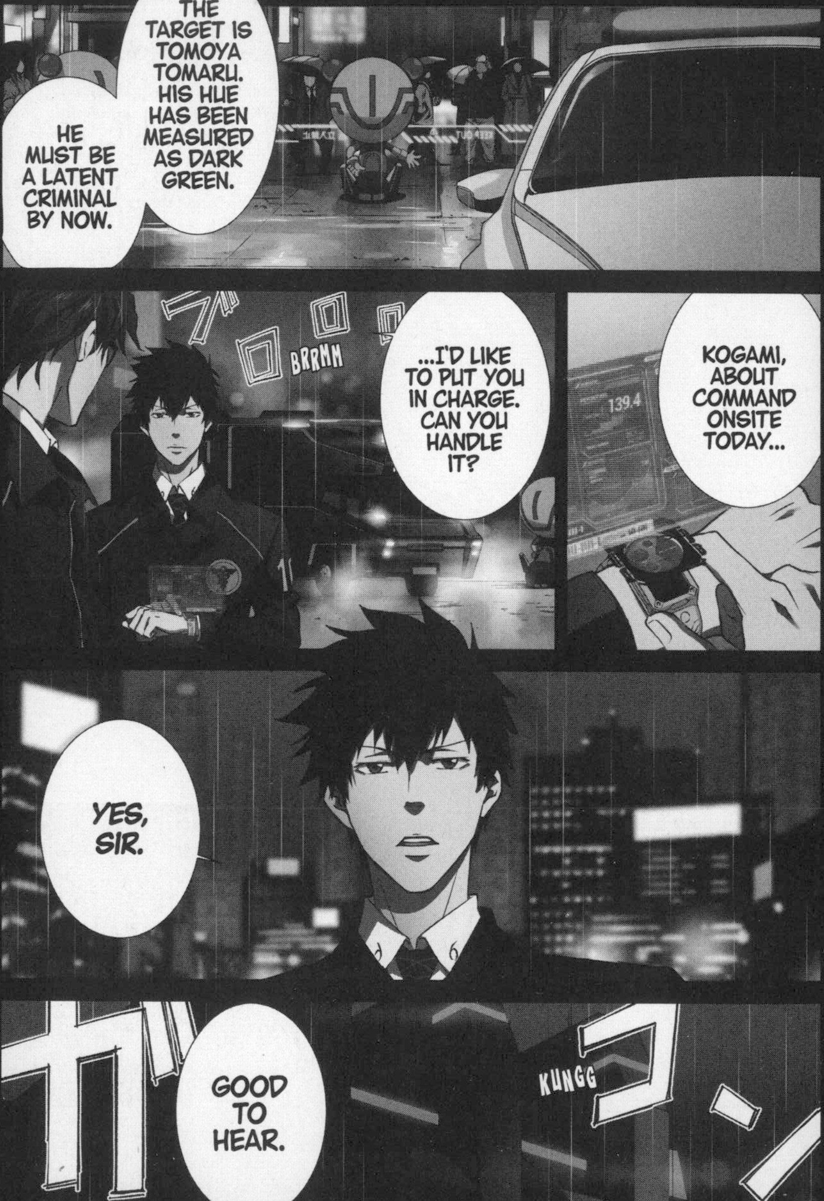
THE TARGET IS TOMOYA TOMARU. HIS HUE HAS BEEN MEASURED AS DARK GREEN.
HE MUST BE A LATENT CRIMINAL BY NOW.
139.4
KOGAMI, ABOUT COMMAND ONSITE TODAY...
BRRMM
...I'D LIKE TO PUT YOU IN CHARGE. CAN YOU HANDLE IT?
YES, SIR.
KUNGG
GOOD TO HEAR.

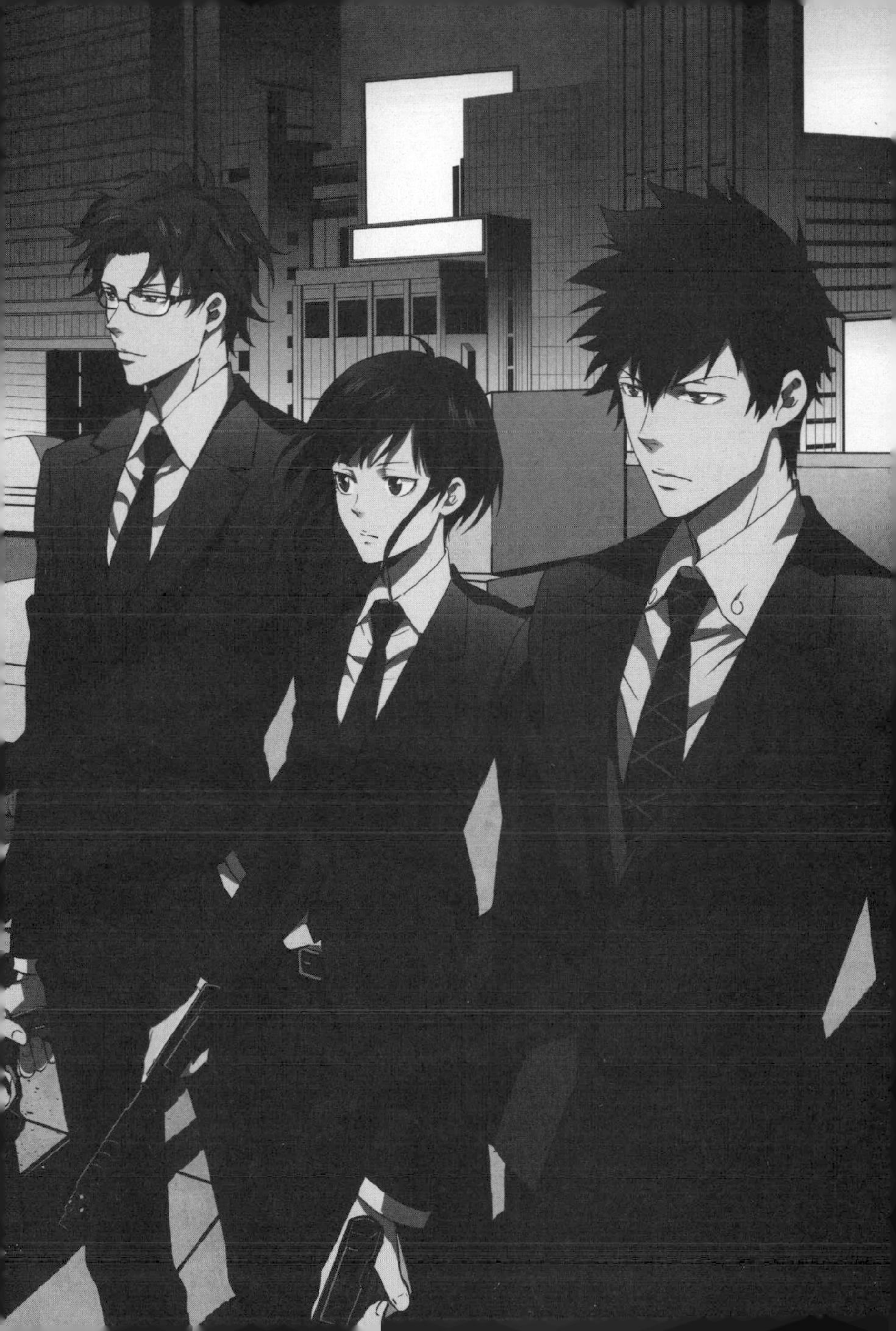

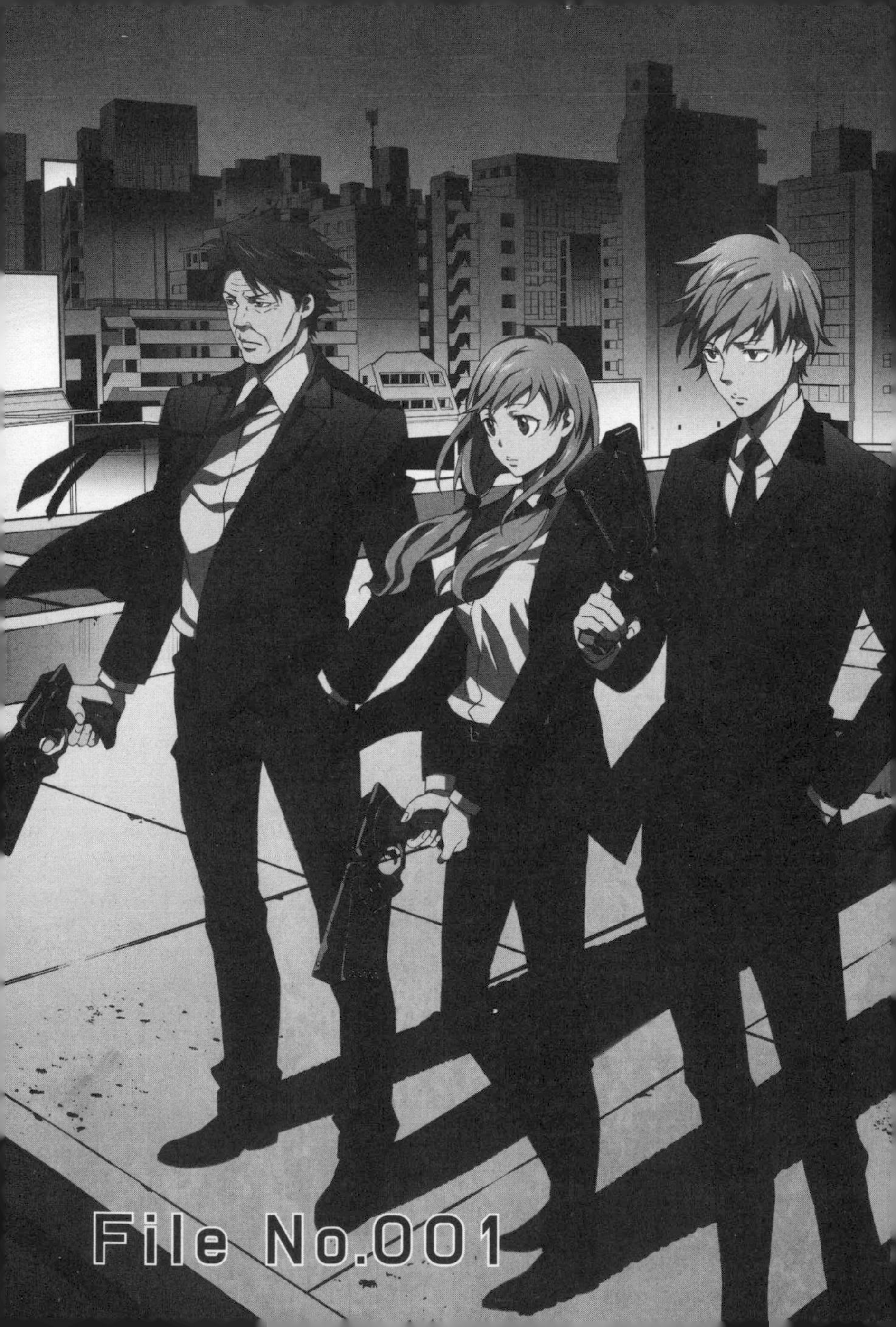
File No.001

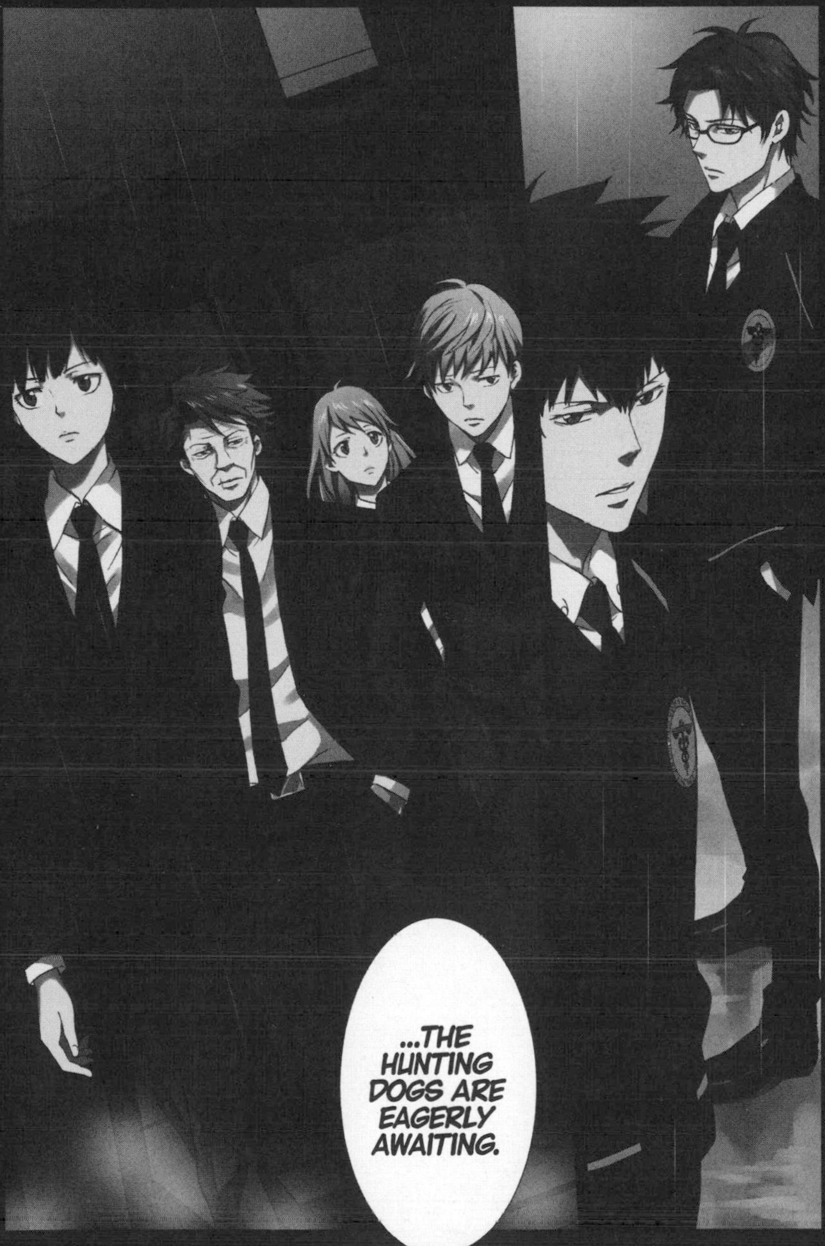
...THE HUNTING DOGS ARE EAGERLY AWAITING.

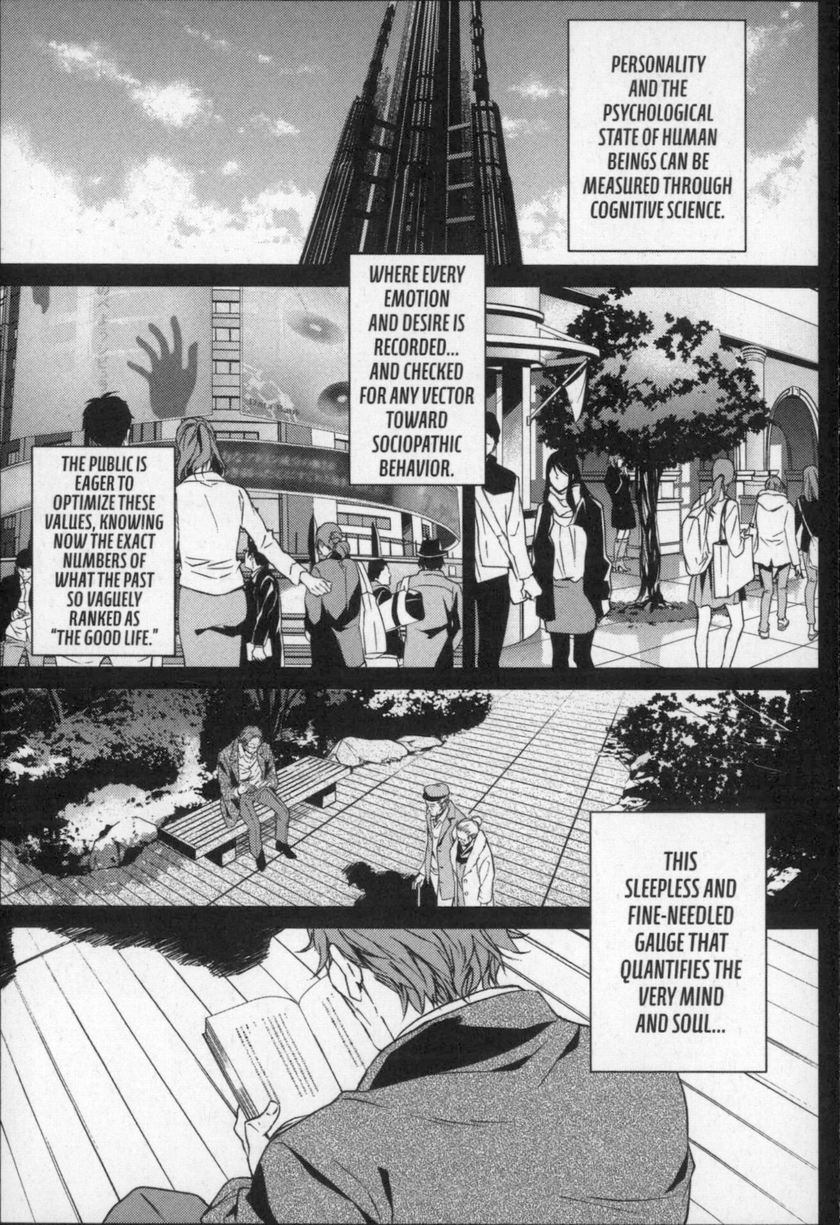
PERSONALITY AND THE PSYCHOLOGICAL STATE OF HUMAN BEINGS CAN BE MEASURED THROUGH COGNITIVE SCIENCE.
WHERE EVERY EMOTION AND DESIRE IS RECORDED... AND CHECKED FOR ANY VECTOR TOWARD SOCIOPATHIC BEHAVIOR.
THE PUBLIC IS EAGER TO OPTIMIZE THESE VALUES, KNOWING NOW THE EXACT NUMBERS OF WHAT THE PAST SO VAGUELY RANKED AS "THE GOOD LIFE."
THIS SLEEPLESS AND FINE-NEEDLED GAUGE THAT QUANTIFIES THE VERY MIND AND SOUL...

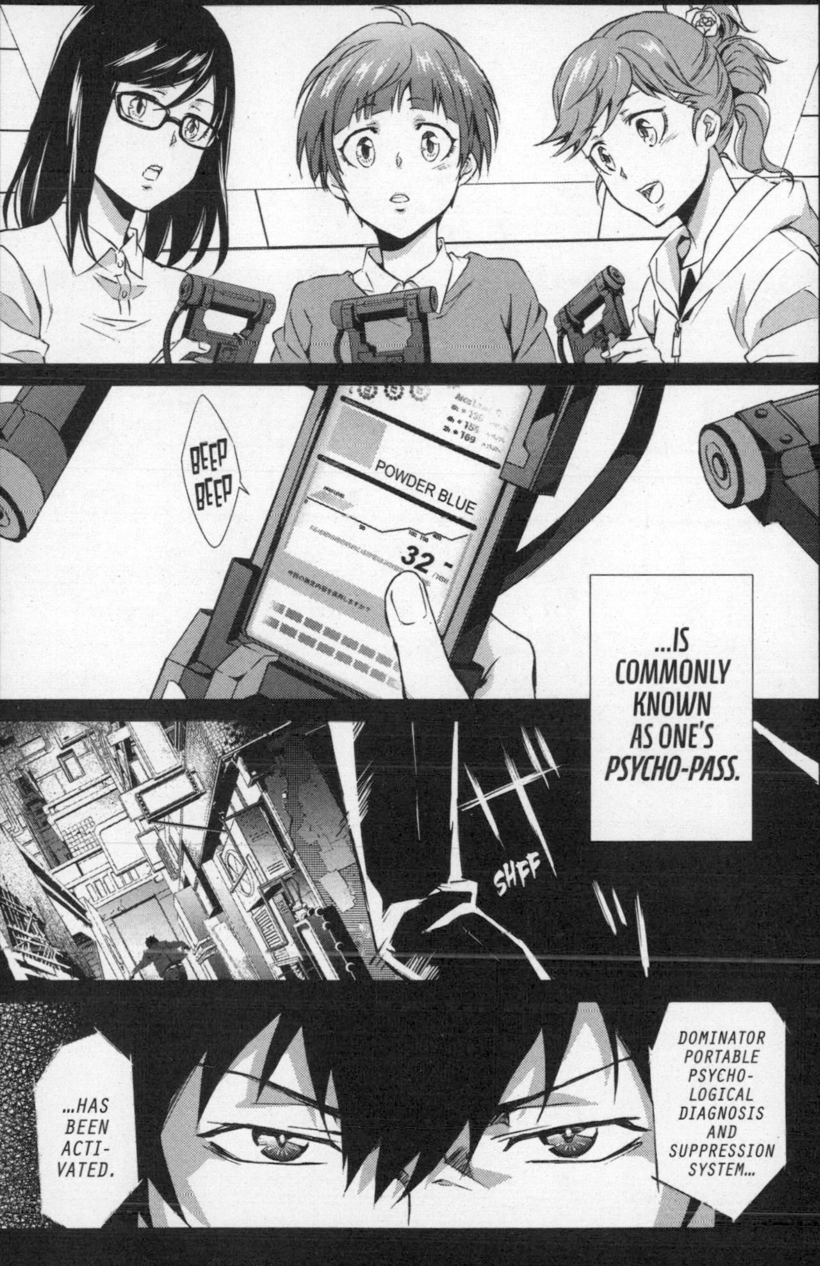
POWDER BLUE
32 -
BEEP BEEP
...IS COMMONLY KNOWN AS ONE'S *PSYCHO-PASS.*
SHFF
DOMINATOR PORTABLE PSYCHO-LOGICAL DIAGNOSIS AND SUPPRESSION SYSTEM...
...HAS BEEN ACTI-VATED.

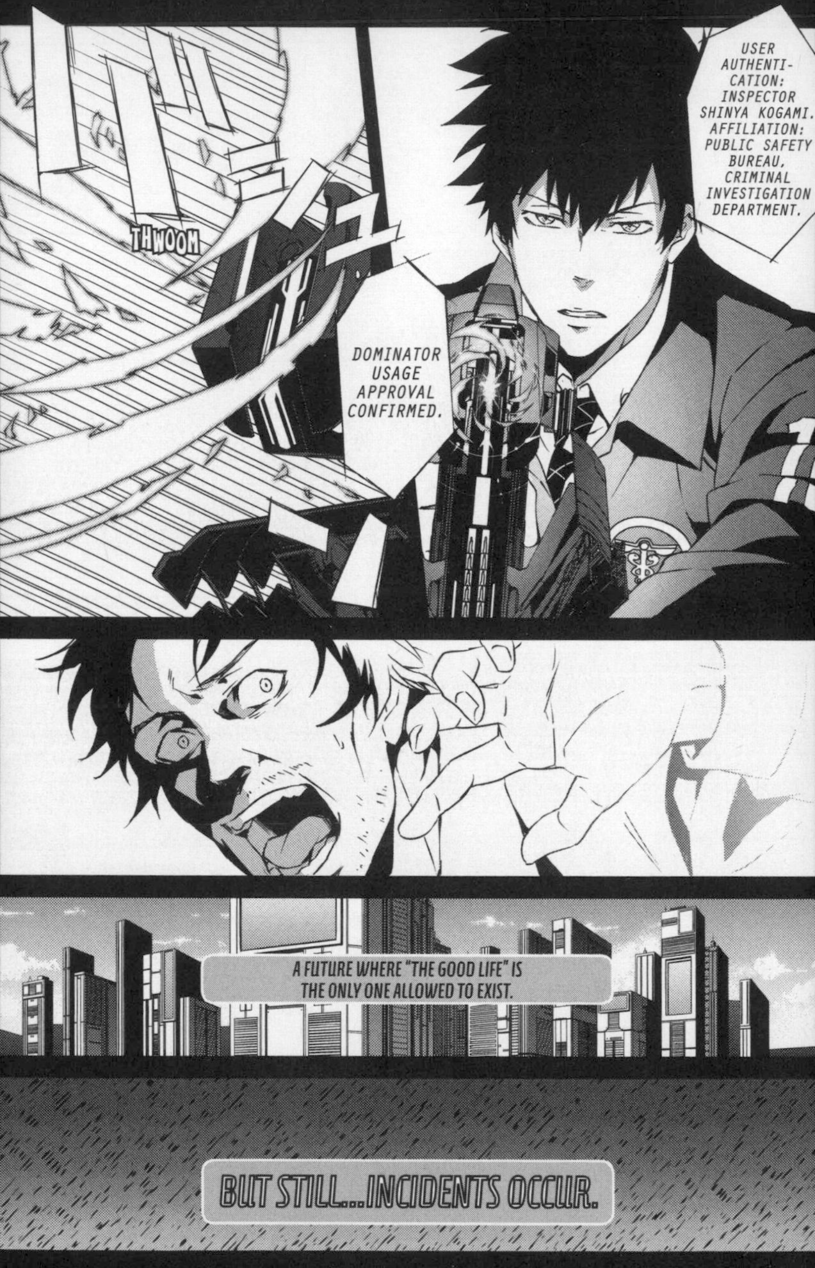
USER AUTHENTI-CATION: INSPECTOR SHINYA KOGAMI. AFFILIATION: PUBLIC SAFETY BUREAU, CRIMINAL INVESTIGATION DEPARTMENT.
DOMINATOR USAGE APPROVAL CONFIRMED.
THWOOM
A FUTURE WHERE "THE GOOD LIFE" IS THE ONLY ONE ALLOWED TO EXIST.
BUT STILL...INCIDENTS OCCUR.

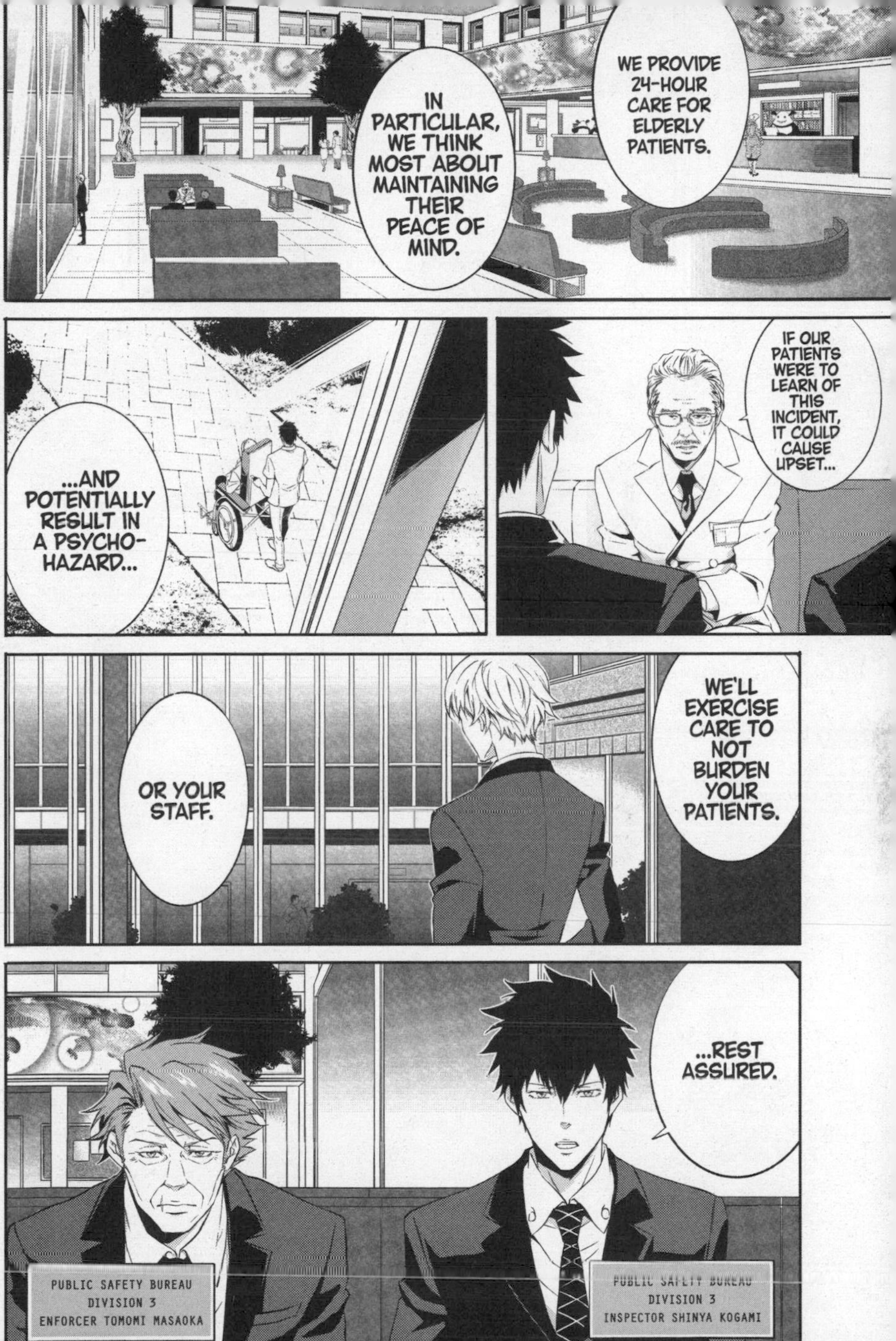
WE PROVIDE 24-HOUR CARE FOR ELDERLY PATIENTS.
IN PARTICULAR, WE THINK MOST ABOUT MAINTAINING THEIR PEACE OF MIND.
IF OUR PATIENTS WERE TO LEARN OF THIS INCIDENT, IT COULD CAUSE UPSET...
...AND POTENTIALLY RESULT IN A PSYCHO-HAZARD...
WE'LL EXERCISE CARE TO NOT BURDEN YOUR PATIENTS.
OR YOUR STAFF.
...REST ASSURED.
PUBLIC SAFETY BUREAU DIVISION 3 INSPECTOR SHINYA KOGAMI
PUBLIC SAFETY BUREAU DIVISION 3 ENFORCER TOMOMI MASAOKA

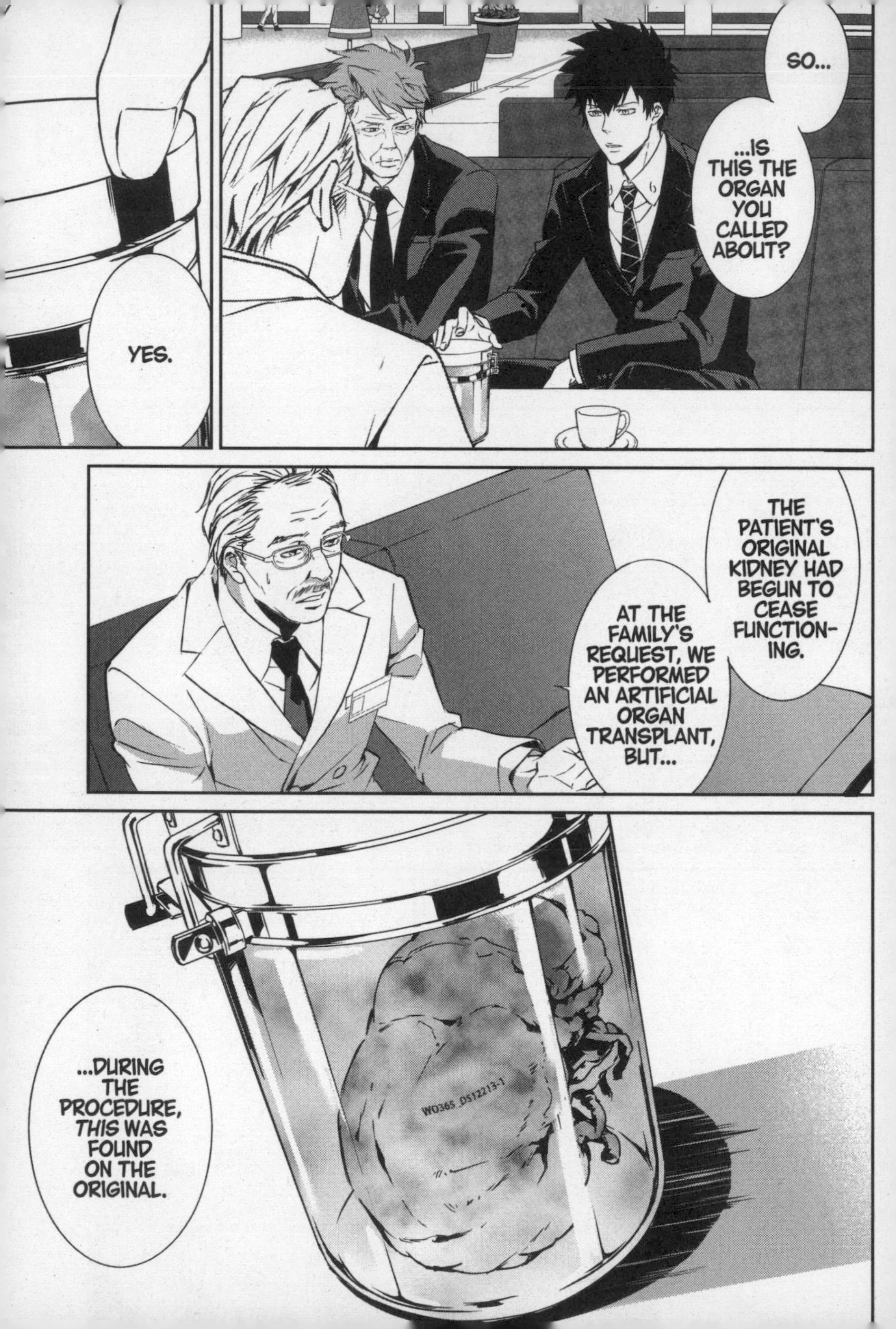
SO...
...IS THIS THE ORGAN YOU CALLED ABOUT?
YES.
THE PATIENT'S ORIGINAL KIDNEY HAD BEGUN TO CEASE FUNCTIONING.
AT THE FAMILY'S REQUEST, WE PERFORMED AN ARTIFICIAL ORGAN TRANSPLANT, BUT...
...DURING THE PROCEDURE, *THIS* WAS FOUND ON THE ORIGINAL.

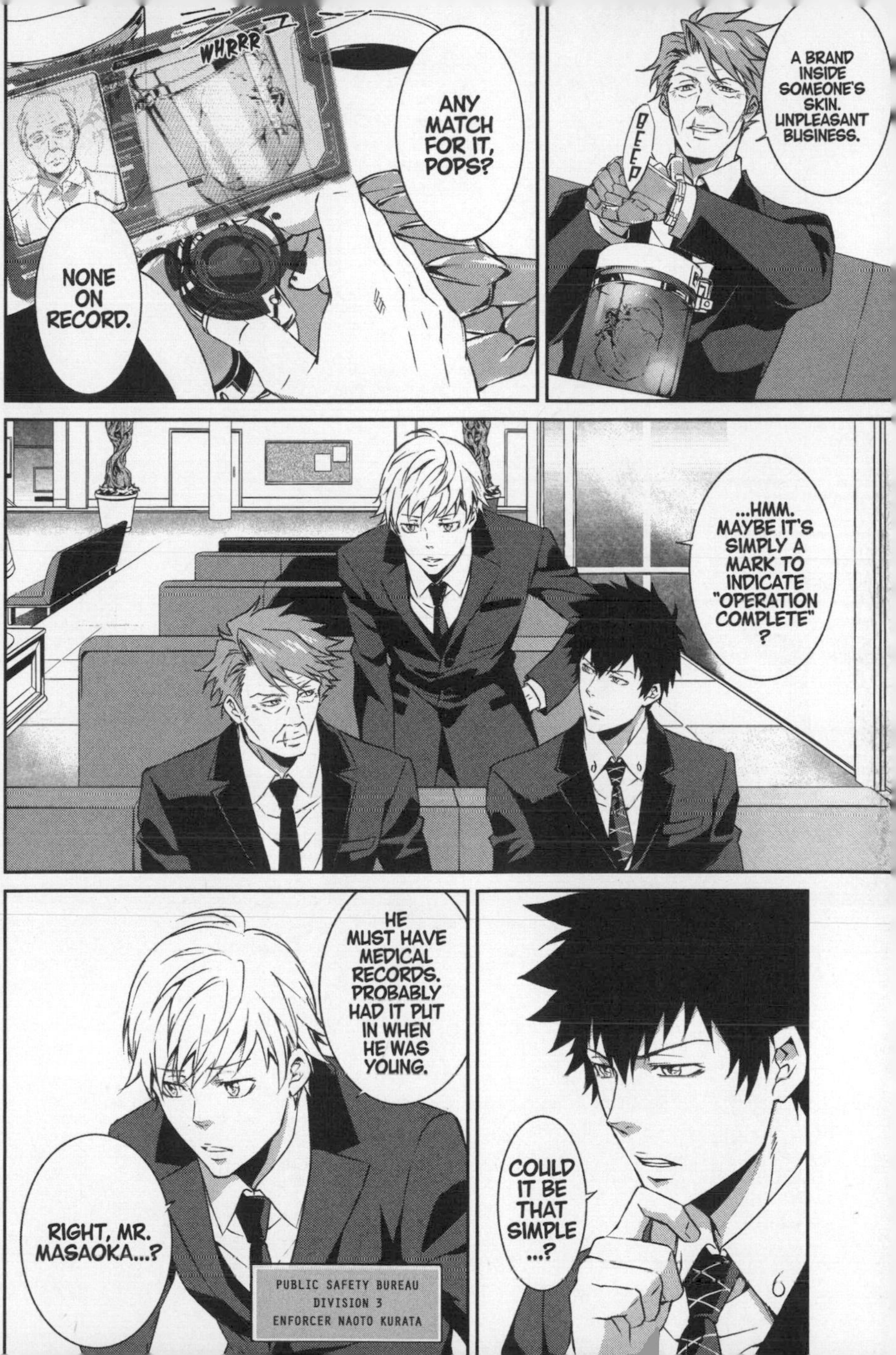
A BRAND INSIDE SOMEONE'S SKIN. UNPLEASANT BUSINESS.
BEEP
WHRRR
ANY MATCH FOR IT, POPS?
NONE ON RECORD.
...HMM. MAYBE IT'S SIMPLY A MARK TO INDICATE "OPERATION COMPLETE"?
COULD IT BE THAT SIMPLE...?
HE MUST HAVE MEDICAL RECORDS. PROBABLY HAD IT PUT IN WHEN HE WAS YOUNG.
RIGHT, MR. MASAOKA...?
PUBLIC SAFETY BUREAU DIVISION 3 ENFORCER NAOTO KURATA

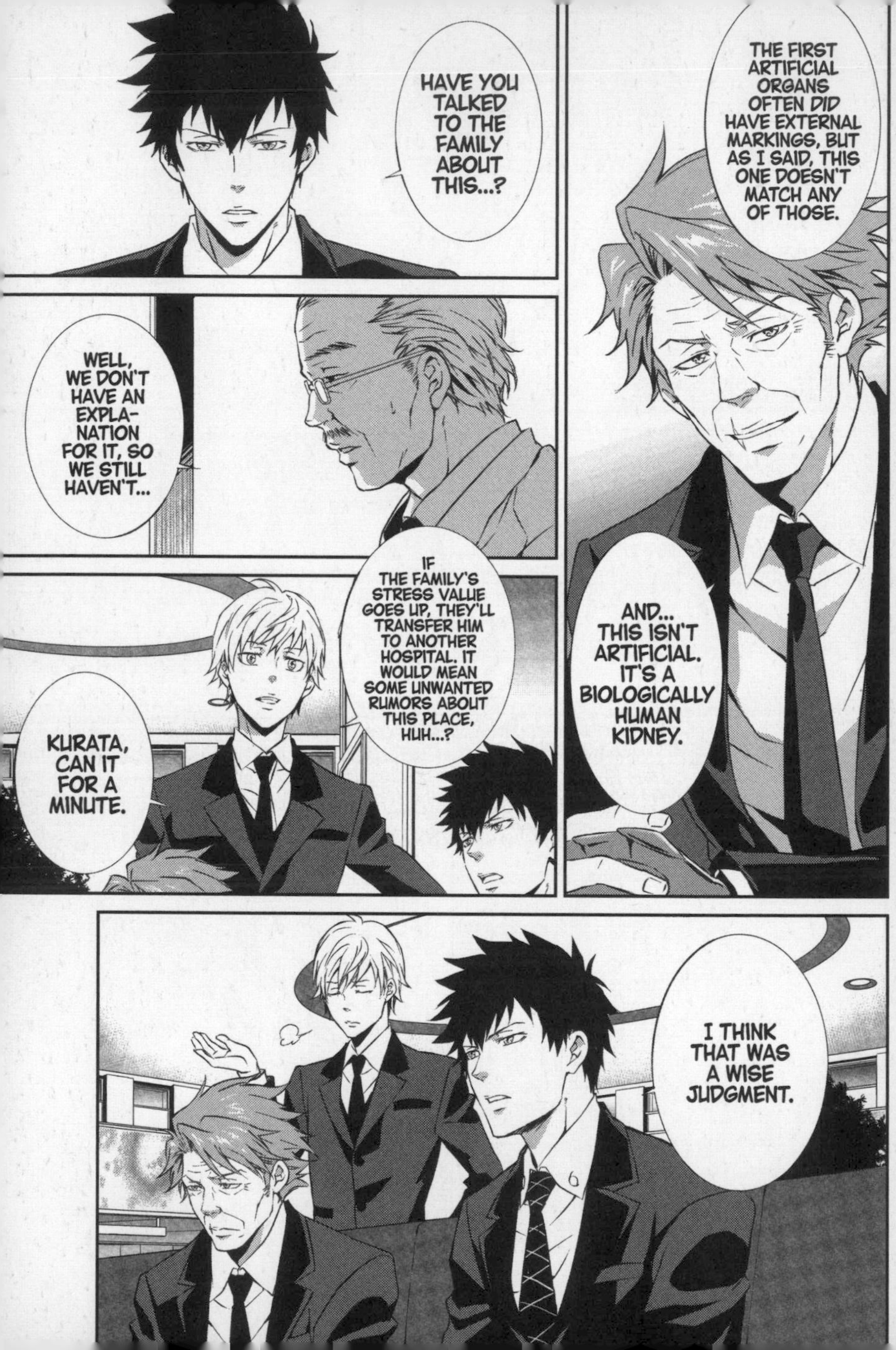
THE FIRST ARTIFICIAL ORGANS OFTEN DID HAVE EXTERNAL MARKINGS, BUT AS I SAID, THIS ONE DOESN'T MATCH ANY OF THOSE.
AND... THIS ISN'T ARTIFICIAL. IT'S A BIOLOGICALLY HUMAN KIDNEY.
HAVE YOU TALKED TO THE FAMILY ABOUT THIS...?
WELL, WE DON'T HAVE AN EXPLA-NATION FOR IT, SO WE STILL HAVEN'T...
IF THE FAMILY'S STRESS VALUE GOES UP, THEY'LL TRANSFER HIM TO ANOTHER HOSPITAL. IT WOULD MEAN SOME UNWANTED RUMORS ABOUT THIS PLACE, HUH...?
KURATA, CAN IT FOR A MINUTE.
I THINK THAT WAS A WISE JUDGMENT.

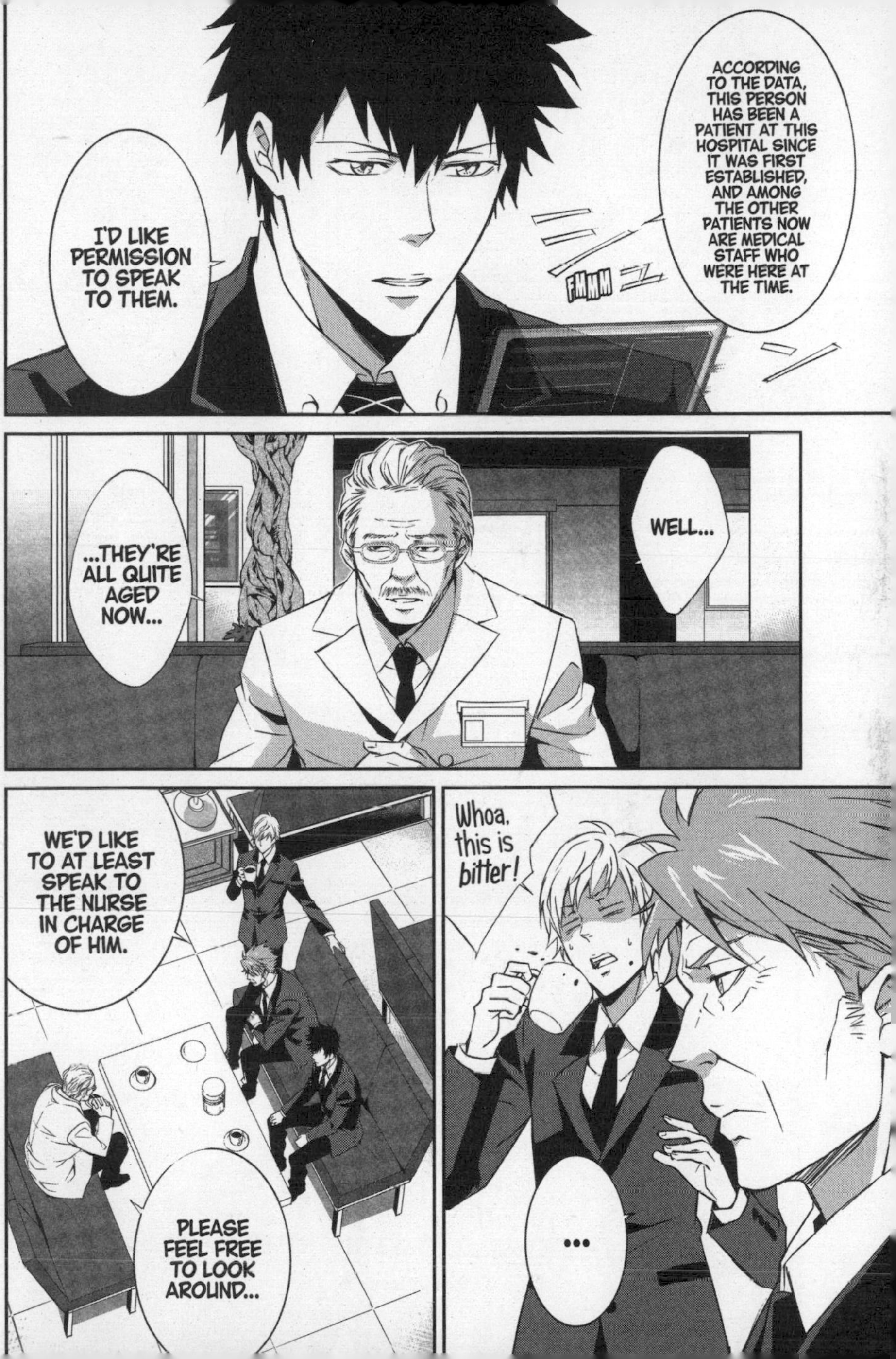
ACCORDING TO THE DATA, THIS PERSON HAS BEEN A PATIENT AT THIS HOSPITAL SINCE IT WAS FIRST ESTABLISHED, AND AMONG THE OTHER PATIENTS NOW ARE MEDICAL STAFF WHO WERE HERE AT THE TIME.
FMMM
I'D LIKE PERMISSION TO SPEAK TO THEM.
WELL...
...THEY'RE ALL QUITE AGED NOW...
Whoa, this is *bitter*!
...
WE'D LIKE TO AT LEAST SPEAK TO THE NURSE IN CHARGE OF HIM.
PLEASE FEEL FREE TO LOOK AROUND...

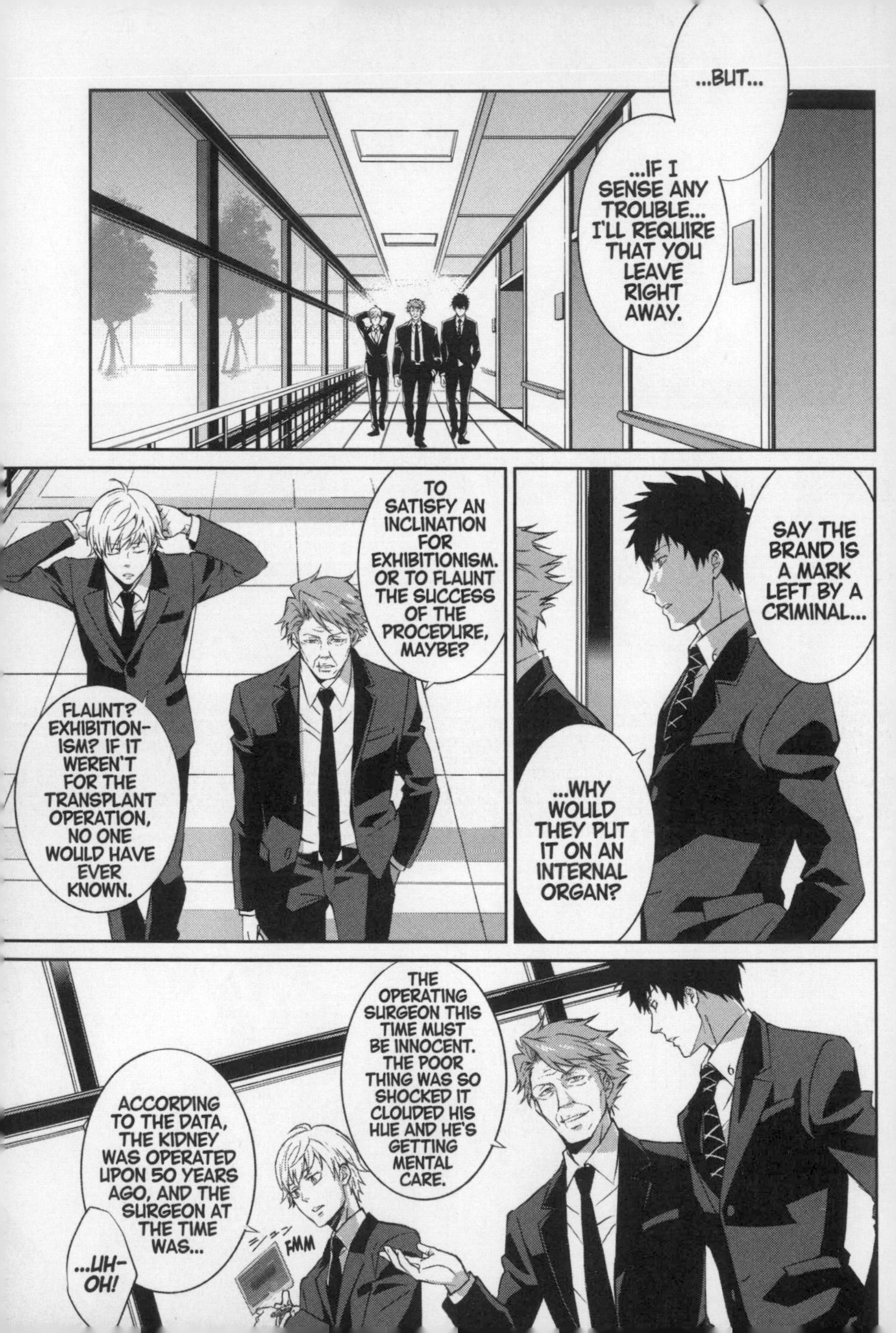
...BUT...
...IF I SENSE ANY TROUBLE... I'LL REQUIRE THAT YOU LEAVE RIGHT AWAY.
SAY THE BRAND IS A MARK LEFT BY A CRIMINAL...
...WHY WOULD THEY PUT IT ON AN INTERNAL ORGAN?
TO SATISFY AN INCLINATION FOR EXHIBITIONISM. OR TO FLAUNT THE SUCCESS OF THE PROCEDURE, MAYBE?
FLAUNT? EXHIBITION-ISM? IF IT WEREN'T FOR THE TRANSPLANT OPERATION, NO ONE WOULD HAVE EVER KNOWN.
THE OPERATING SURGEON THIS TIME MUST BE INNOCENT. THE POOR THING WAS SO SHOCKED IT CLOUDED HIS HUE AND HE'S GETTING MENTAL CARE.
ACCORDING TO THE DATA, THE KIDNEY WAS OPERATED UPON 50 YEARS AGO, AND THE SURGEON AT THE TIME WAS...
FMM
...UH-OH!

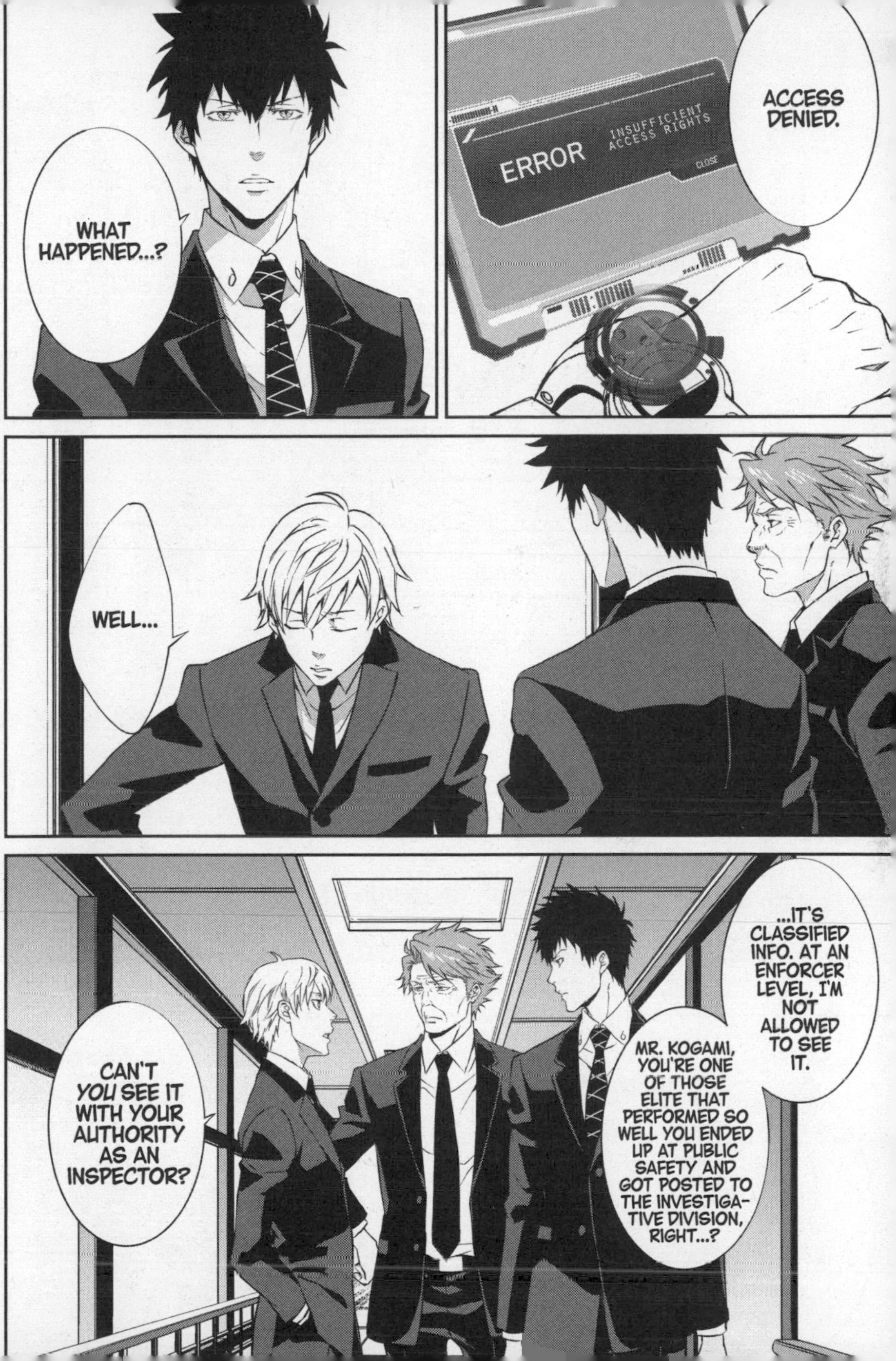
ACCESS DENIED.
ERROR
INSUFFICIENT ACCESS RIGHTS
CLOSE
WHAT HAPPENED...?
WELL...
...IT'S CLASSIFIED INFO. AT AN ENFORCER LEVEL, I'M NOT ALLOWED TO SEE IT.
MR. KOGAMI, YOU'RE ONE OF THOSE ELITE THAT PERFORMED SO WELL YOU ENDED UP AT PUBLIC SAFETY AND GOT POSTED TO THE INVESTIGA-TIVE DIVISION, RIGHT...?
CAN'T *YOU* SEE IT WITH YOUR AUTHORITY AS AN INSPECTOR?

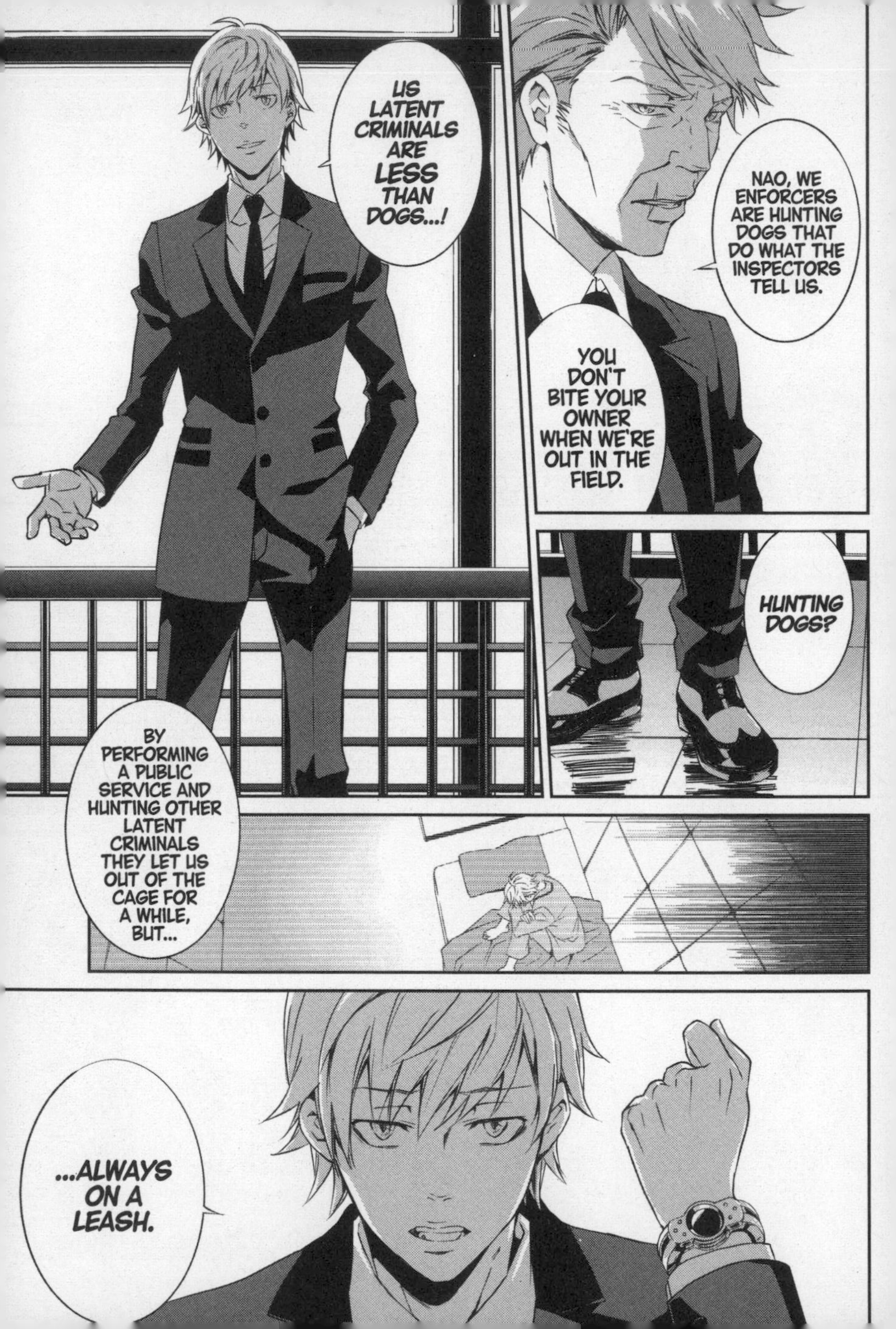
NAO, WE ENFORCERS ARE HUNTING DOGS THAT DO WHAT THE INSPECTORS TELL US.
YOU DON'T BITE YOUR OWNER WHEN WE'RE OUT IN THE FIELD.
HUNTING DOGS?
US LATENT CRIMINALS ARE LESS THAN DOGS...!
BY PERFORMING A PUBLIC SERVICE AND HUNTING OTHER LATENT CRIMINALS THEY LET US OUT OF THE CAGE FOR A WHILE, BUT...
...ALWAYS ON A LEASH.

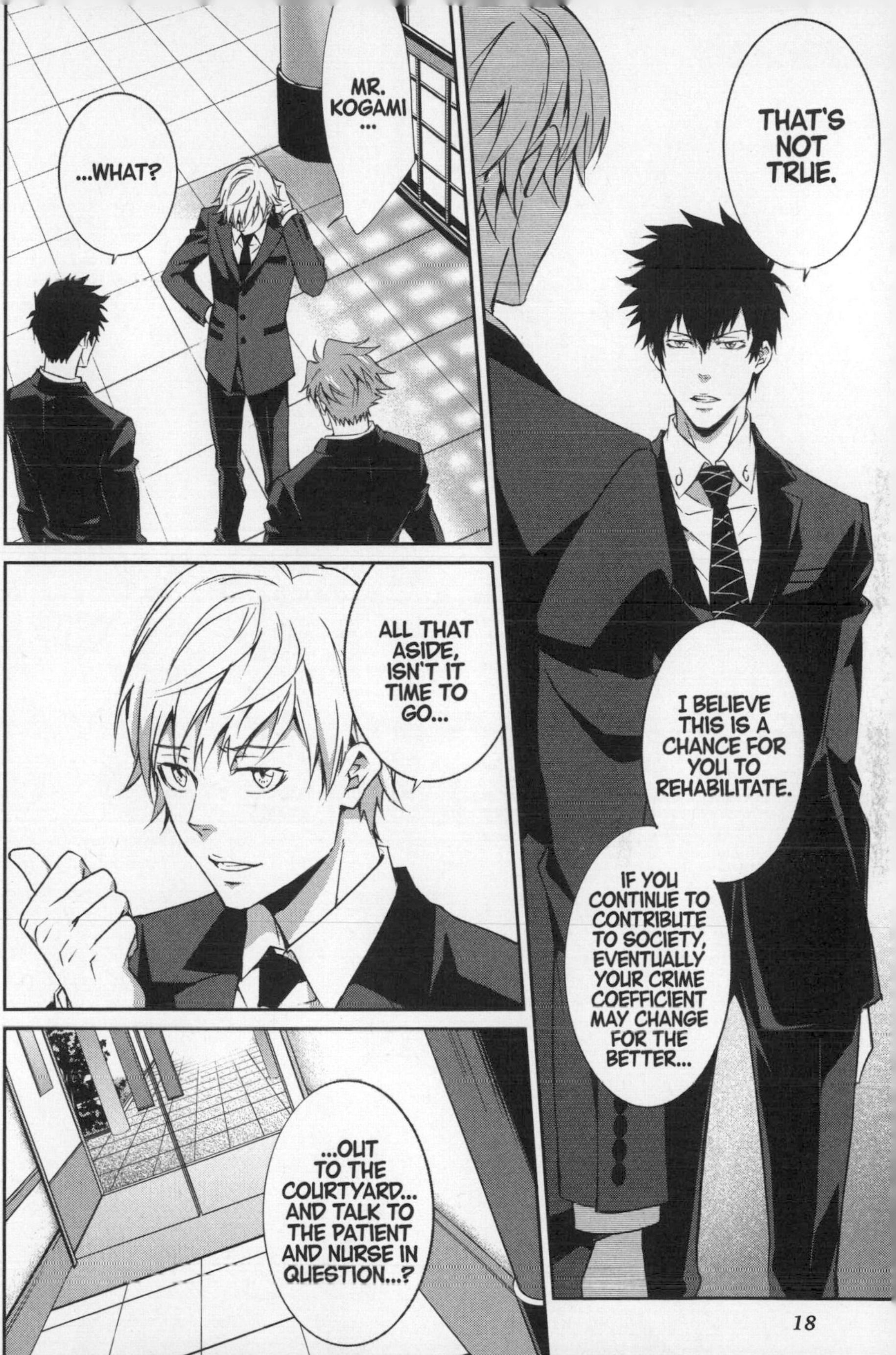
THAT'S NOT TRUE.
I BELIEVE THIS IS A CHANCE FOR YOU TO REHABILITATE.
IF YOU CONTINUE TO CONTRIBUTE TO SOCIETY, EVENTUALLY YOUR CRIME COEFFICIENT MAY CHANGE FOR THE BETTER...
MR. KOGAMI ...
...WHAT?
ALL THAT ASIDE, ISN'T IT TIME TO GO...
...OUT TO THE COURTYARD... AND TALK TO THE PATIENT AND NURSE IN QUESTION...?

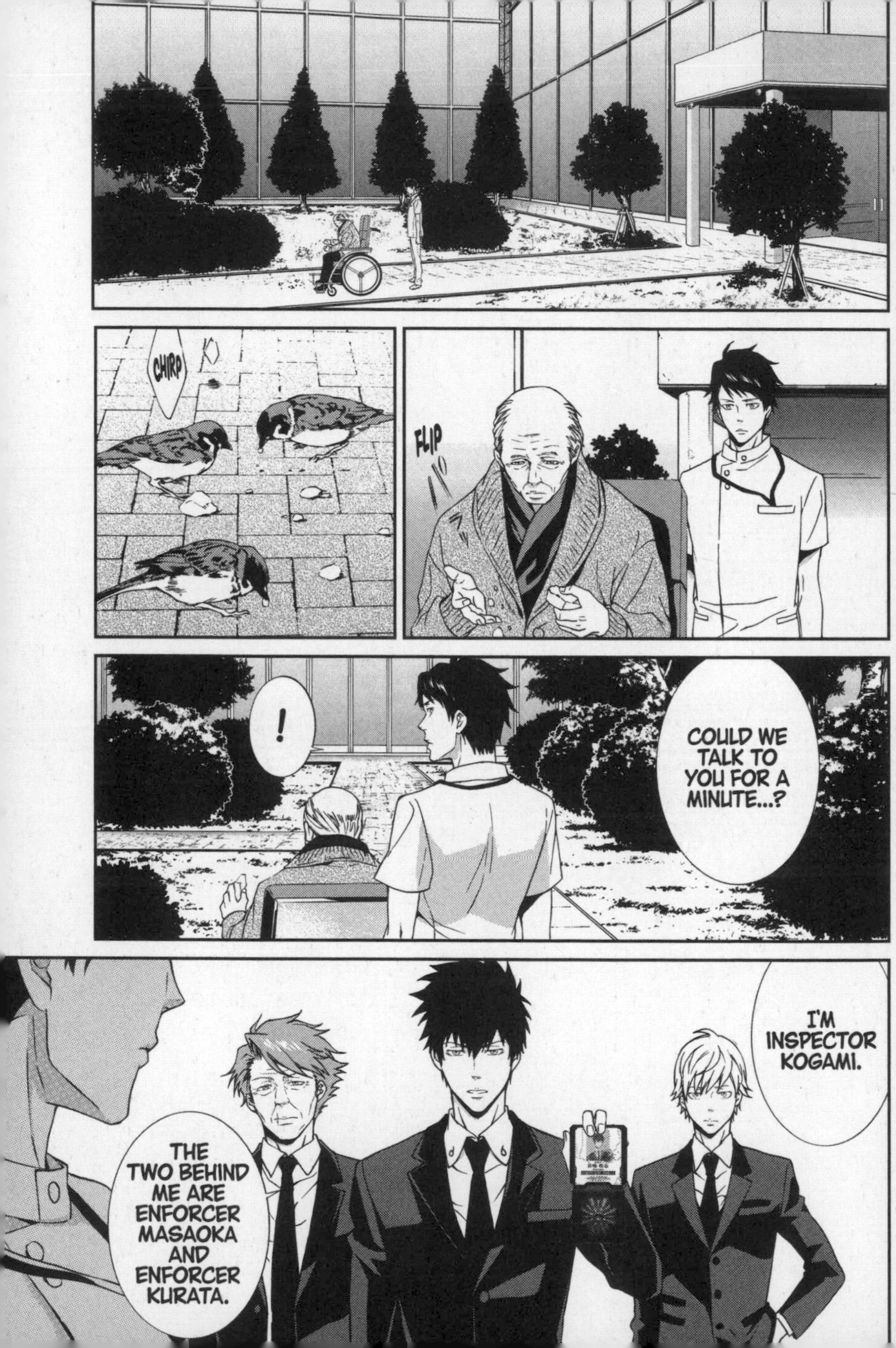

FLIP
CHIRP
COULD WE TALK TO YOU FOR A MINUTE...?
!
I'M INSPECTOR KOGAMI.
THE TWO BEHIND ME ARE ENFORCER MASAOKA AND ENFORCER KURATA.

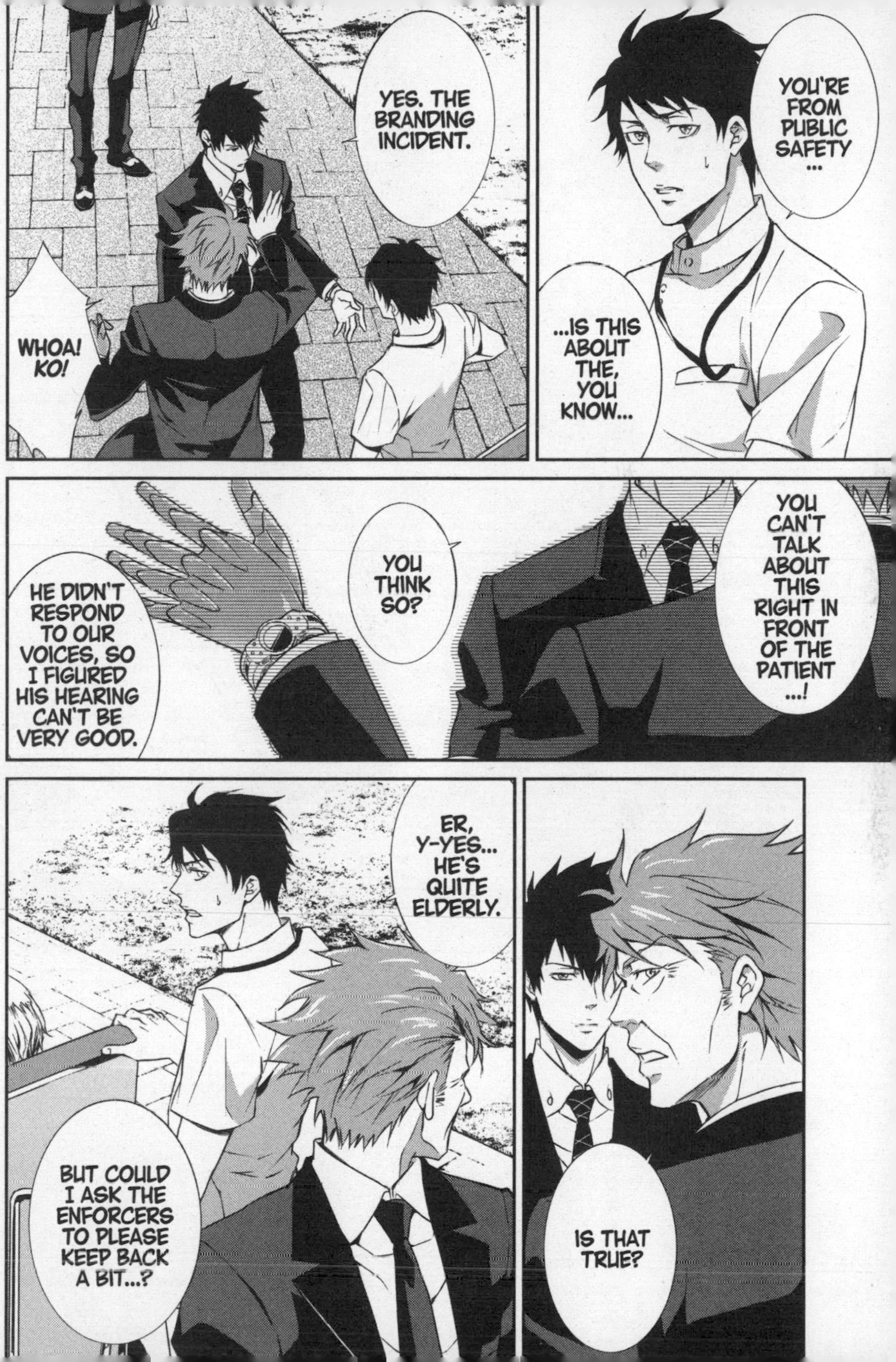
YOU'RE FROM PUBLIC SAFETY ...
...IS THIS ABOUT THE, YOU KNOW...
YES. THE BRANDING INCIDENT.
WHOA! KO!
YOU CAN'T TALK ABOUT THIS RIGHT IN FRONT OF THE PATIENT ...!
YOU THINK SO?
HE DIDN'T RESPOND TO OUR VOICES, SO I FIGURED HIS HEARING CAN'T BE VERY GOOD.
IS THAT TRUE?
ER, Y-YES... HE'S QUITE ELDERLY.
BUT COULD I ASK THE ENFORCERS TO PLEASE KEEP BACK A BIT...?

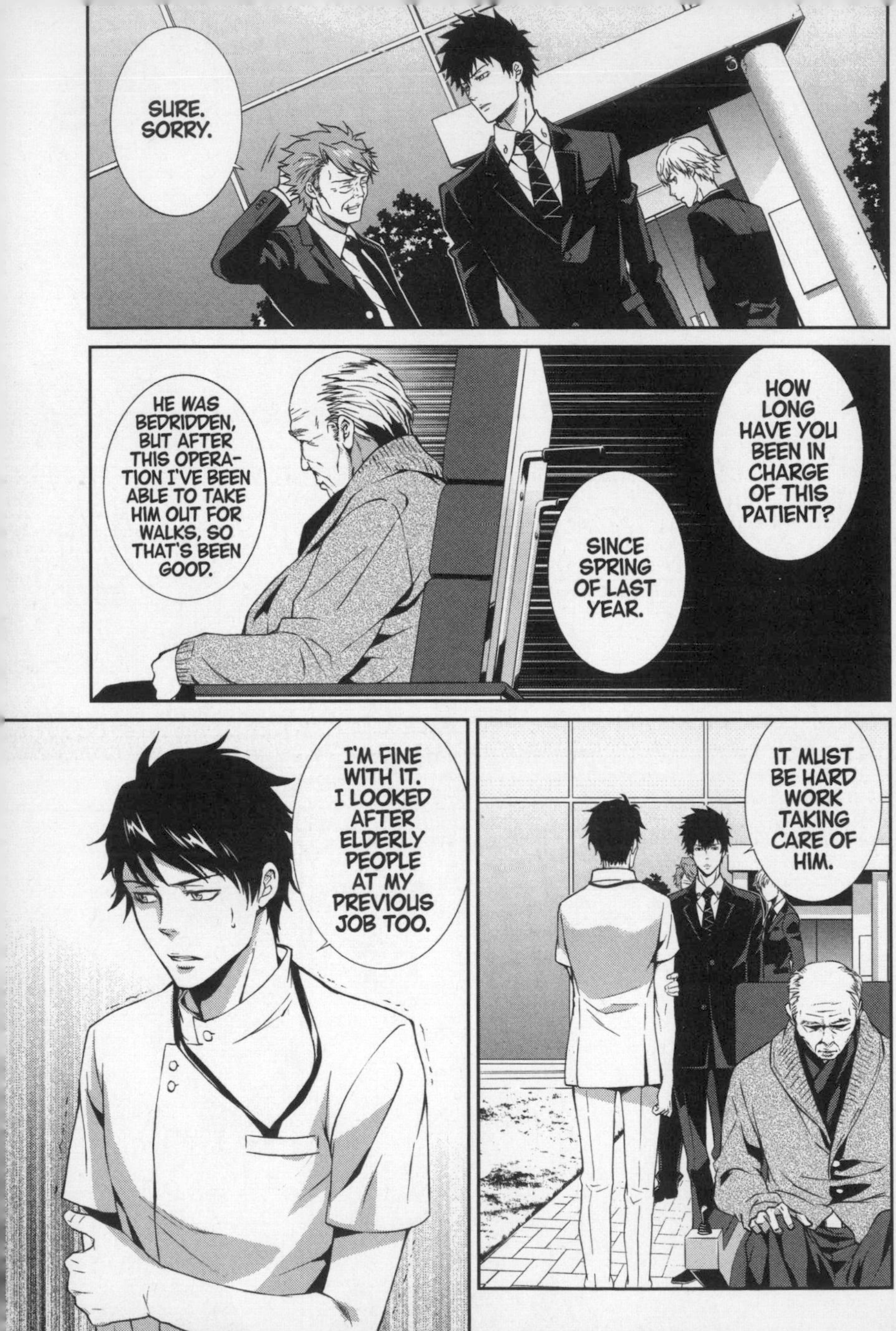
SURE. SORRY.
HOW LONG HAVE YOU BEEN IN CHARGE OF THIS PATIENT?
SINCE SPRING OF LAST YEAR.
HE WAS BEDRIDDEN, BUT AFTER THIS OPERATION I'VE BEEN ABLE TO TAKE HIM OUT FOR WALKS, SO THAT'S BEEN GOOD.
IT MUST BE HARD WORK TAKING CARE OF HIM.
I'M FINE WITH IT. I LOOKED AFTER ELDERLY PEOPLE AT MY PREVIOUS JOB TOO.

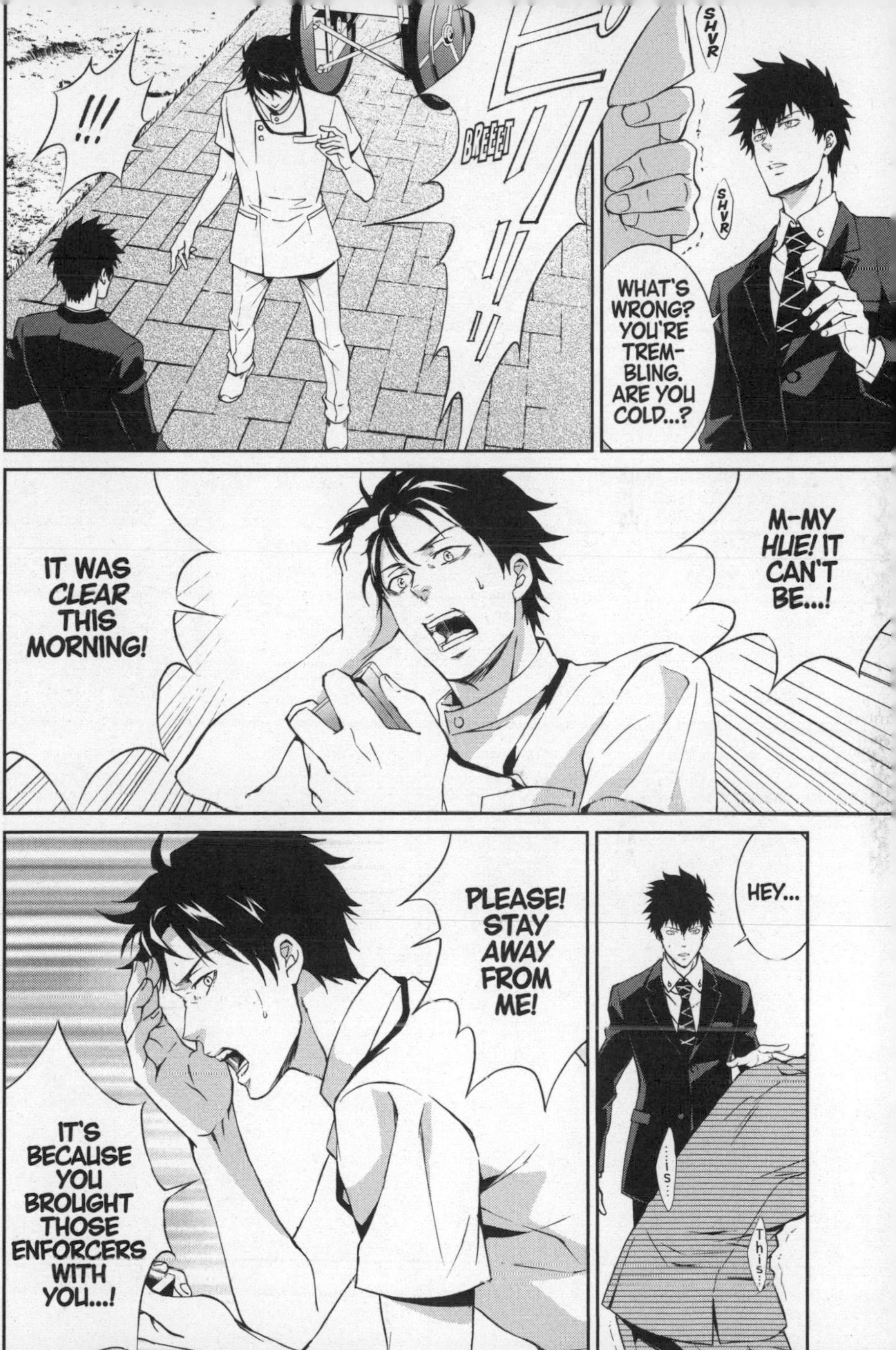
SHVR
SHVR
WHAT'S WRONG? YOU'RE TREM-BLING. ARE YOU COLD...?
BREEET
!!!
M-MY HUE! IT CAN'T BE...!
IT WAS CLEAR THIS MORNING!
HEY...
This...
...is...
PLEASE! STAY AWAY FROM ME!
IT'S BECAUSE YOU BROUGHT THOSE ENFORCERS WITH YOU...!

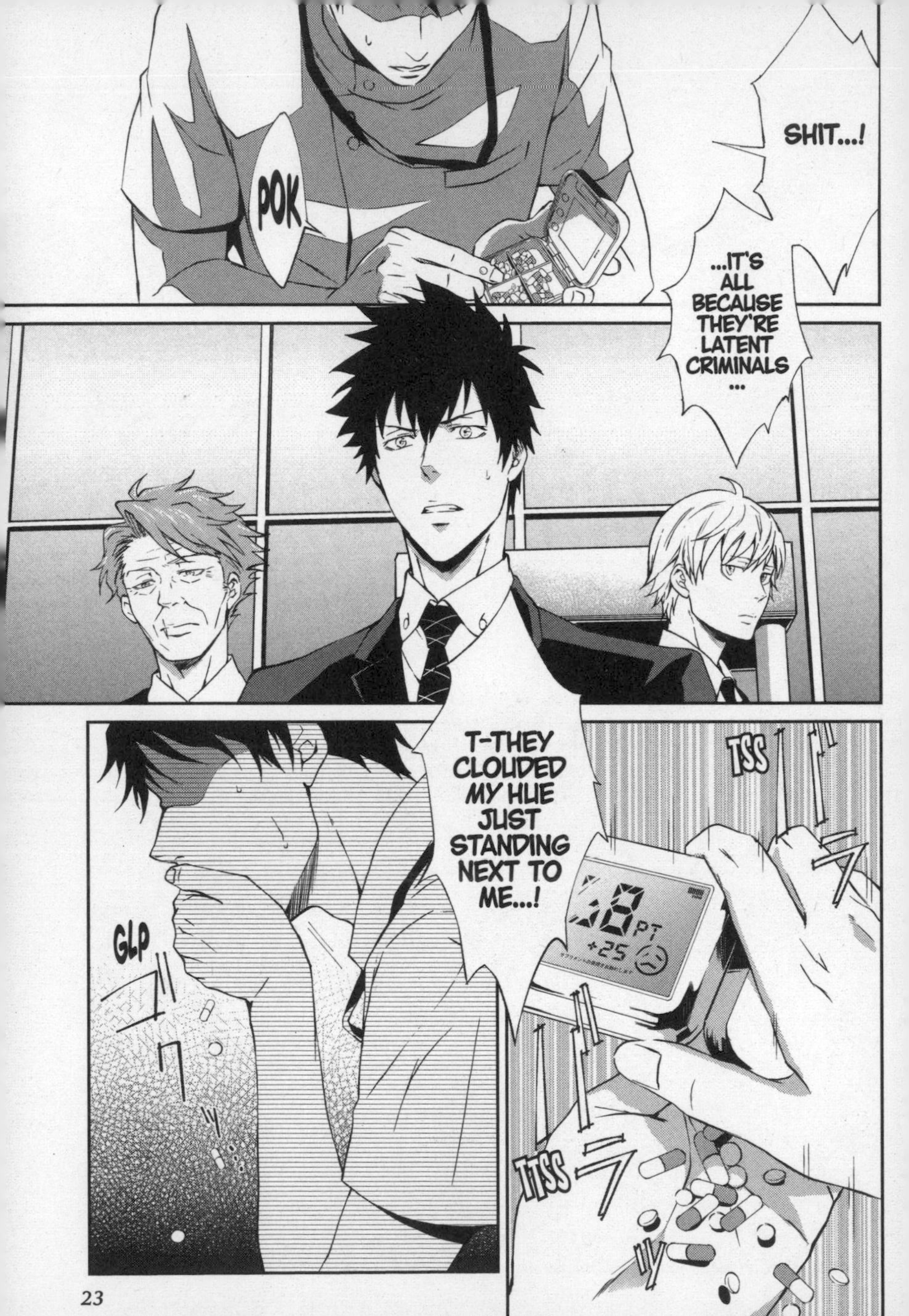
SHIT...!
POK
...IT'S ALL BECAUSE THEY'RE LATENT CRIMINALS ...
TSS
T-THEY CLOUDED MY HUE JUST STANDING NEXT TO ME...!
TTSS
GLP

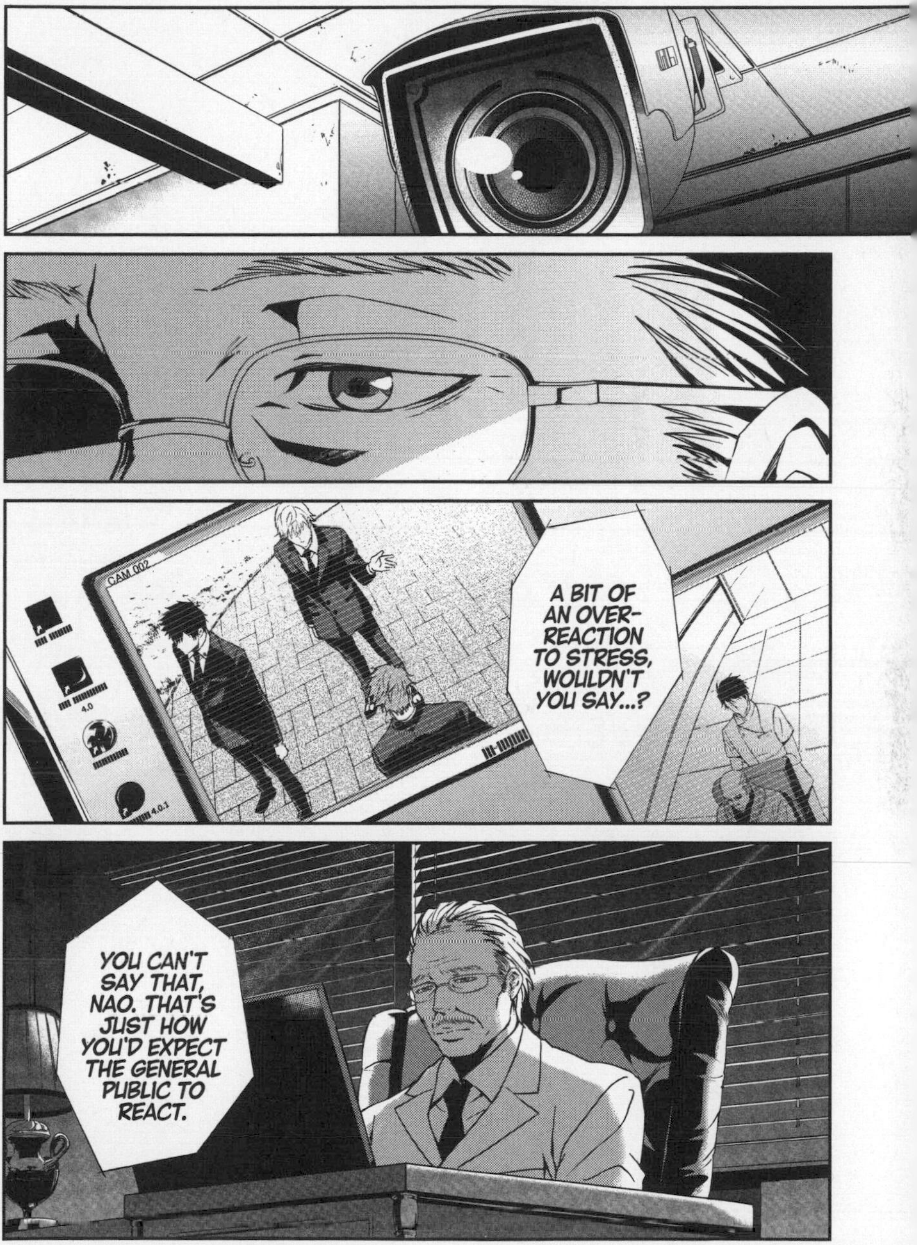
CAM 002
A BIT OF AN OVER-REACTION TO STRESS, WOULDN'T YOU SAY...?
YOU CAN'T SAY THAT, NAO. THAT'S JUST HOW YOU'D EXPECT THE GENERAL PUBLIC TO REACT.

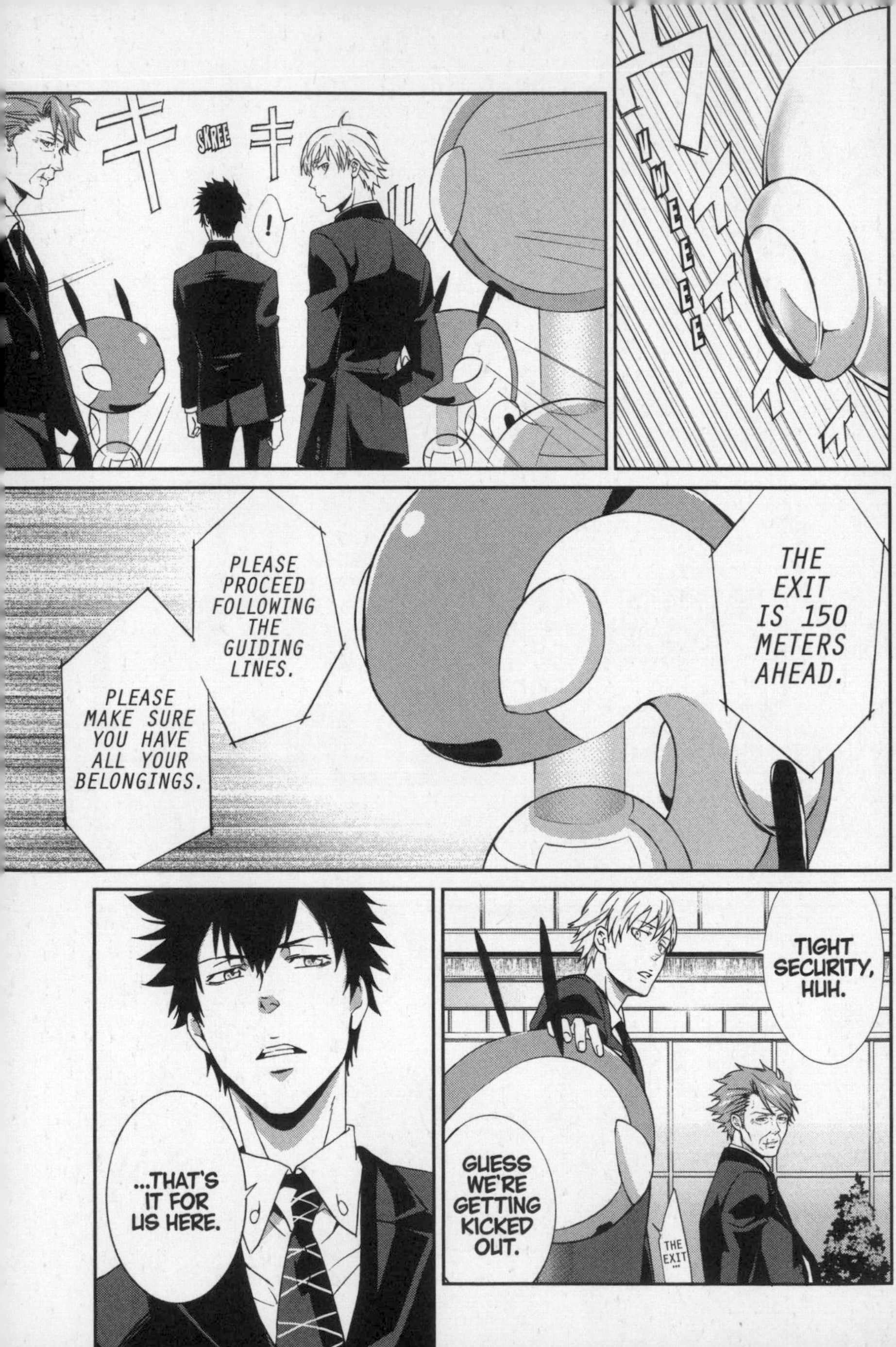
UWEEEE
SKREE
!
THE EXIT IS 150 METERS AHEAD.
PLEASE PROCEED FOLLOWING THE GUIDING LINES.
PLEASE MAKE SURE YOU HAVE ALL YOUR BELONGINGS.
TIGHT SECURITY, HUH.
GUESS WE'RE GETTING KICKED OUT.
THE EXIT...
...THAT'S IT FOR US HERE.

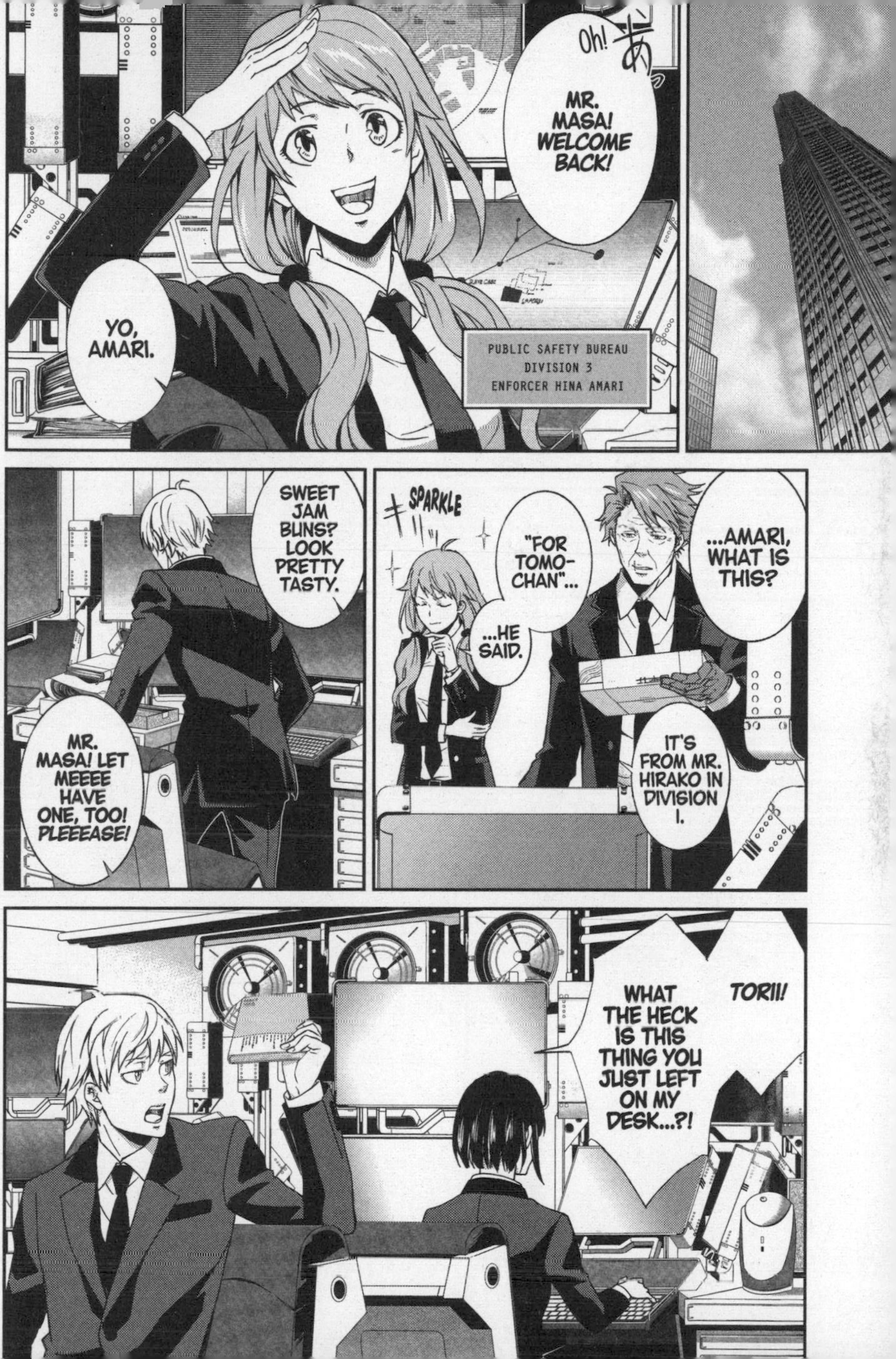
Oh! あ
MR. MASA! WELCOME BACK!
PUBLIC SAFETY BUREAU DIVISION 3 ENFORCER HINA AMARI
YO, AMARI.
...AMARI, WHAT IS THIS?
"FOR TOMO-CHAN"...
SPARKLE
...HE SAID.
IT'S FROM MR. HIRAKO IN DIVISION I.
SWEET JAM BUNS? LOOK PRETTY TASTY.
MR. MASA! LET MEEEE HAVE ONE, TOO! PLEEEASE!
TORII!
WHAT THE HECK IS THIS THING YOU JUST LEFT ON MY DESK...?!

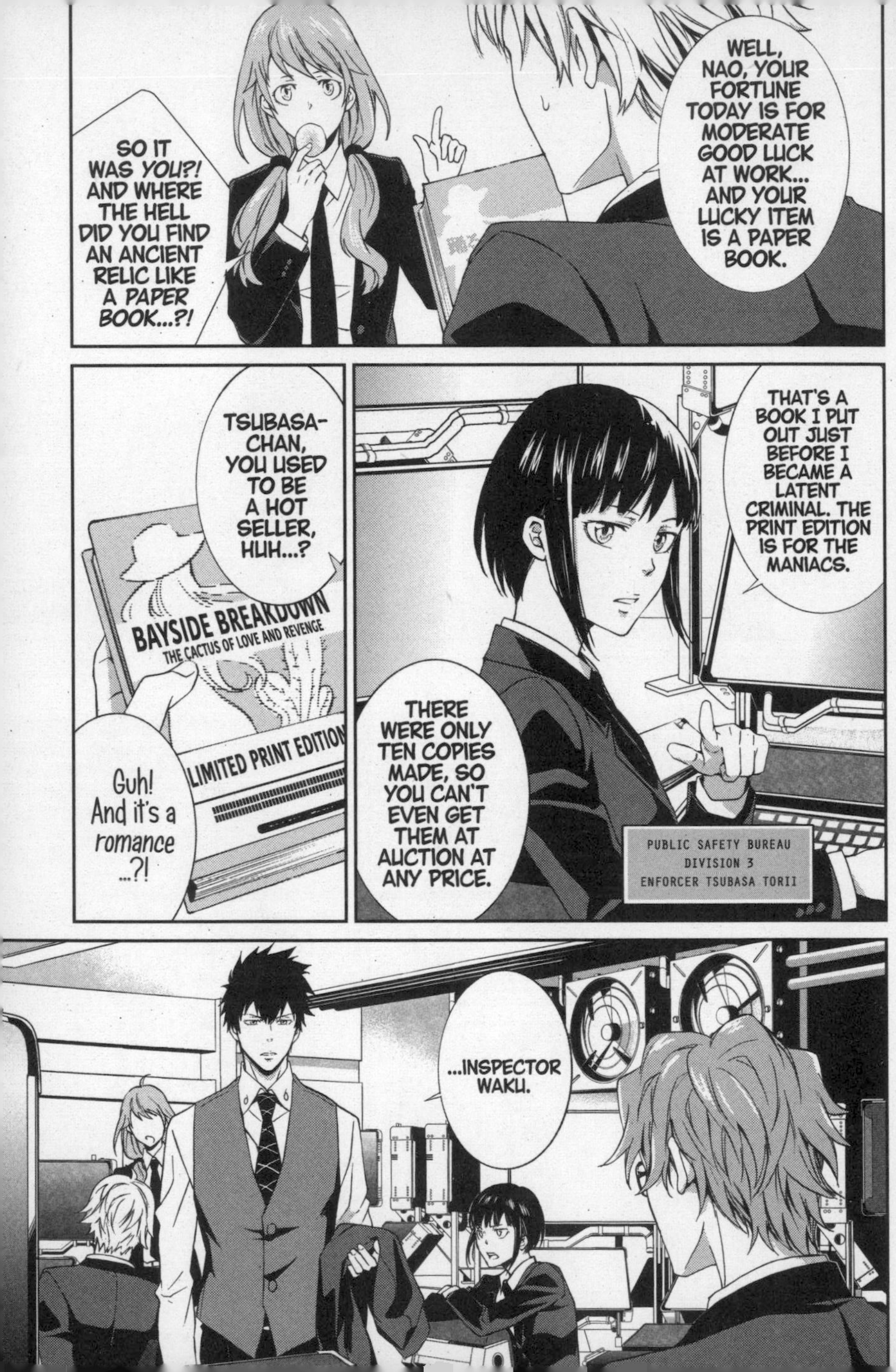
WELL, NAO, YOUR FORTUNE TODAY IS FOR MODERATE GOOD LUCK AT WORK... AND YOUR LUCKY ITEM IS A PAPER BOOK.
SO IT WAS *YOU*?! AND WHERE THE HELL DID YOU FIND AN ANCIENT RELIC LIKE A PAPER BOOK...?!
THAT'S A BOOK I PUT OUT JUST BEFORE I BECAME A LATENT CRIMINAL. THE PRINT EDITION IS FOR THE MANIACS.
THERE WERE ONLY TEN COPIES MADE, SO YOU CAN'T EVEN GET THEM AT AUCTION AT ANY PRICE.
PUBLIC SAFETY BUREAU DIVISION 3 ENFORCER TSUBASA TORII
TSUBASA-CHAN, YOU USED TO BE A HOT SELLER, HUH...?
BAYSIDE BREAKDOWN
THE CACTUS OF LOVE AND REVENGE
LIMITED PRINT EDITION
Guh! And it's a romance ...?!
...INSPECTOR WAKU.

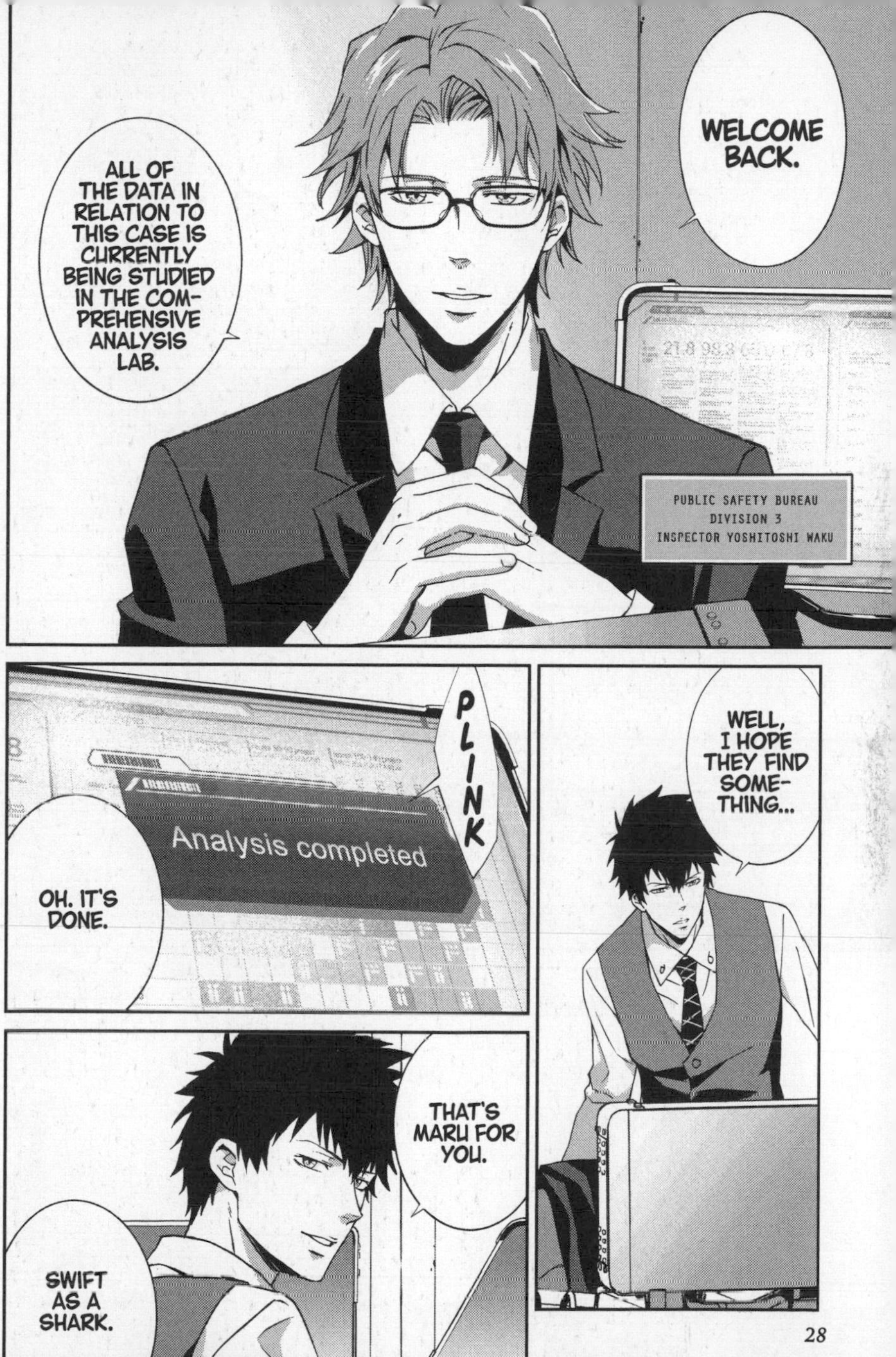
WELCOME BACK.
ALL OF THE DATA IN RELATION TO THIS CASE IS CURRENTLY BEING STUDIED IN THE COMPREHENSIVE ANALYSIS LAB.
PUBLIC SAFETY BUREAU DIVISION 3 INSPECTOR YOSHITOSHI WAKU
WELL, I HOPE THEY FIND SOMETHING...
PLINK
Analysis completed
OH. IT'S DONE.
THAT'S MARU FOR YOU.
SWIFT AS A SHARK.

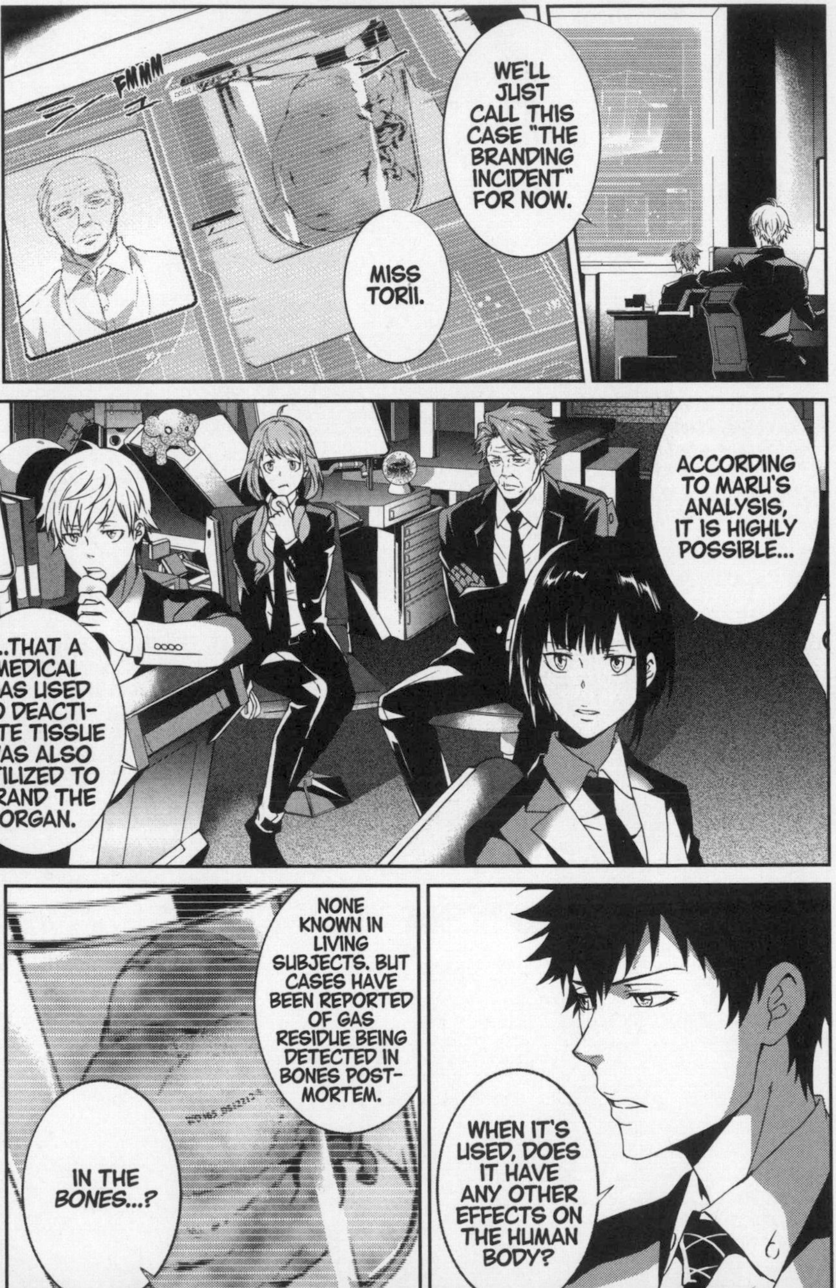
WE'LL JUST CALL THIS CASE "THE BRANDING INCIDENT" FOR NOW.
MISS TORII.
FMMM
ACCORDING TO MARU'S ANALYSIS, IT IS HIGHLY POSSIBLE...
...THAT A MEDICAL GAS USED TO DEACTI-VATE TISSUE WAS ALSO UTILIZED TO BRAND THE ORGAN.
WHEN IT'S USED, DOES IT HAVE ANY OTHER EFFECTS ON THE HUMAN BODY?
NONE KNOWN IN LIVING SUBJECTS. BUT CASES HAVE BEEN REPORTED OF GAS RESIDUE BEING DETECTED IN BONES POST-MORTEM.
IN THE BONES...?

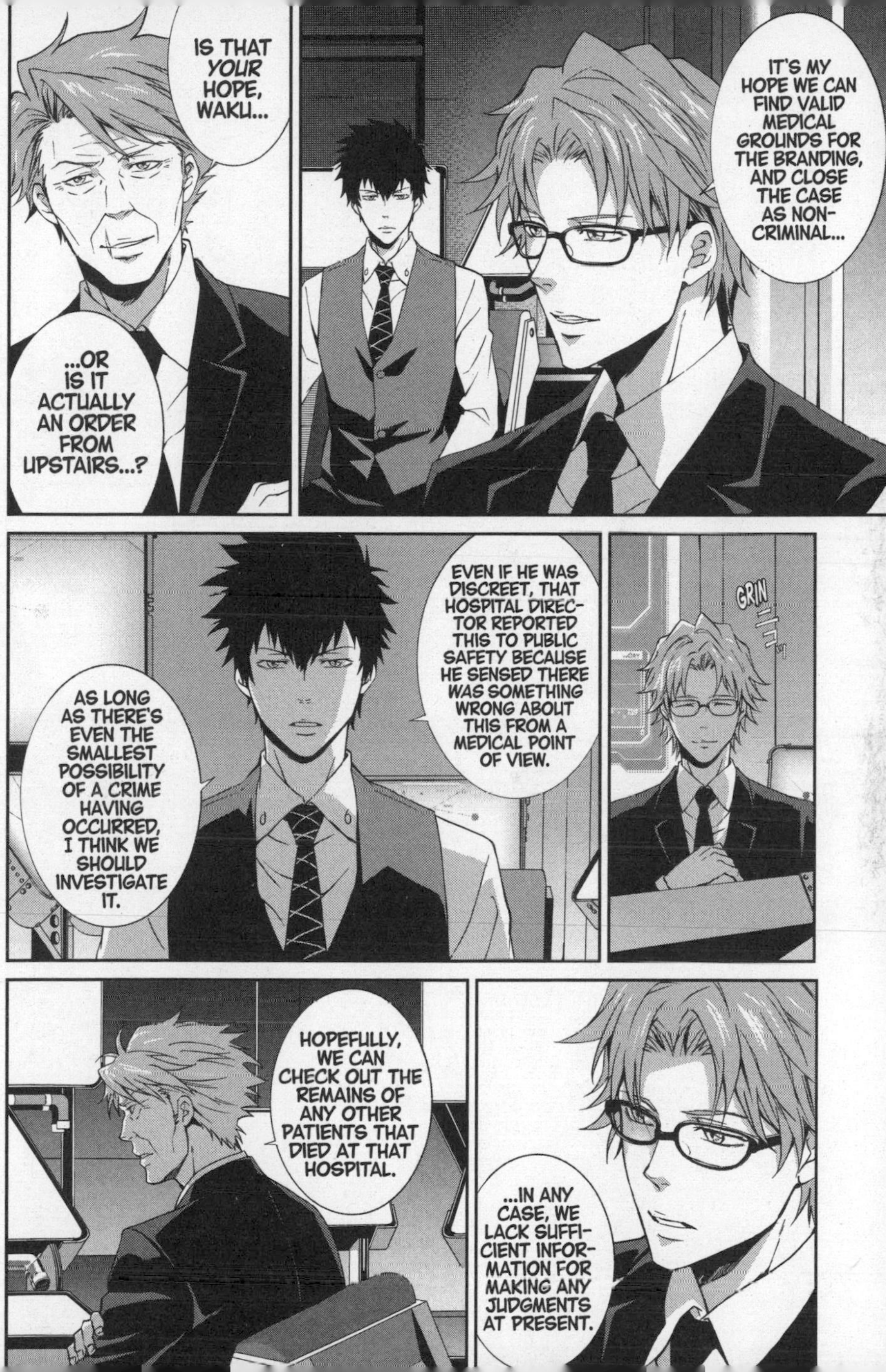
IT'S MY HOPE WE CAN FIND VALID MEDICAL GROUNDS FOR THE BRANDING, AND CLOSE THE CASE AS NON-CRIMINAL...
IS THAT *YOUR* HOPE, WAKU...
...OR IS IT ACTUALLY AN ORDER FROM UPSTAIRS...?
GRIN
EVEN IF HE WAS DISCREET, THAT HOSPITAL DIRECTOR REPORTED THIS TO PUBLIC SAFETY BECAUSE HE SENSED THERE WAS SOMETHING WRONG ABOUT THIS FROM A MEDICAL POINT OF VIEW.
AS LONG AS THERE'S EVEN THE SMALLEST POSSIBILITY OF A CRIME HAVING OCCURRED, I THINK WE SHOULD INVESTIGATE IT.
...IN ANY CASE, WE LACK SUFFICIENT INFORMATION FOR MAKING ANY JUDGMENTS AT PRESENT.
HOPEFULLY, WE CAN CHECK OUT THE REMAINS OF ANY OTHER PATIENTS THAT DIED AT THAT HOSPITAL.

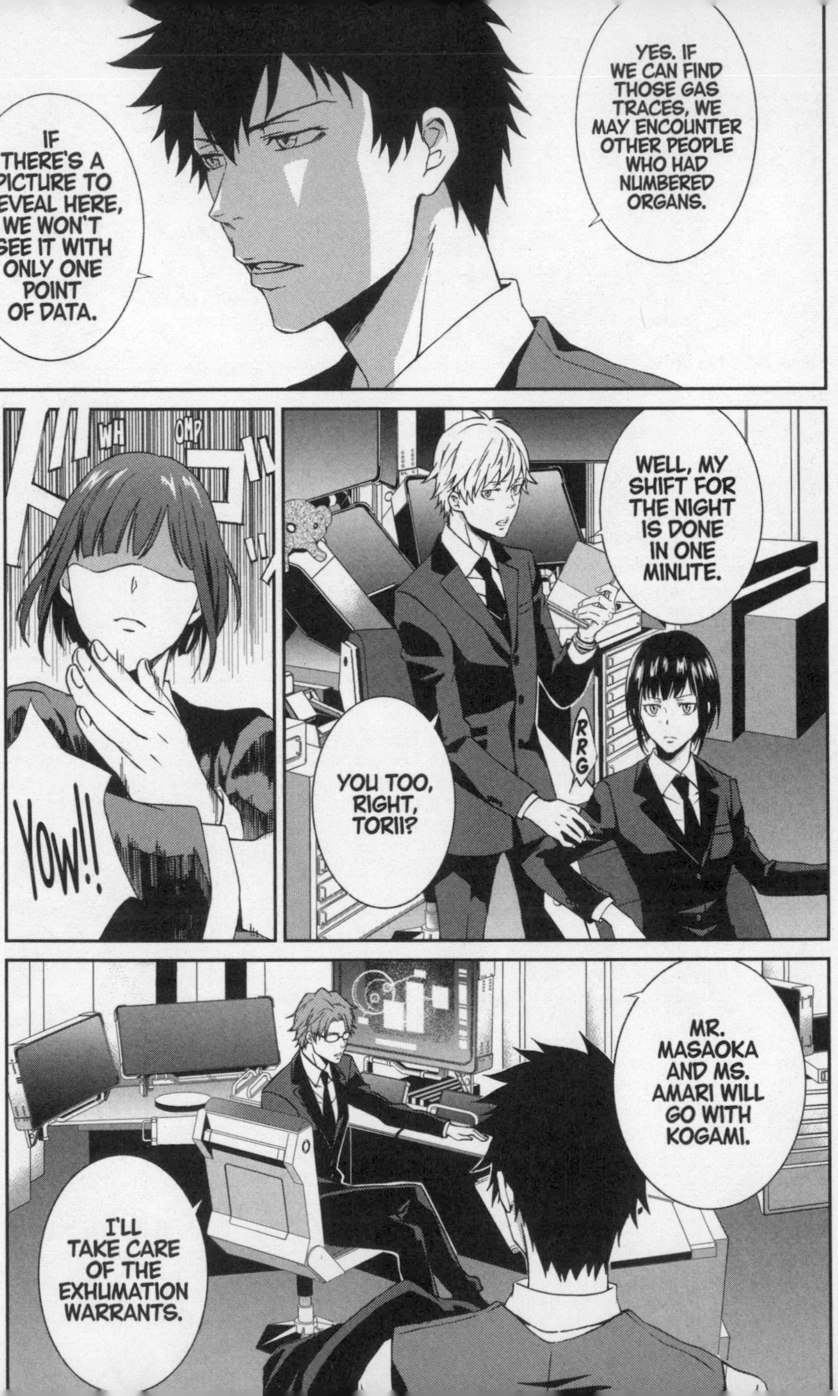
YES. IF WE CAN FIND THOSE GAS TRACES, WE MAY ENCOUNTER OTHER PEOPLE WHO HAD NUMBERED ORGANS.
IF THERE'S A PICTURE TO REVEAL HERE, WE WON'T SEE IT WITH ONLY ONE POINT OF DATA.
WELL, MY SHIFT FOR THE NIGHT IS DONE IN ONE MINUTE.
RRG
YOU TOO, RIGHT, TORII?
WHOMP
YOW!!
MR. MASAOKA AND MS. AMARI WILL GO WITH KOGAMI.
I'LL TAKE CARE OF THE EXHUMATION WARRANTS.

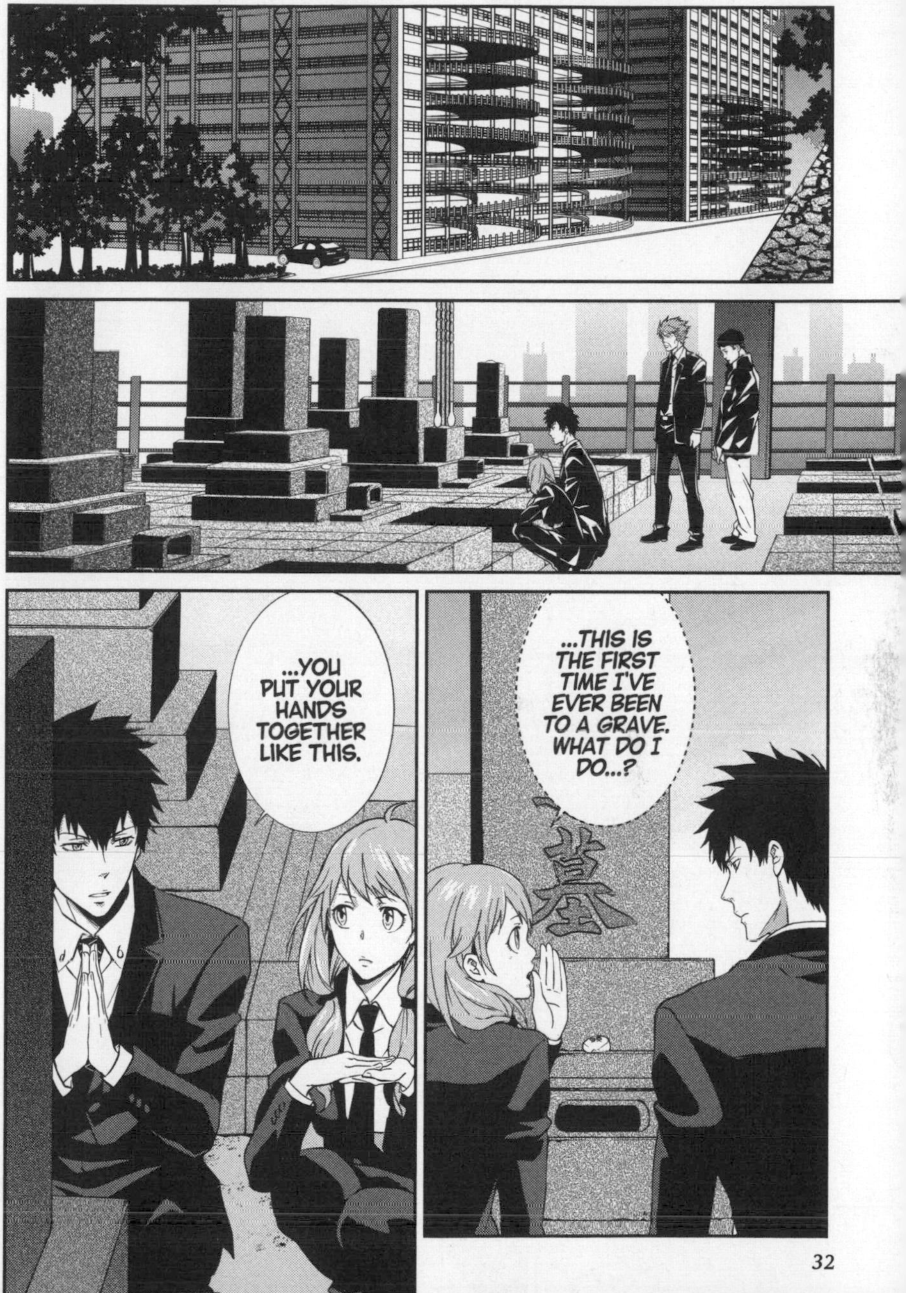
...THIS IS THE FIRST TIME I'VE EVER BEEN TO A GRAVE. WHAT DO I DO...?
墓
...YOU PUT YOUR HANDS TOGETHER LIKE THIS.

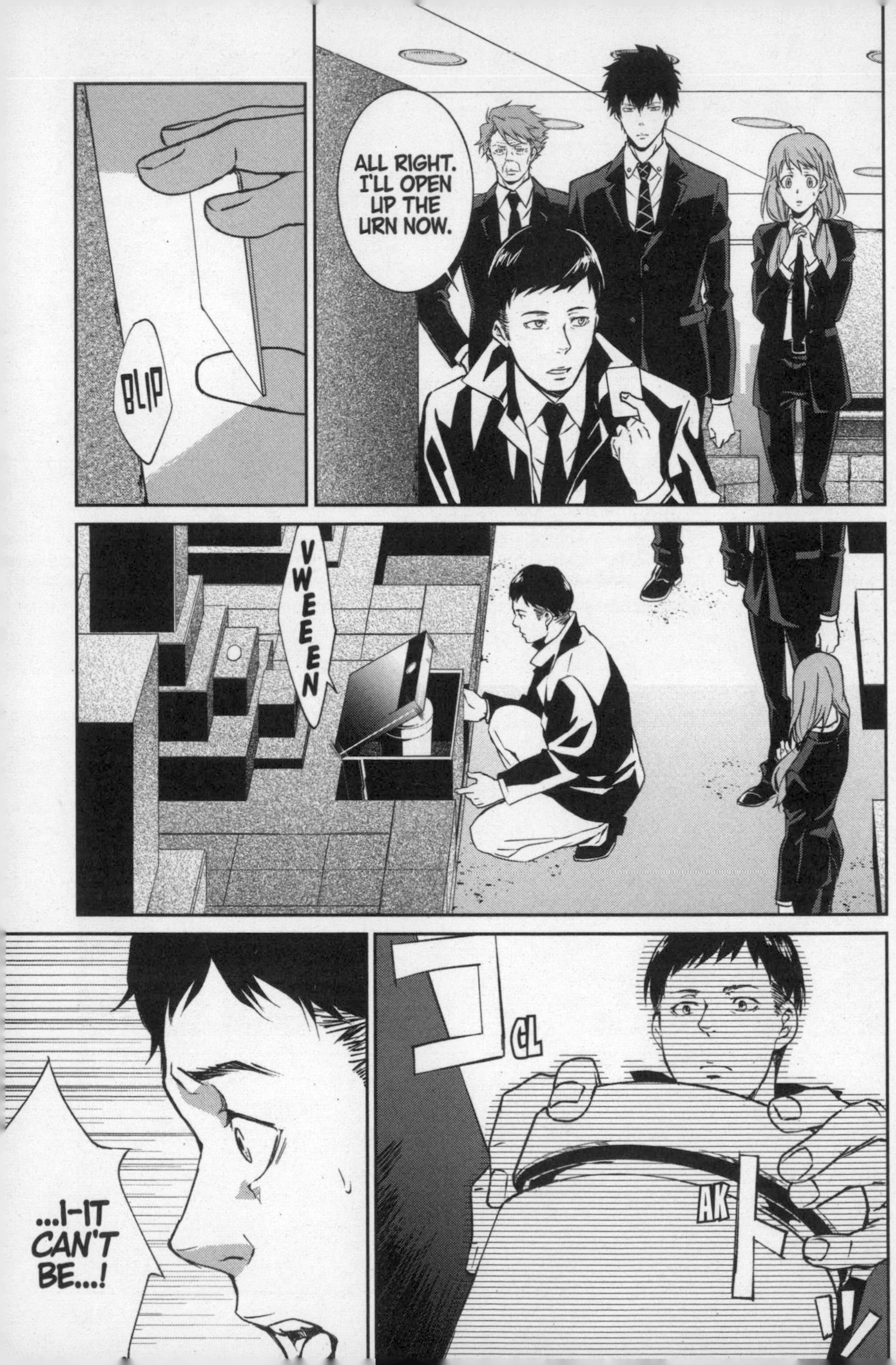
ALL RIGHT. I'LL OPEN UP THE URN NOW.
BLIP
VWEEEEN
CL
AK
...I-IT CAN'T BE...!

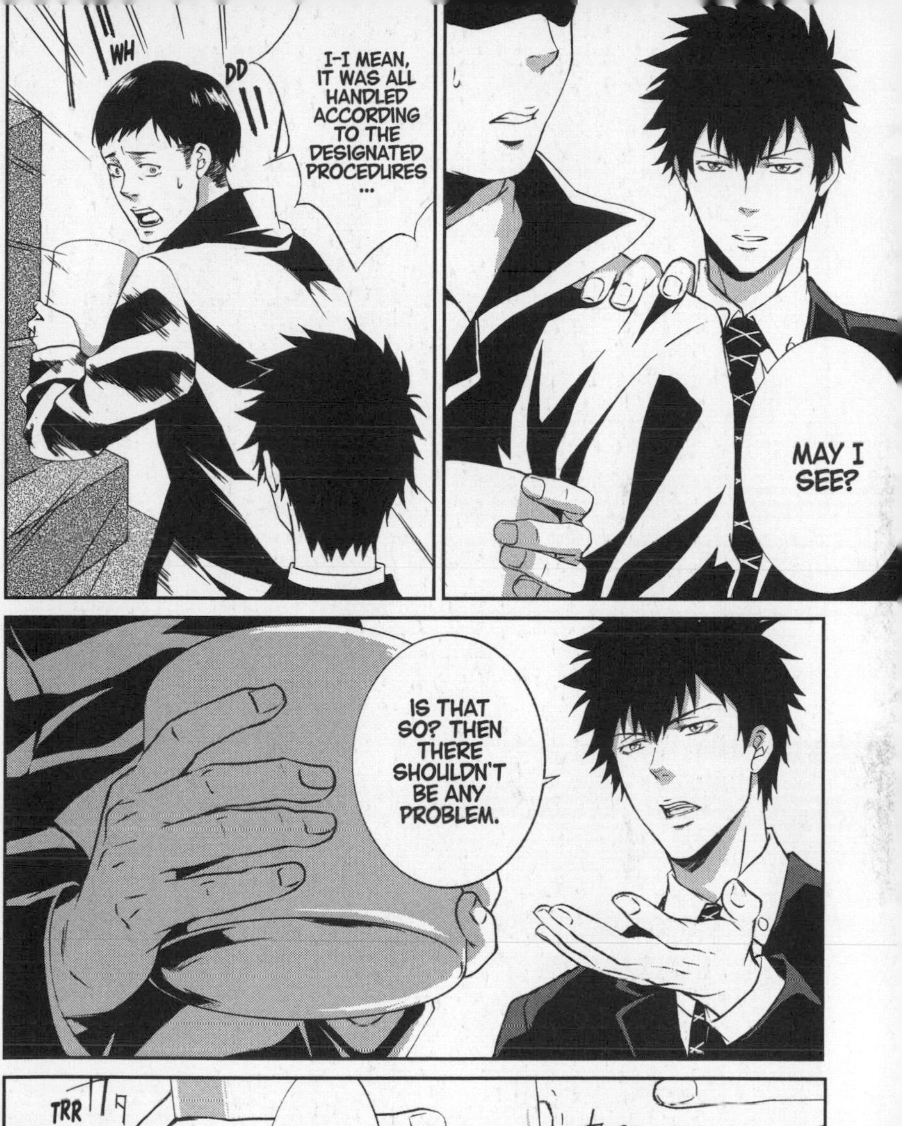
MAY I SEE?
WH
DD
I-I MEAN, IT WAS ALL HANDLED ACCORDING TO THE DESIGNATED PROCEDURES ...
IS THAT SO? THEN THERE SHOULDN'T BE ANY PROBLEM.
TRR
I...
TRR
TRR
...I'M NOT RESPONSIBLE ...

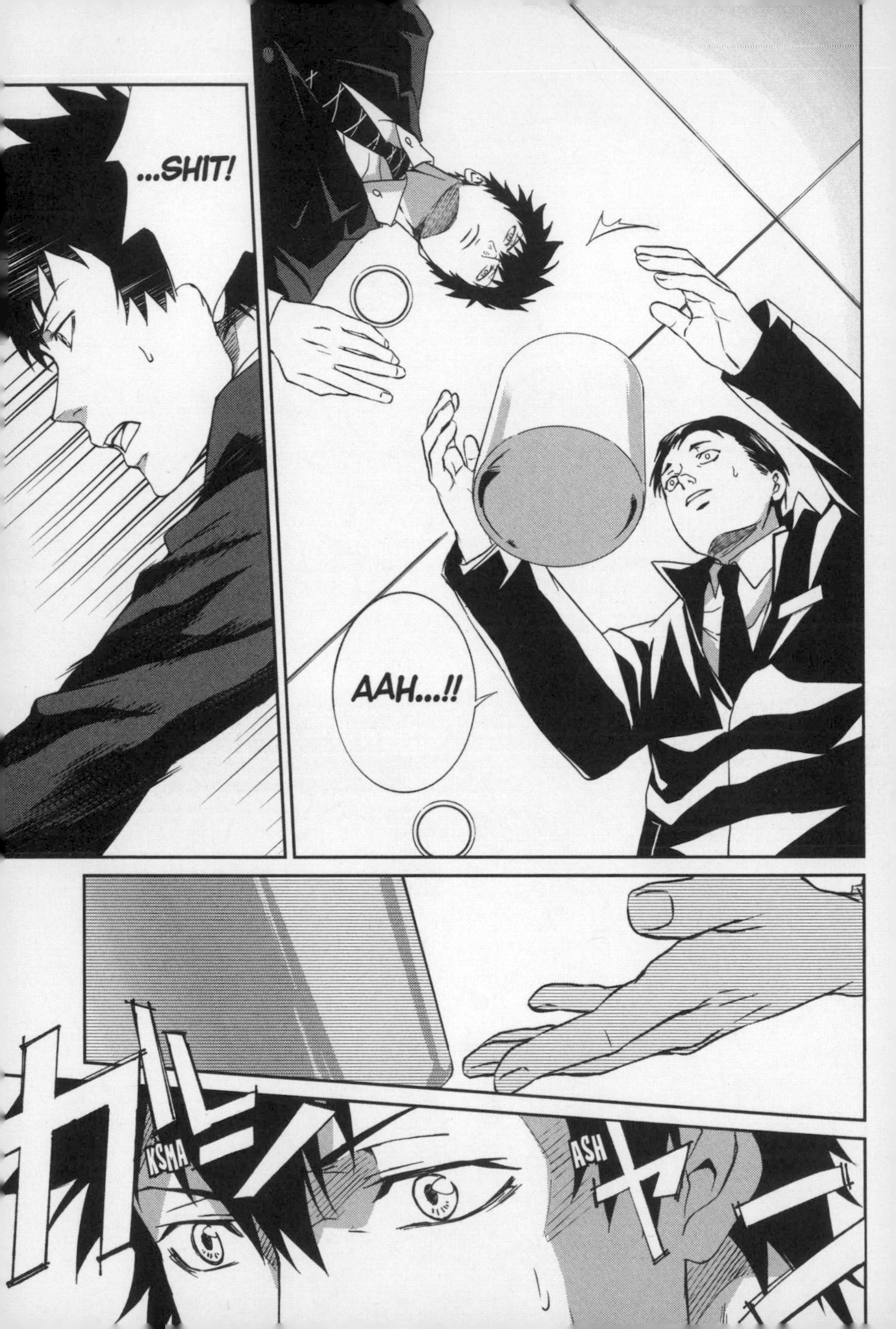
AAH...!!
...SHIT!
KSMA
ASH

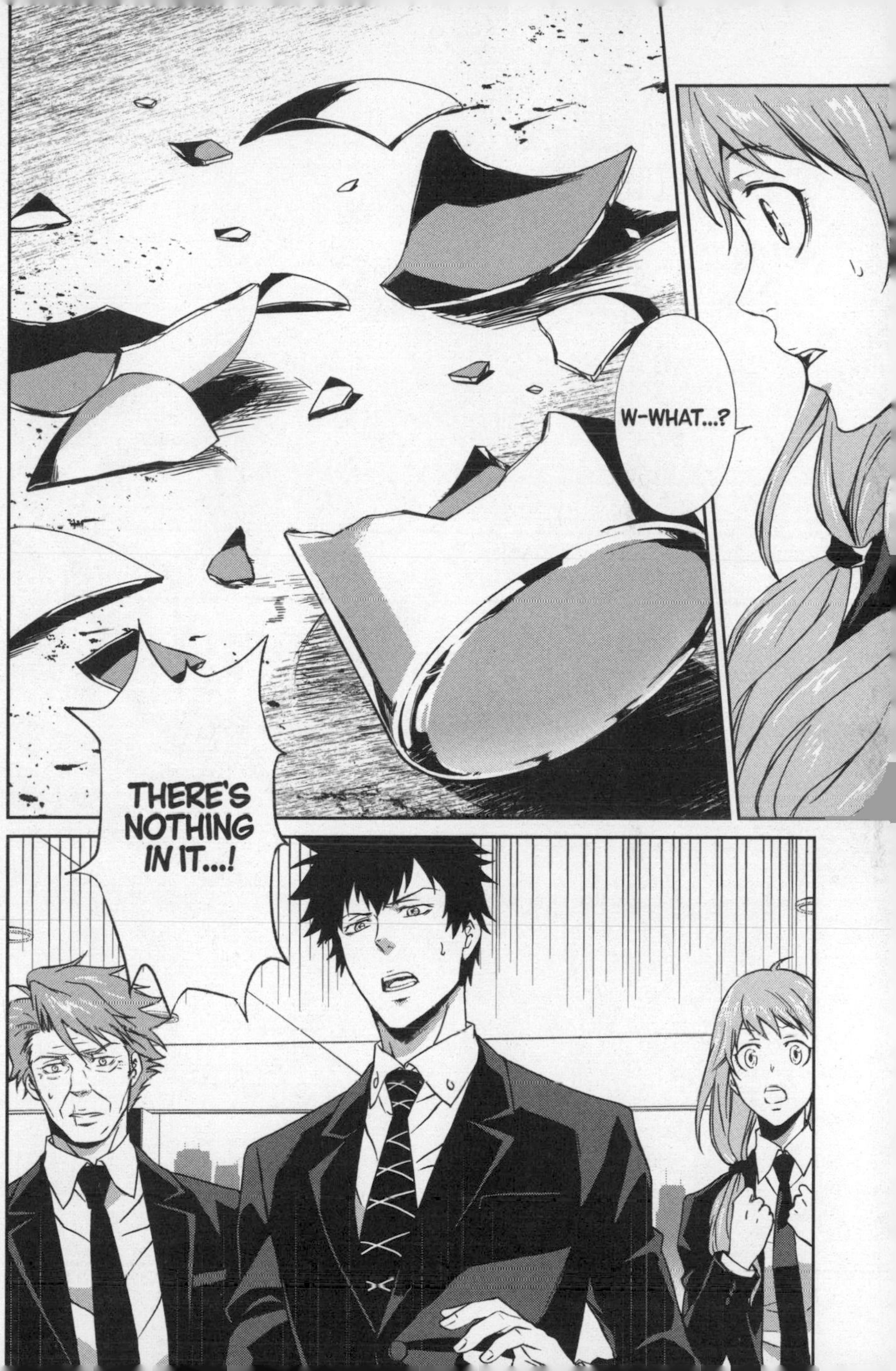
W-WHAT...?
THERE'S NOTHING IN IT...!

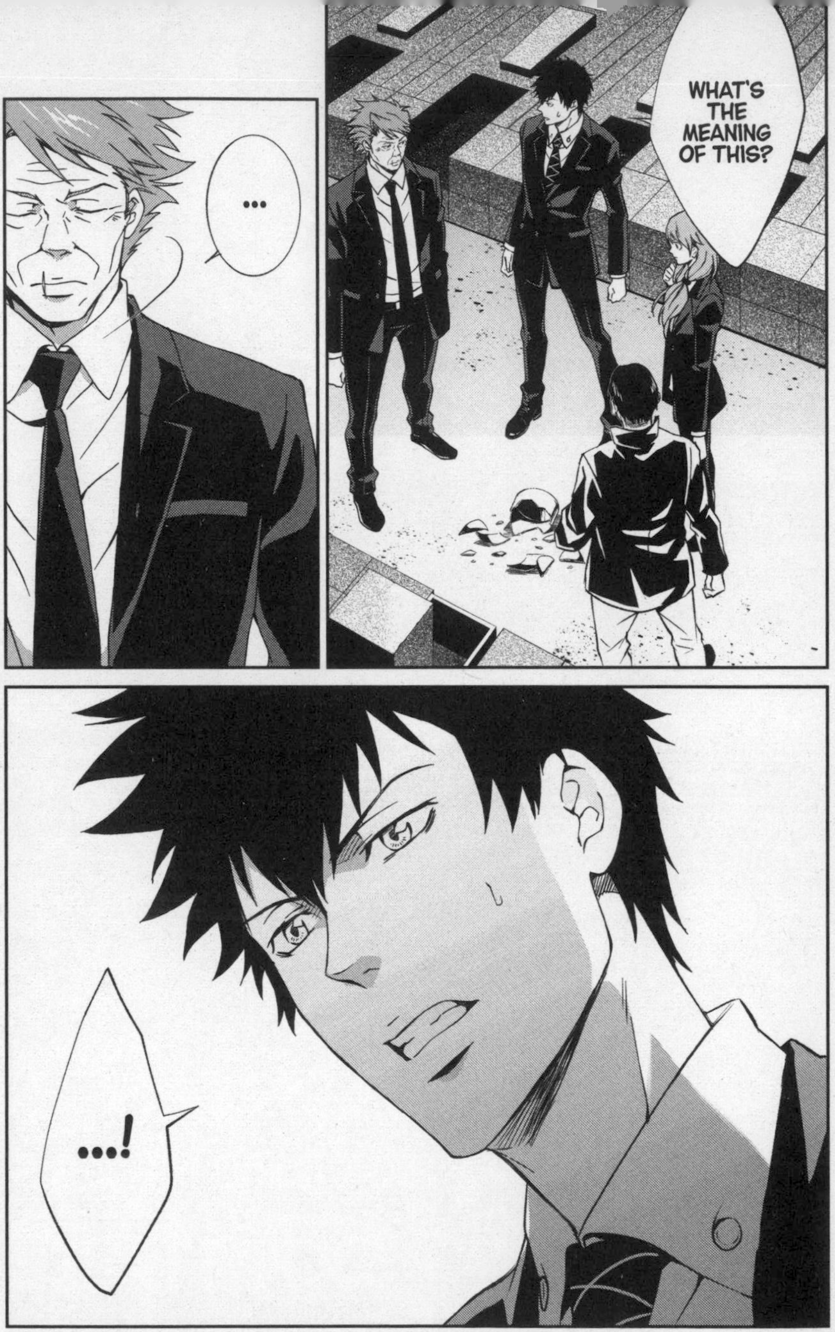
WHAT'S THE MEANING OF THIS?
...
...!

PSYCHO-PASS

監視官 狡噛慎也

INSPECTOR SHINYA KOUGAMI

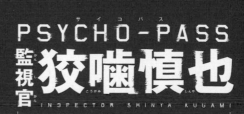

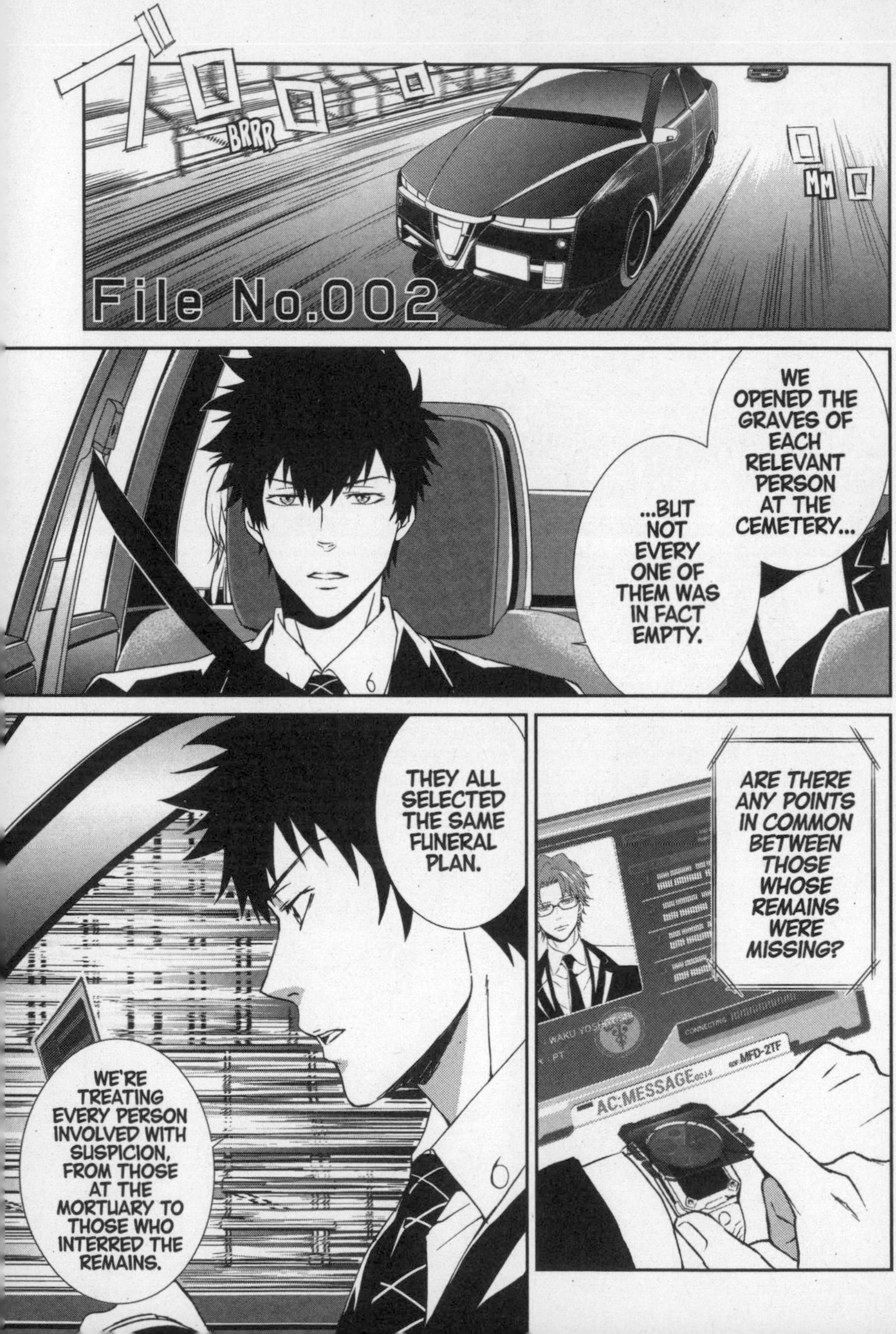
BRRR
MM
File No.002
WE OPENED THE GRAVES OF EACH RELEVANT PERSON AT THE CEMETERY...
...BUT NOT EVERY ONE OF THEM WAS IN FACT EMPTY.
ARE THERE ANY POINTS IN COMMON BETWEEN THOSE WHOSE REMAINS WERE MISSING?
AC:MESSAGE
MFD-2TF
THEY ALL SELECTED THE SAME FUNERAL PLAN.
WE'RE TREATING EVERY PERSON INVOLVED WITH SUSPICION, FROM THOSE AT THE MORTUARY TO THOSE WHO INTERRED THE REMAINS.

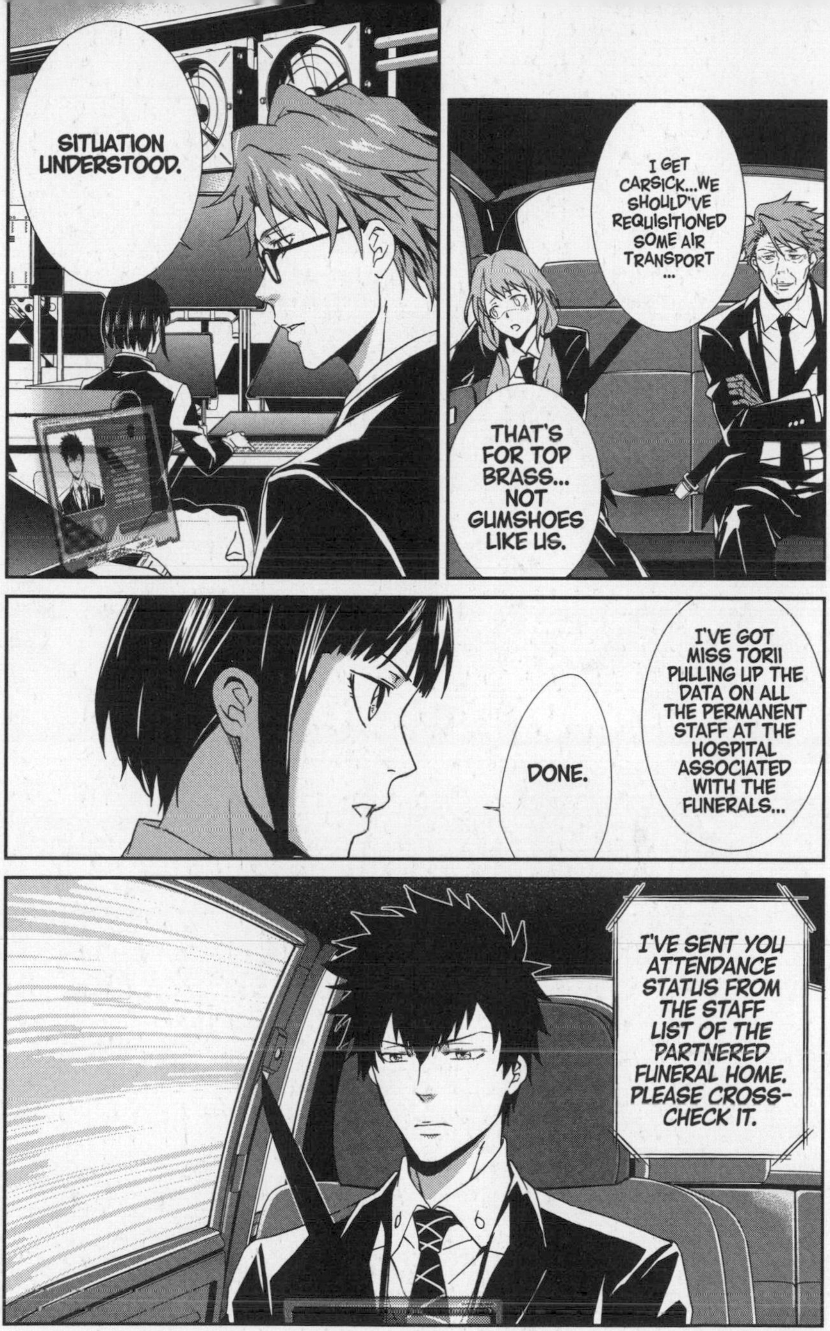
I GET CARSICK...WE SHOULD'VE REQUISITIONED SOME AIR TRANSPORT ...
THAT'S FOR TOP BRASS... NOT GUMSHOES LIKE US.
SITUATION UNDERSTOOD.
I'VE GOT MISS TORII PULLING UP THE DATA ON ALL THE PERMANENT STAFF AT THE HOSPITAL ASSOCIATED WITH THE FUNERALS...
DONE.
I'VE SENT YOU ATTENDANCE STATUS FROM THE STAFF LIST OF THE PARTNERED FUNERAL HOME. PLEASE CROSS-CHECK IT.

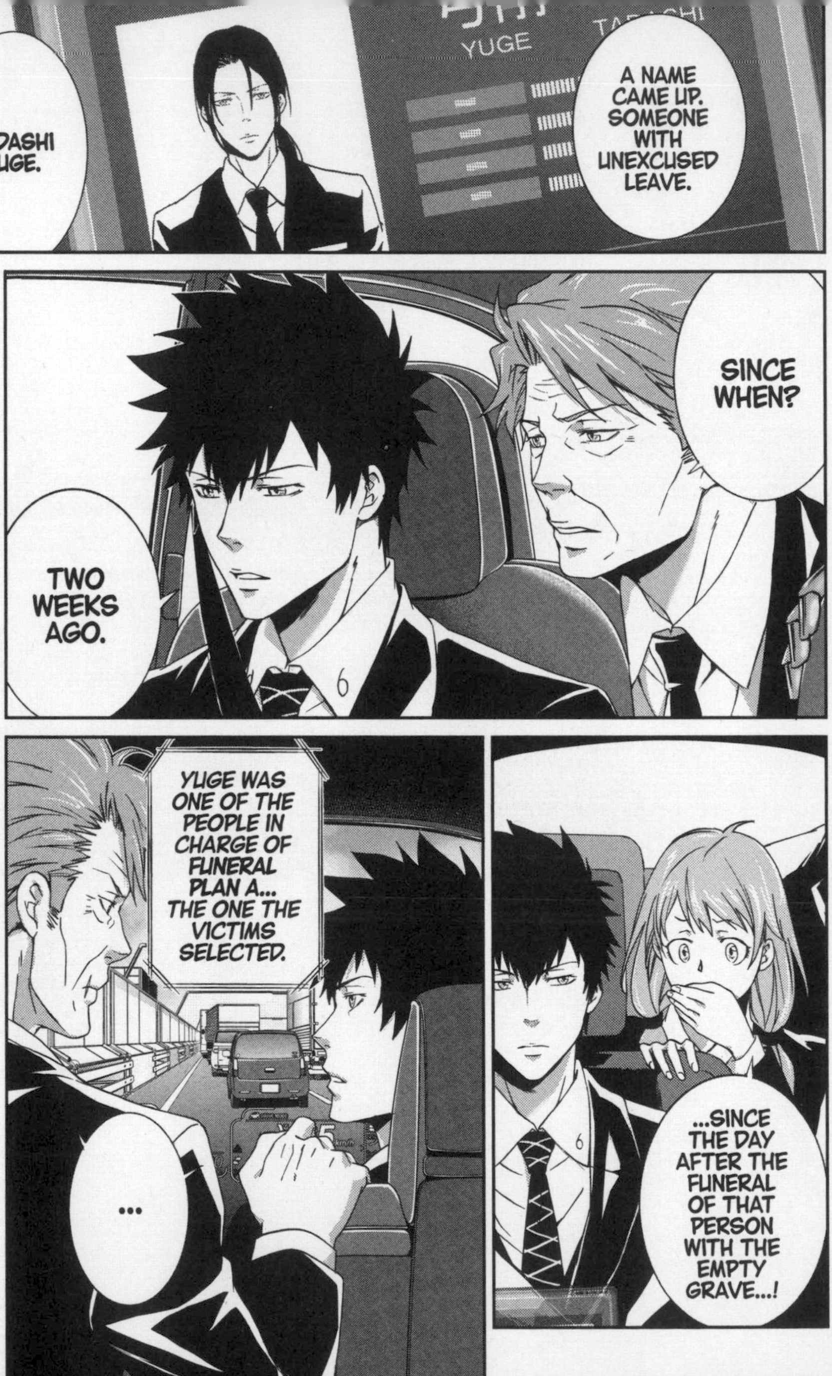
YUGE
A NAME CAME UP. SOMEONE WITH UNEXCUSED LEAVE.
TADASHI YUGE.
SINCE WHEN?
TWO WEEKS AGO.
...SINCE THE DAY AFTER THE FUNERAL OF THAT PERSON WITH THE EMPTY GRAVE...!
YUGE WAS ONE OF THE PEOPLE IN CHARGE OF FUNERAL PLAN A... THE ONE THE VICTIMS SELECTED.
...

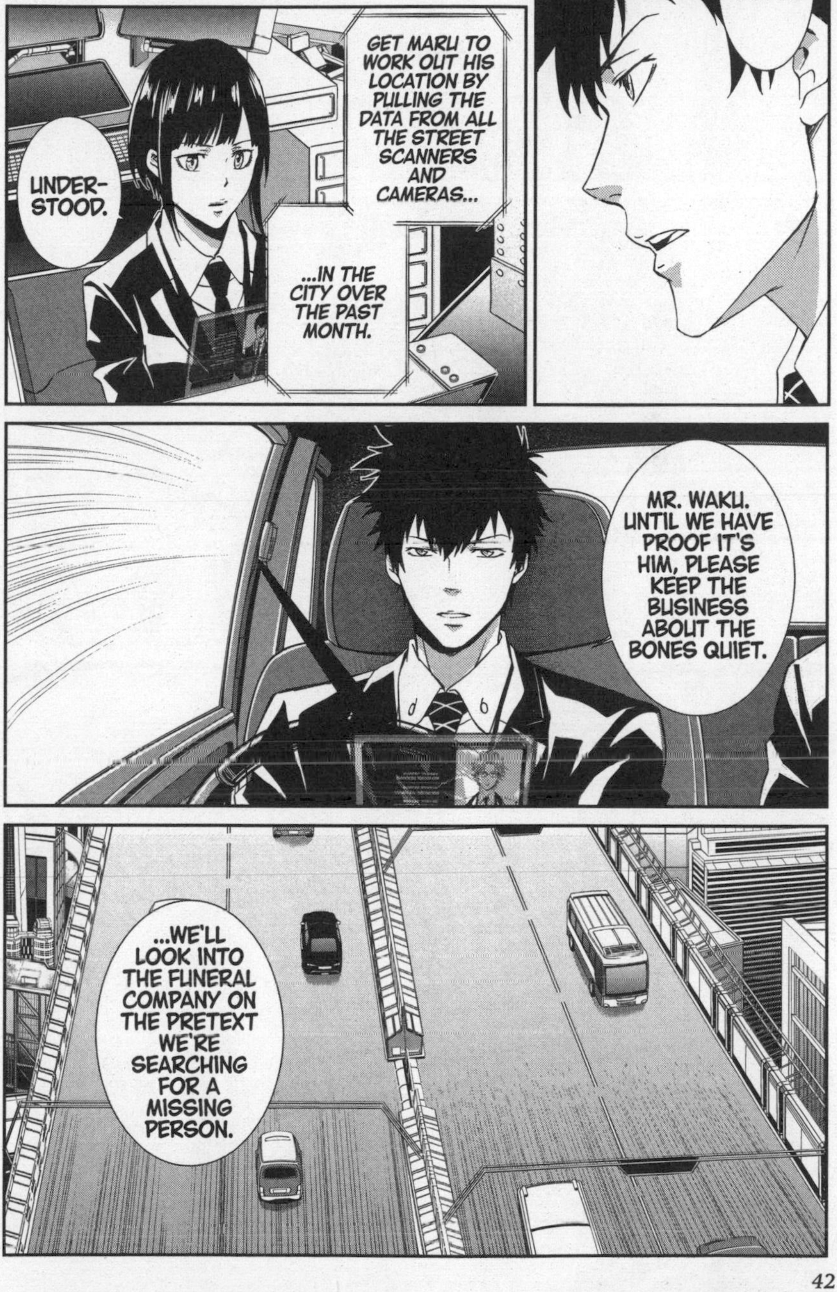
TORII.
GET MARU TO WORK OUT HIS LOCATION BY PULLING THE DATA FROM ALL THE STREET SCANNERS AND CAMERAS...
...IN THE CITY OVER THE PAST MONTH.
UNDER-STOOD.
MR. WAKU. UNTIL WE HAVE PROOF IT'S HIM, PLEASE KEEP THE BUSINESS ABOUT THE BONES QUIET.
...WE'LL LOOK INTO THE FUNERAL COMPANY ON THE PRETEXT WE'RE SEARCHING FOR A MISSING PERSON.

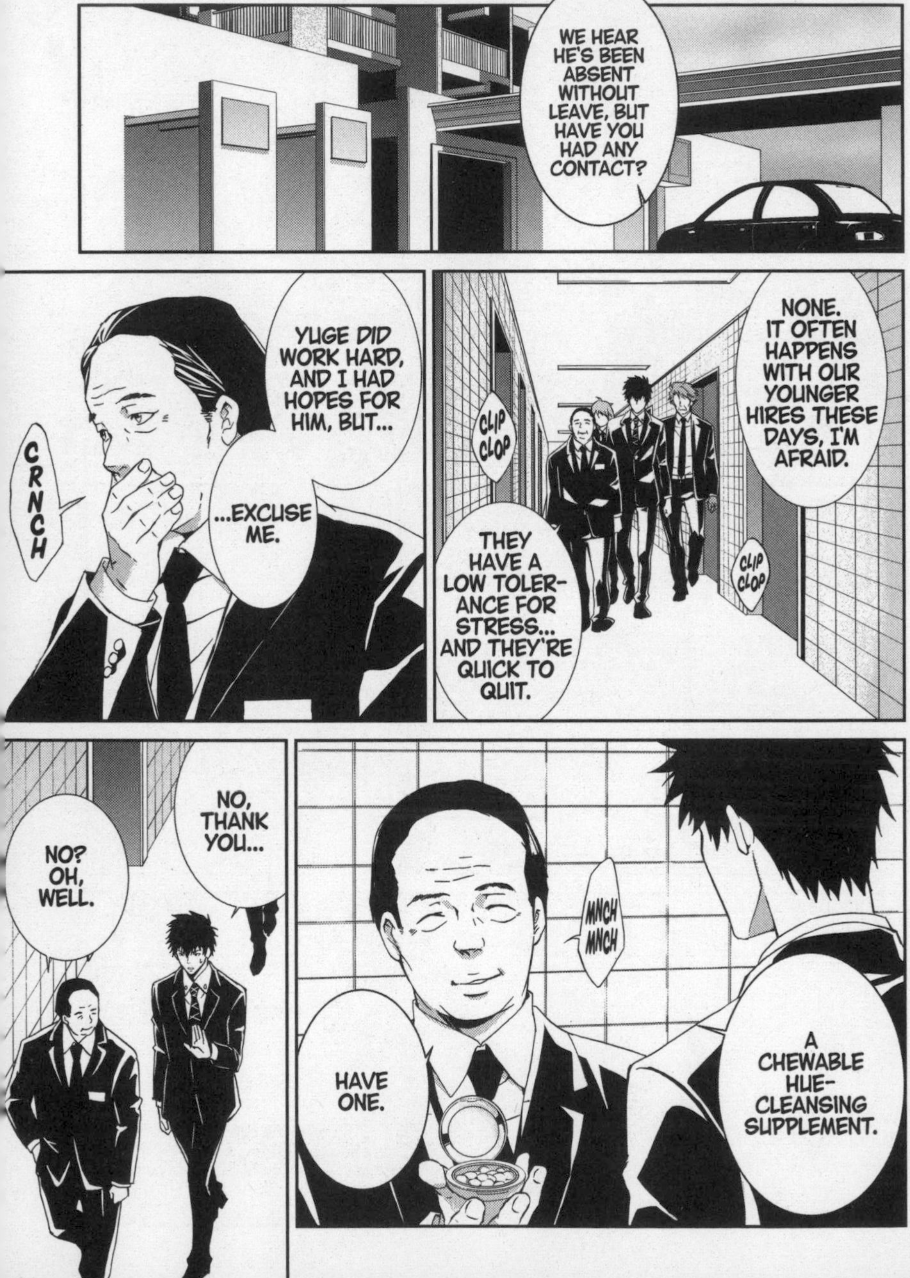
WE HEAR HE'S BEEN ABSENT WITHOUT LEAVE, BUT HAVE YOU HAD ANY CONTACT?
NONE. IT OFTEN HAPPENS WITH OUR YOUNGER HIRES THESE DAYS, I'M AFRAID.
CLIP CLOP
CLIP CLOP
THEY HAVE A LOW TOLER-ANCE FOR STRESS... AND THEY'RE QUICK TO QUIT.
YUGE DID WORK HARD, AND I HAD HOPES FOR HIM, BUT...
...EXCUSE ME.
CRNCH
A CHEWABLE HUE-CLEANSING SUPPLEMENT.
MNCH MNCH
HAVE ONE.
NO, THANK YOU...
NO? OH, WELL.

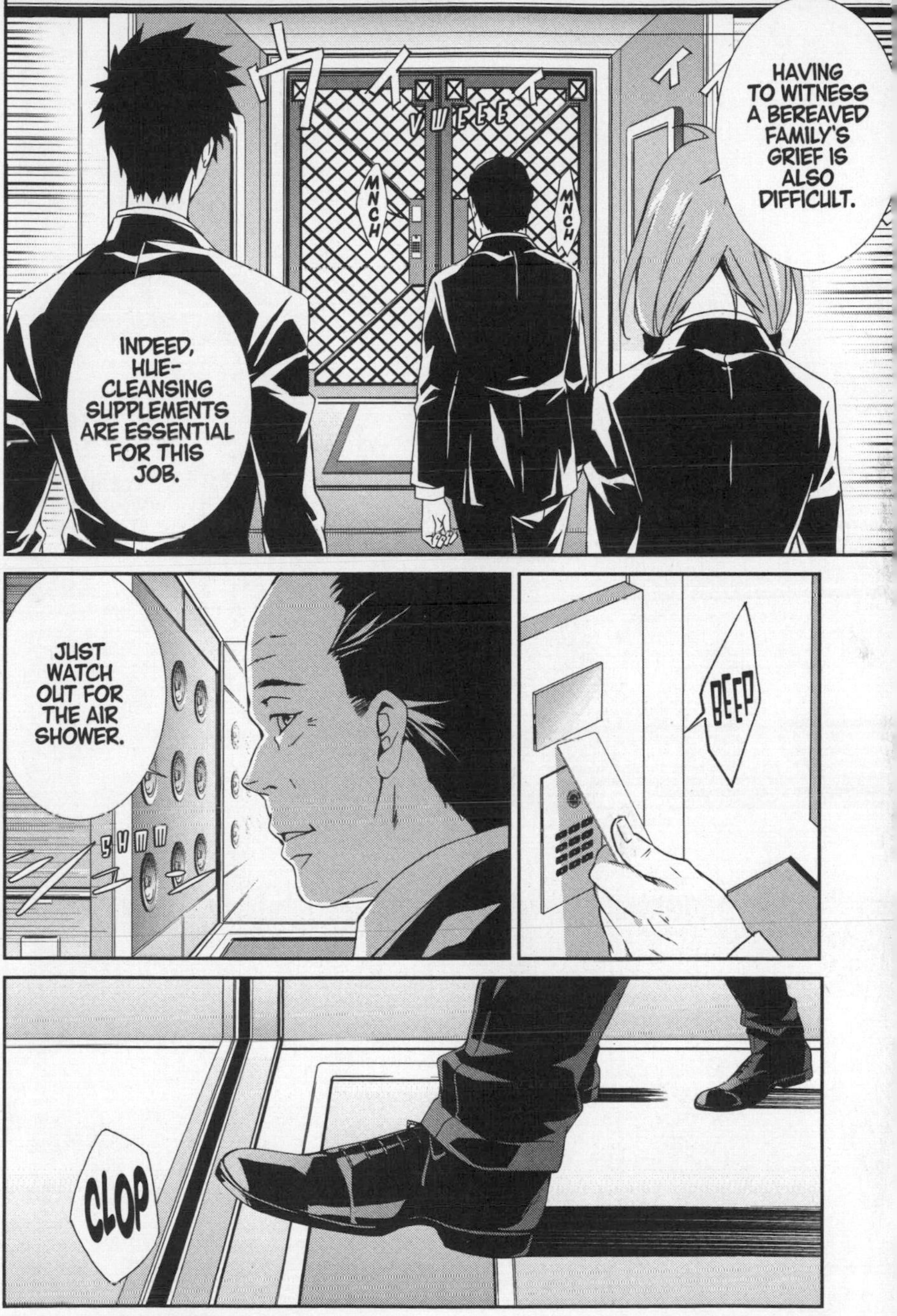
HAVING TO WITNESS A BEREAVED FAMILY'S GRIEF IS ALSO DIFFICULT.
VWEEE
MNCH
MNCH
INDEED, HUE-CLEANSING SUPPLEMENTS ARE ESSENTIAL FOR THIS JOB.
BEEP
JUST WATCH OUT FOR THE AIR SHOWER.
SHMM
CLOP

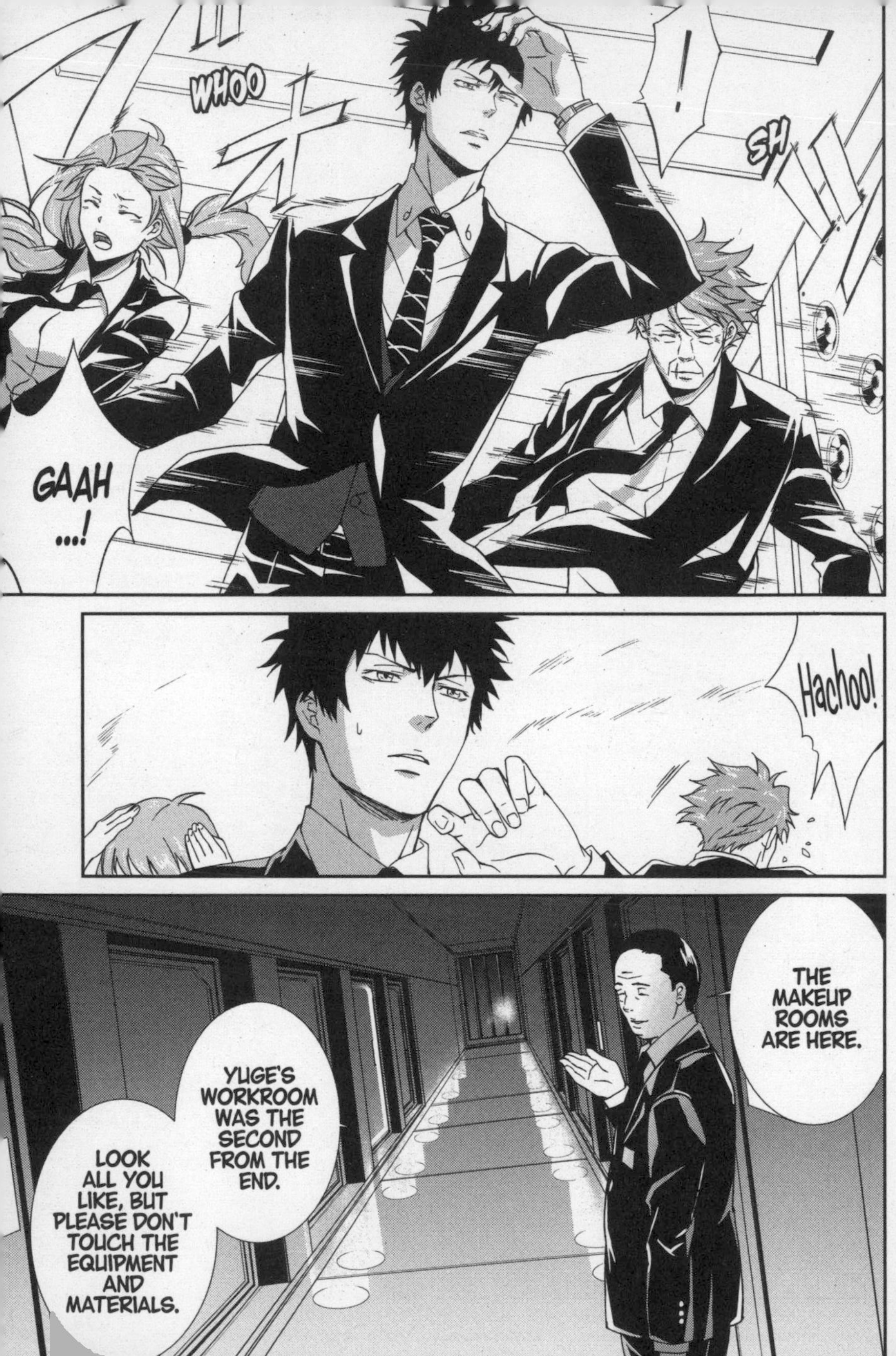
SH
!
WHOO
GAAH ...!
Hachoo!
THE MAKEUP ROOMS ARE HERE.
YUGE'S WORKROOM WAS THE SECOND FROM THE END.
LOOK ALL YOU LIKE, BUT PLEASE DON'T TOUCH THE EQUIPMENT AND MATERIALS.

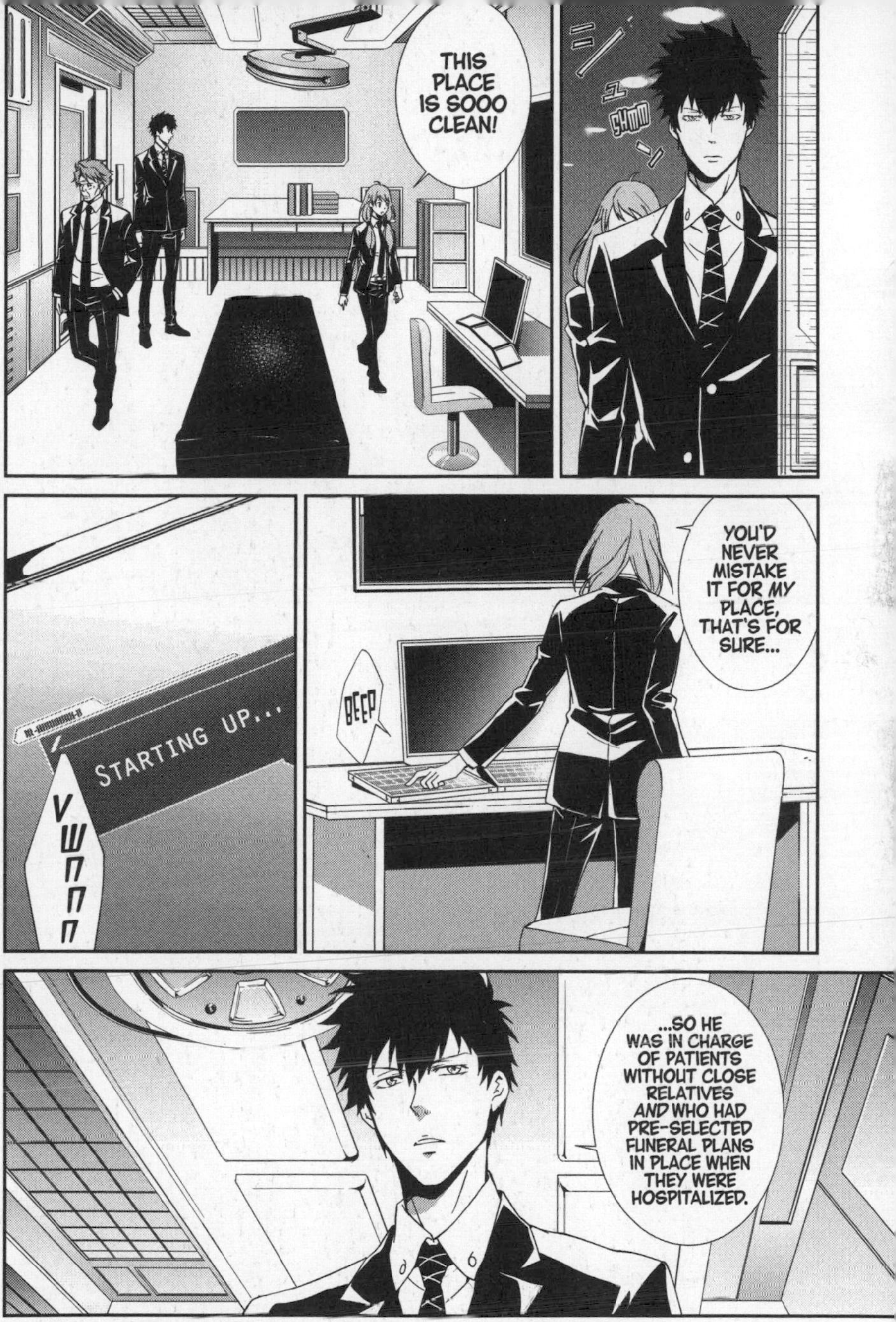
SHOM
THIS PLACE IS SOOO CLEAN!
YOU'D NEVER MISTAKE IT FOR MY PLACE, THAT'S FOR SURE...
BEEP
STARTING UP...
VWNNNN
...SO HE WAS IN CHARGE OF PATIENTS WITHOUT CLOSE RELATIVES AND WHO HAD PRE-SELECTED FUNERAL PLANS IN PLACE WHEN THEY WERE HOSPITALIZED.

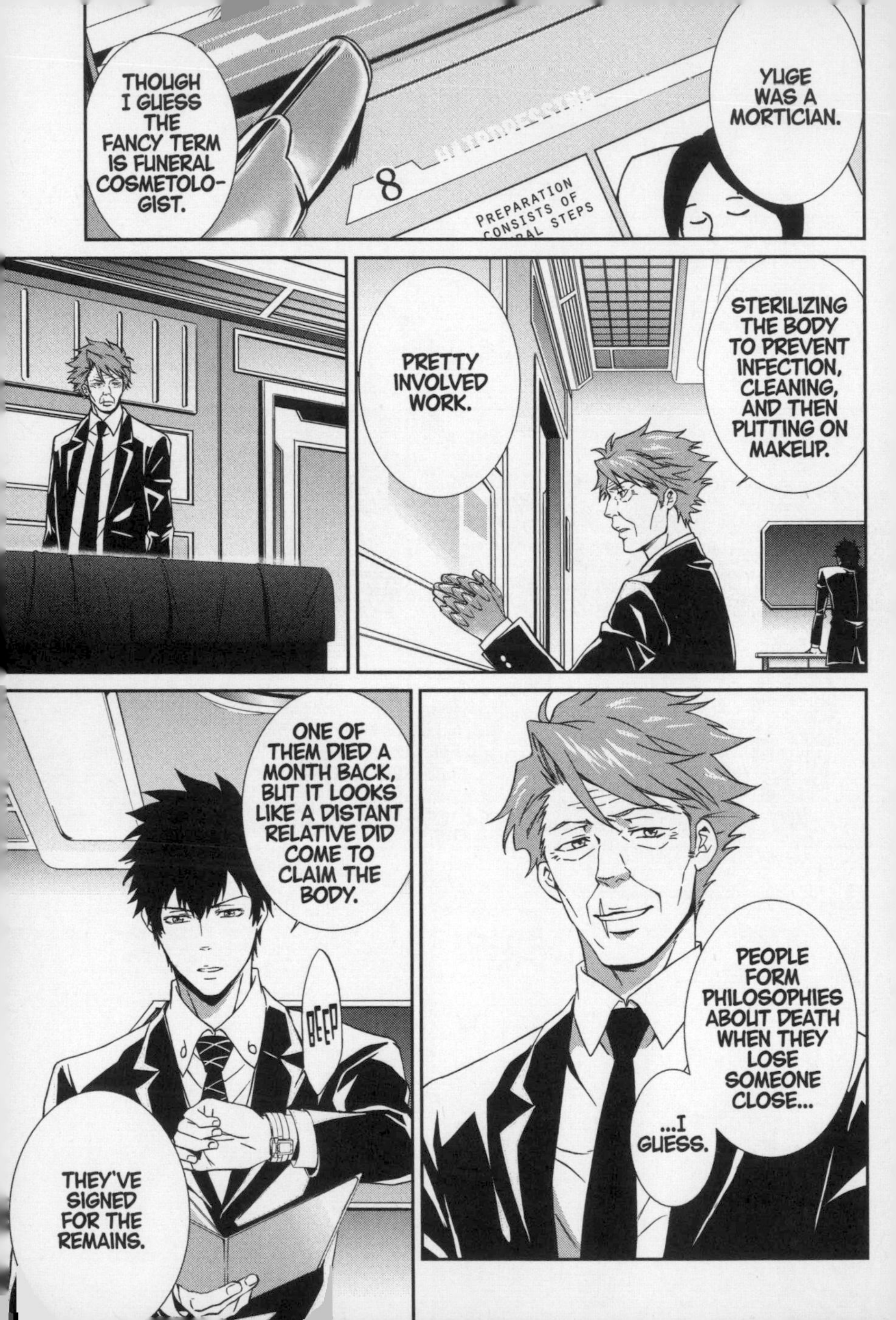
YUGE WAS A MORTICIAN.
THOUGH I GUESS THE FANCY TERM IS FUNERAL COSMETOLOGIST.
8
PREPARATION CONSISTS OF
STERILIZING THE BODY TO PREVENT INFECTION, CLEANING, AND THEN PUTTING ON MAKEUP.
PRETTY INVOLVED WORK.
PEOPLE FORM PHILOSOPHIES ABOUT DEATH WHEN THEY LOSE SOMEONE CLOSE...
...I GUESS.
ONE OF THEM DIED A MONTH BACK, BUT IT LOOKS LIKE A DISTANT RELATIVE DID COME TO CLAIM THE BODY.
BEEP
THEY'VE SIGNED FOR THE REMAINS.

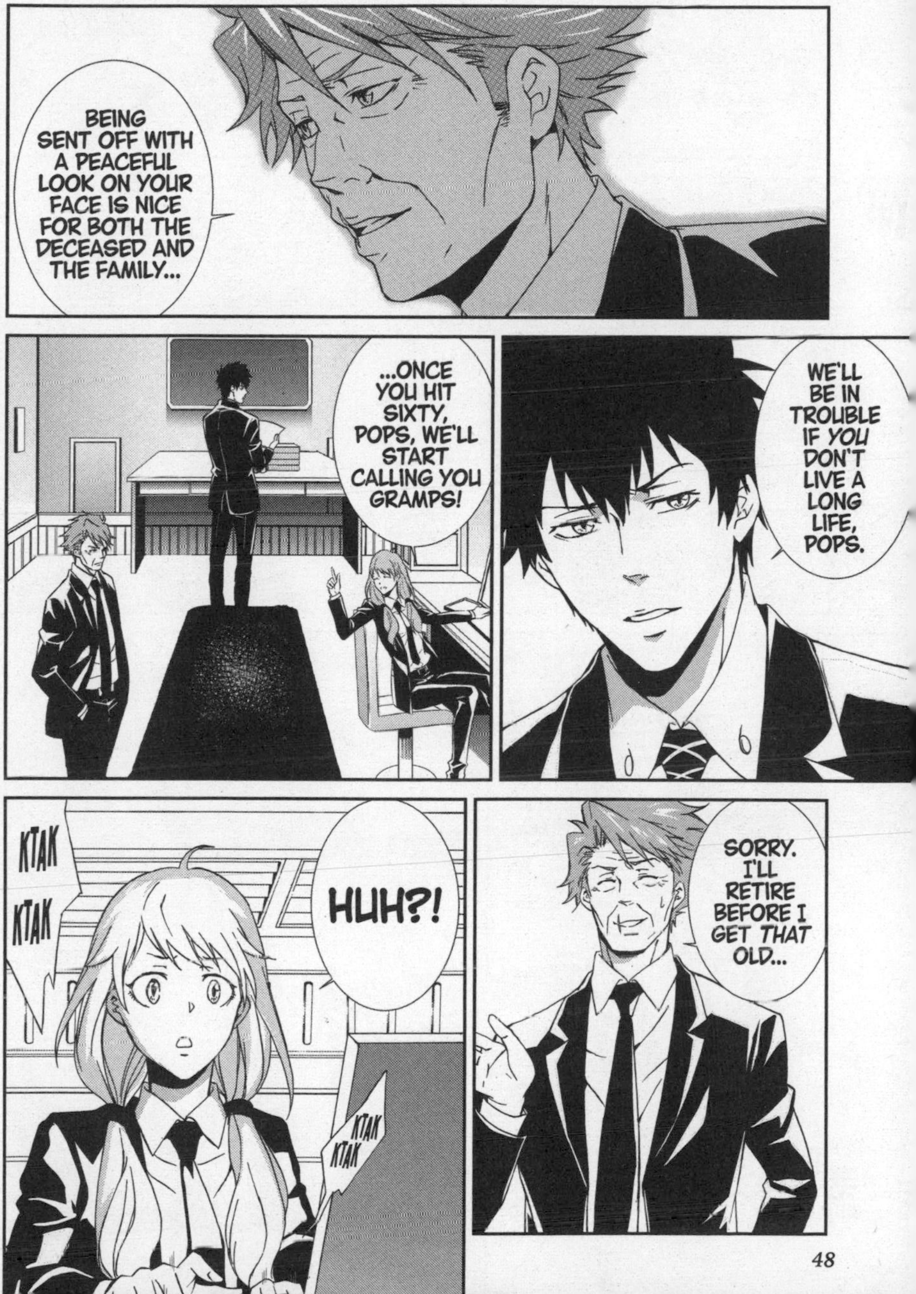
BEING SENT OFF WITH A PEACEFUL LOOK ON YOUR FACE IS NICE FOR BOTH THE DECEASED AND THE FAMILY...
WE'LL BE IN TROUBLE IF *YOU* DON'T LIVE A LONG LIFE, POPS.
...ONCE YOU HIT SIXTY, POPS, WE'LL START CALLING YOU GRAMPS!
SORRY. I'LL RETIRE BEFORE I GET *THAT* OLD...
HUH?!
KTAK KTAK
KTAK KTAK

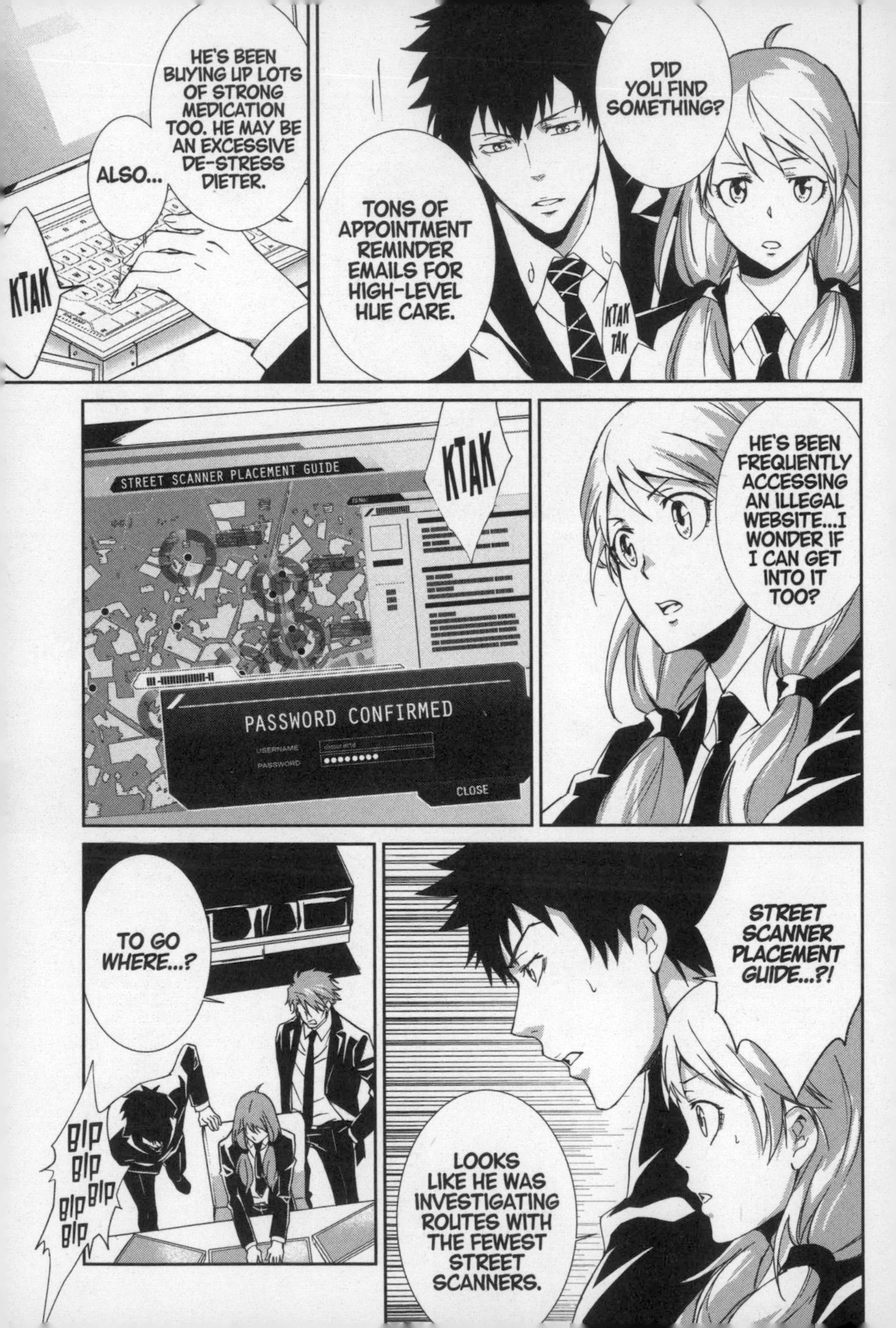
DID YOU FIND SOMETHING?
TONS OF APPOINTMENT REMINDER EMAILS FOR HIGH-LEVEL HUE CARE.
KTAK TAK
HE'S BEEN BUYING UP LOTS OF STRONG MEDICATION TOO. HE MAY BE AN EXCESSIVE DE-STRESS DIETER.
ALSO...
KTAK
HE'S BEEN FREQUENTLY ACCESSING AN ILLEGAL WEBSITE...I WONDER IF I CAN GET INTO IT TOO?
KTAK
STREET SCANNER PLACEMENT GUIDE
PASSWORD CONFIRMED
USERNAME
PASSWORD
CLOSE
STREET SCANNER PLACEMENT GUIDE...?!
LOOKS LIKE HE WAS INVESTIGATING ROUTES WITH THE FEWEST STREET SCANNERS.
TO GO WHERE...?
BIP BIP BIP BIP BIP

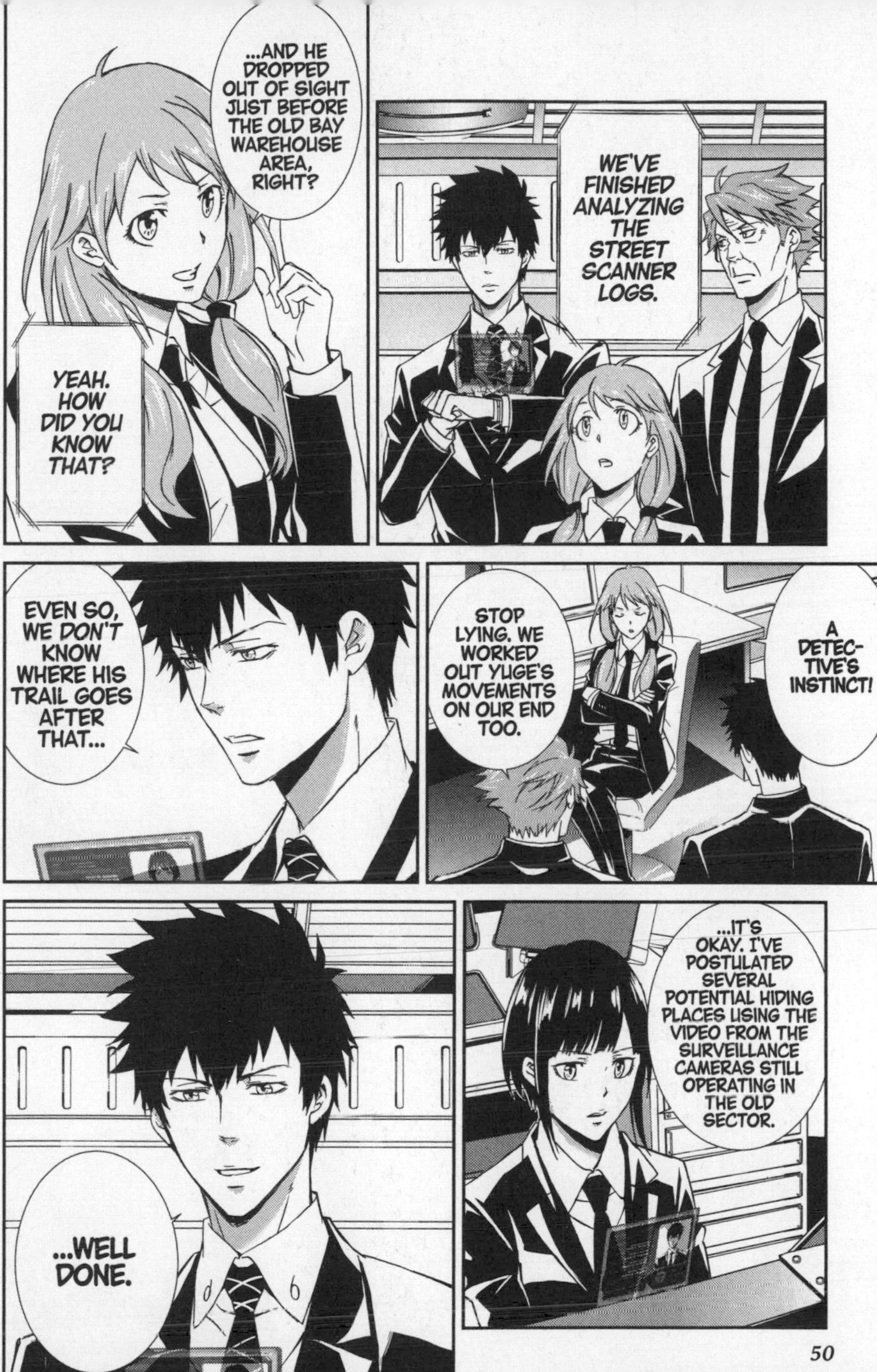

WE'VE FINISHED ANALYZING THE STREET SCANNER LOGS.
...AND HE DROPPED OUT OF SIGHT JUST BEFORE THE OLD BAY WAREHOUSE AREA, RIGHT?
YEAH. HOW DID YOU KNOW THAT?
A DETECTIVE'S INSTINCT!
STOP LYING. WE WORKED OUT YUGE'S MOVEMENTS ON OUR END TOO.
EVEN SO, WE DON'T KNOW WHERE HIS TRAIL GOES AFTER THAT...
...IT'S OKAY. I'VE POSTULATED SEVERAL POTENTIAL HIDING PLACES USING THE VIDEO FROM THE SURVEILLANCE CAMERAS STILL OPERATING IN THE OLD SECTOR.
...WELL DONE.

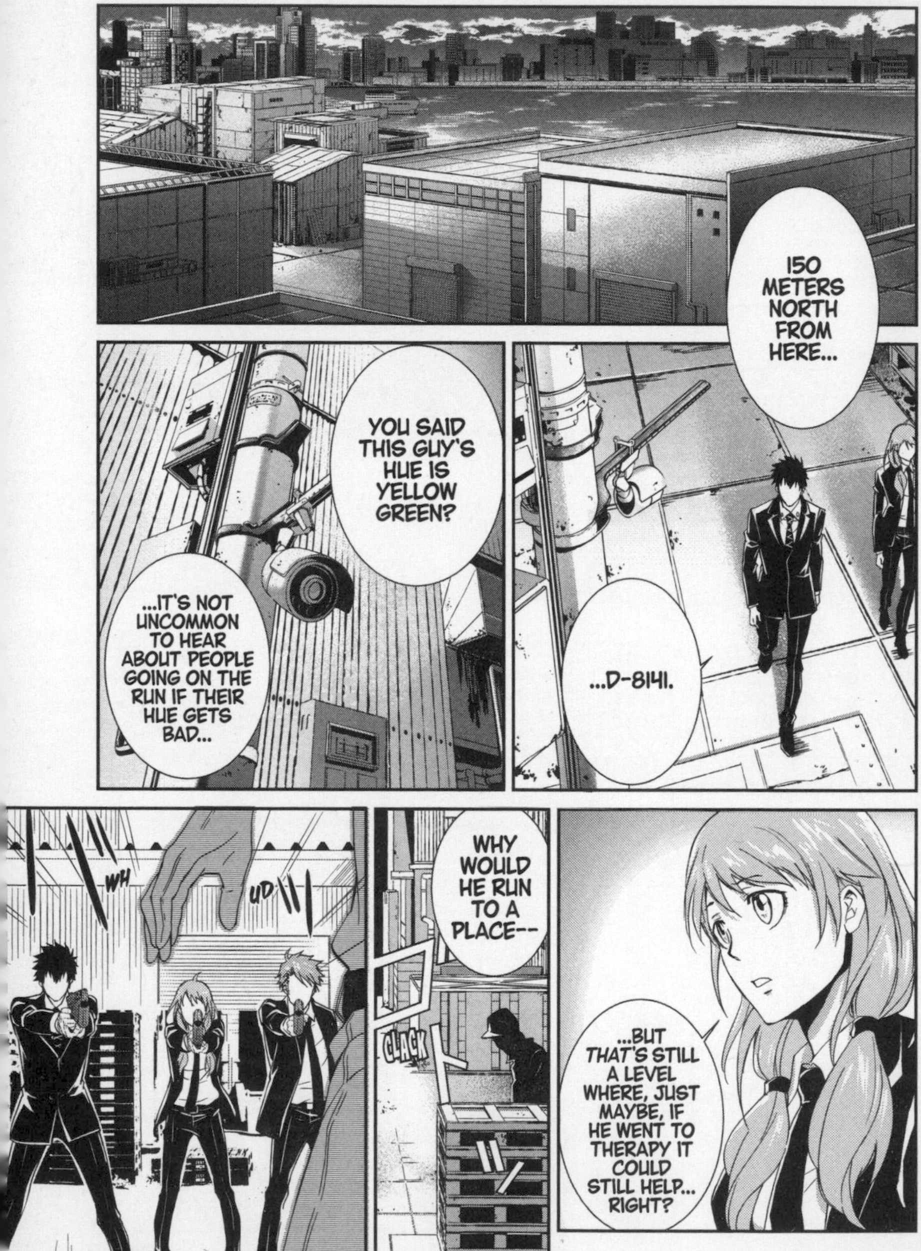
150 METERS NORTH FROM HERE...
...D-8141.
YOU SAID THIS GUY'S HUE IS YELLOW GREEN?
...IT'S NOT UNCOMMON TO HEAR ABOUT PEOPLE GOING ON THE RUN IF THEIR HUE GETS BAD...
...BUT *THAT'S* STILL A LEVEL WHERE, JUST MAYBE, IF HE WENT TO THERAPY IT COULD STILL HELP... RIGHT?
WHY WOULD HE RUN TO A PLACE--
CLACK
WH
UD

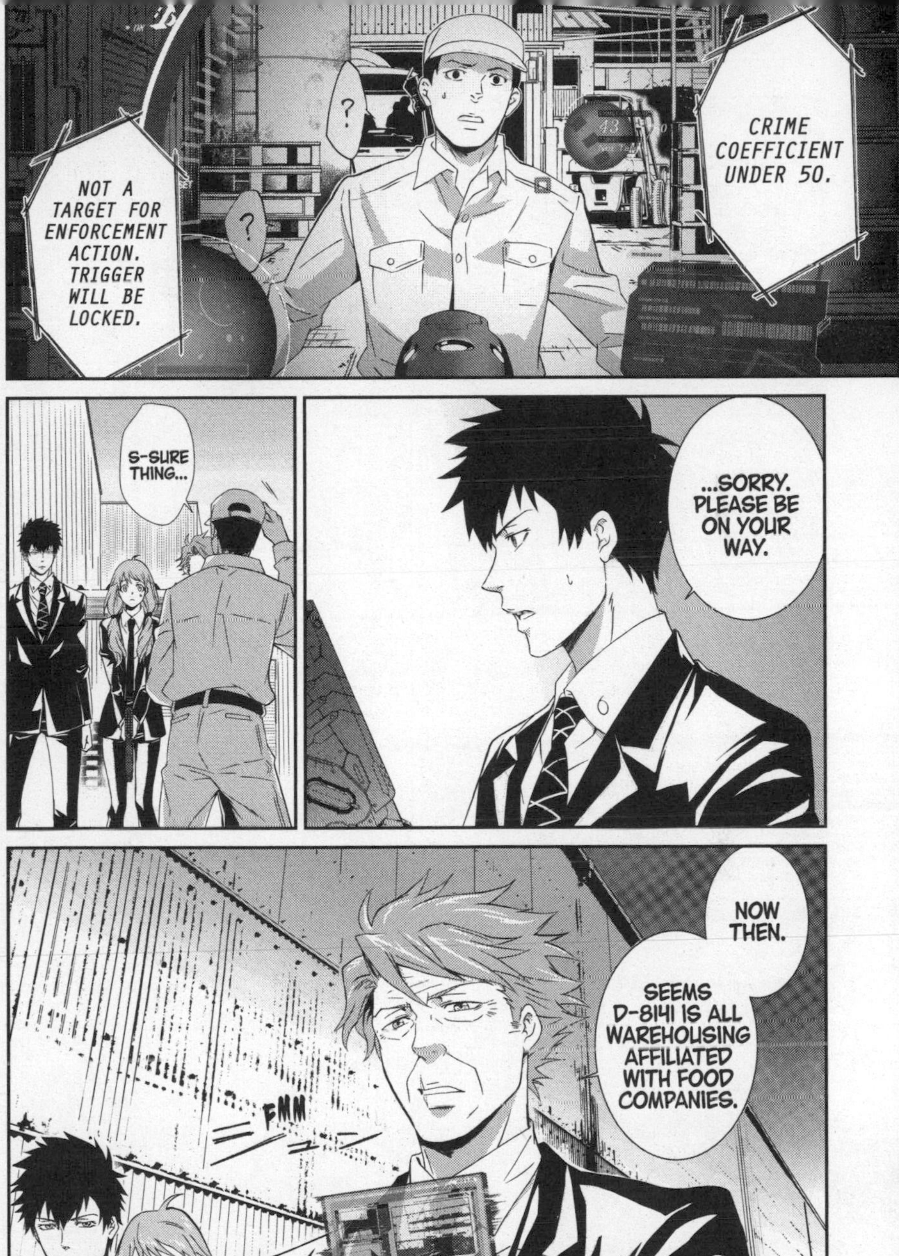
CRIME COEFFICIENT UNDER 50.
?
NOT A TARGET FOR ENFORCEMENT ACTION. TRIGGER WILL BE LOCKED.
?
...SORRY. PLEASE BE ON YOUR WAY.
S-SURE THING...
NOW THEN.
SEEMS D-8141 IS ALL WAREHOUSING AFFILIATED WITH FOOD COMPANIES.
FMM

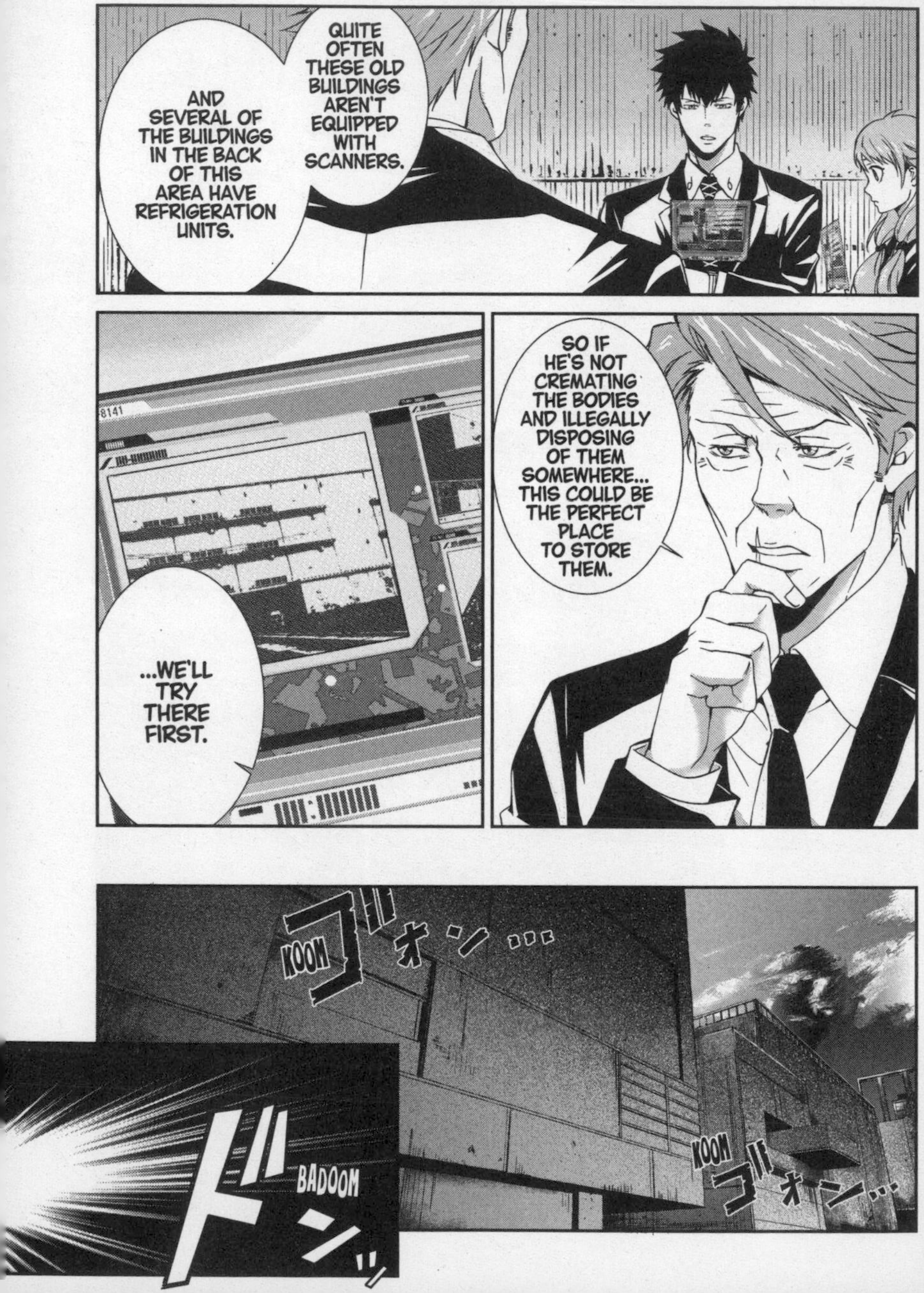
QUITE OFTEN THESE OLD BUILDINGS AREN'T EQUIPPED WITH SCANNERS.
AND SEVERAL OF THE BUILDINGS IN THE BACK OF THIS AREA HAVE REFRIGERATION UNITS.
SO IF HE'S NOT CREMATING THE BODIES AND ILLEGALLY DISPOSING OF THEM SOMEWHERE... THIS COULD BE THE PERFECT PLACE TO STORE THEM.
...WE'LL TRY THERE FIRST.
KOOM
KOOM
BADOOM

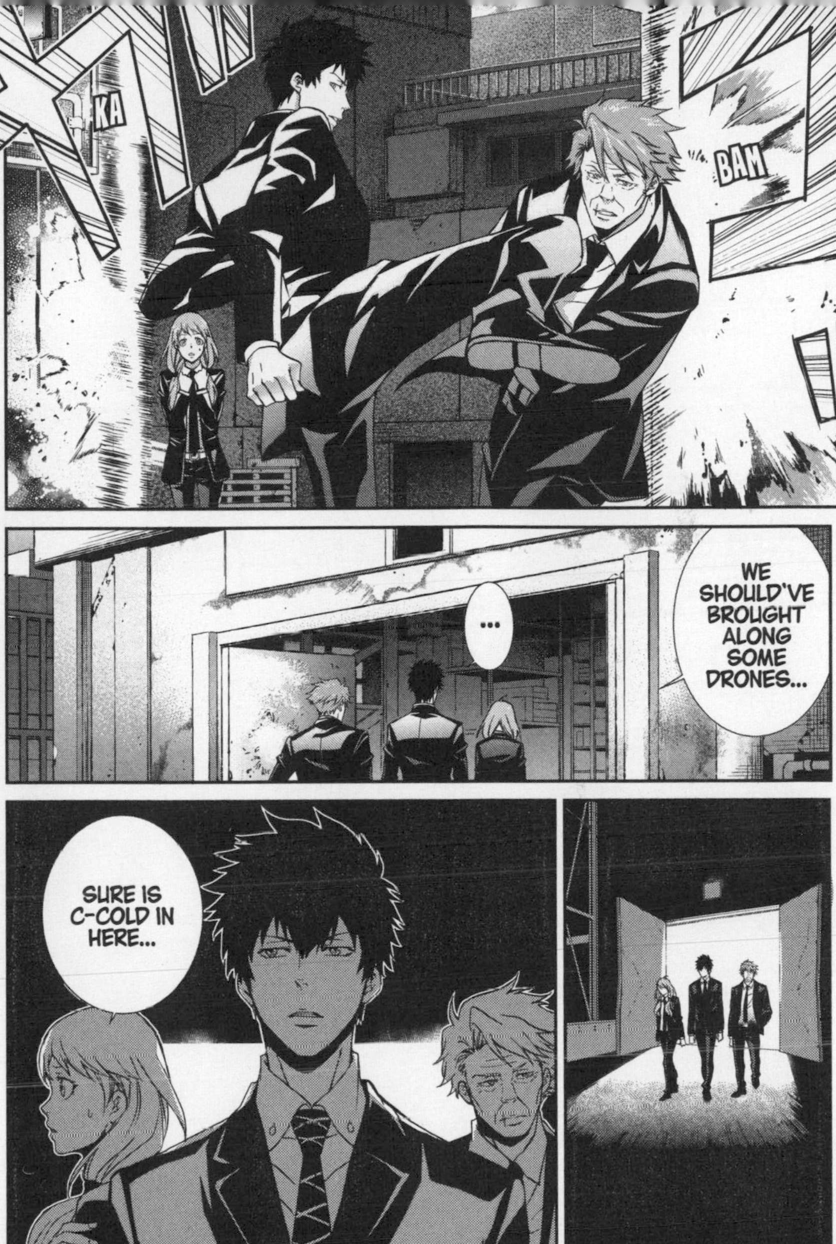
BAM
KA
WE SHOULD'VE BROUGHT ALONG SOME DRONES...
...
SURE IS C-COLD IN HERE...

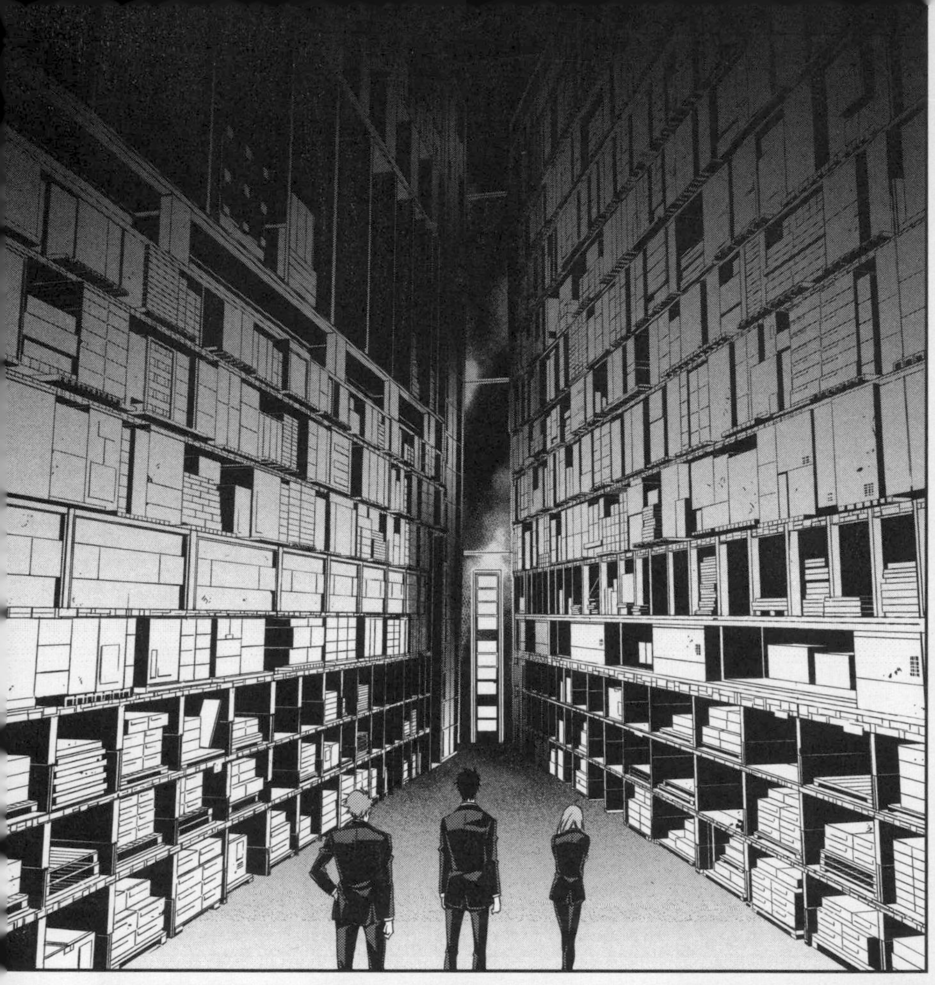

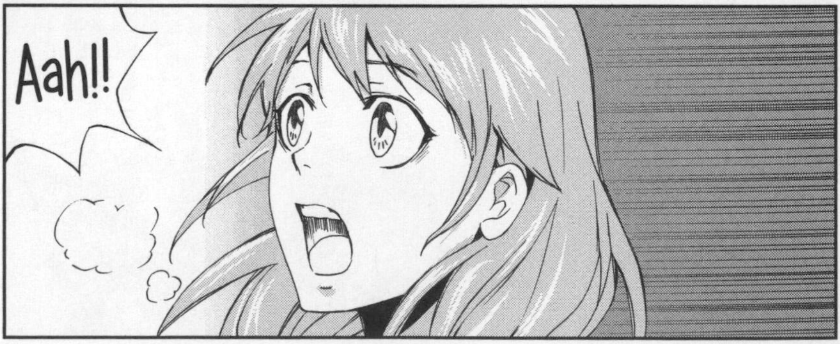
Aah!!

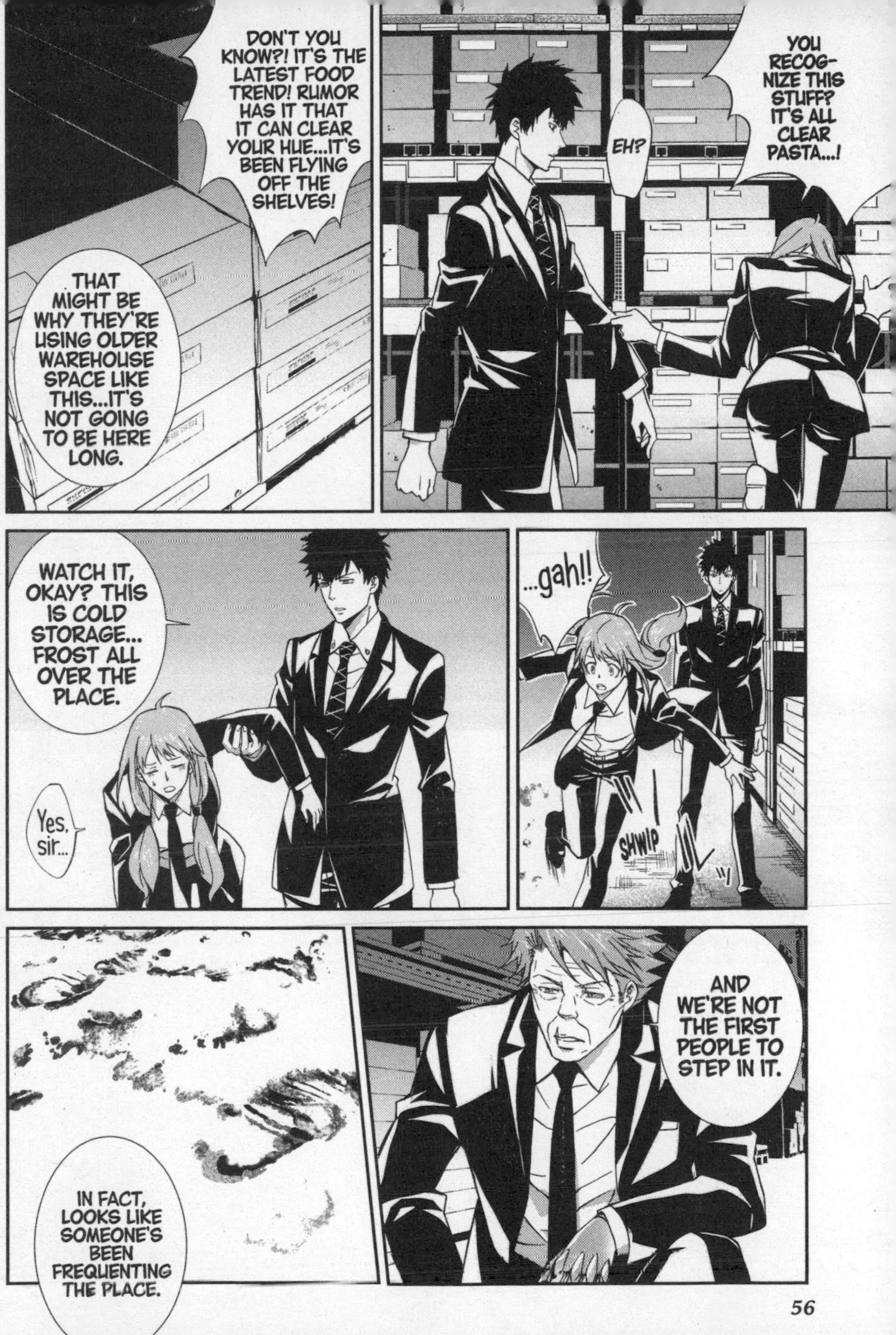
YOU RECOGNIZE THIS STUFF? IT'S ALL CLEAR PASTA...!
EH?
DON'T YOU KNOW?! IT'S THE LATEST FOOD TREND! RUMOR HAS IT THAT IT CAN CLEAR YOUR HUE...IT'S BEEN FLYING OFF THE SHELVES!
THAT MIGHT BE WHY THEY'RE USING OLDER WAREHOUSE SPACE LIKE THIS...IT'S NOT GOING TO BE HERE LONG.
...gah!!
SHWIP
WATCH IT, OKAY? THIS IS COLD STORAGE... FROST ALL OVER THE PLACE.
Yes, sir...
AND WE'RE NOT THE FIRST PEOPLE TO STEP IN IT.
IN FACT, LOOKS LIKE SOMEONE'S BEEN FREQUENTING THE PLACE.

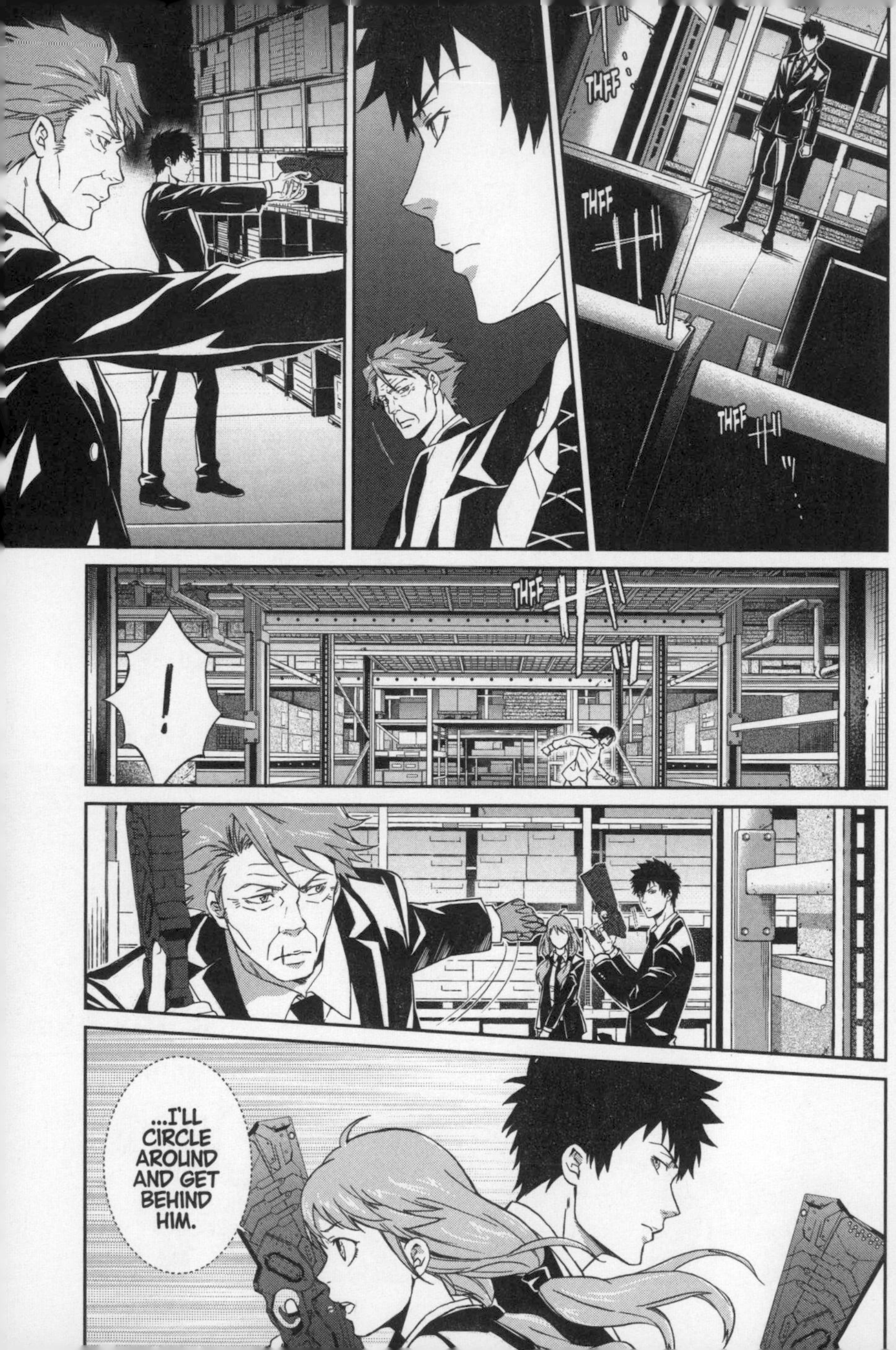
THFF
THFF
THFF
THFF
!
...I'LL CIRCLE AROUND AND GET BEHIND HIM.

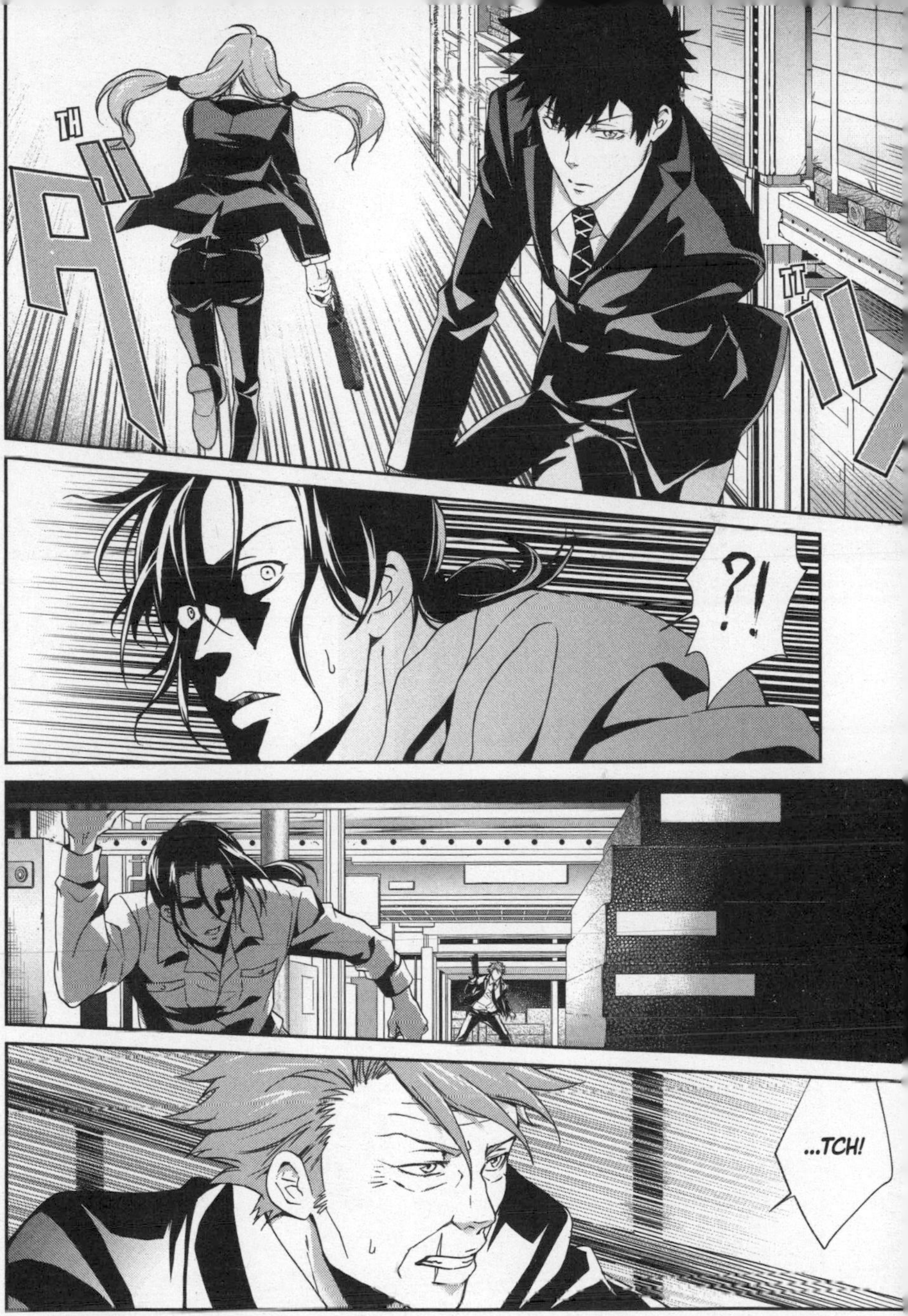
THWAM
TTHUD
?!
...TCH!

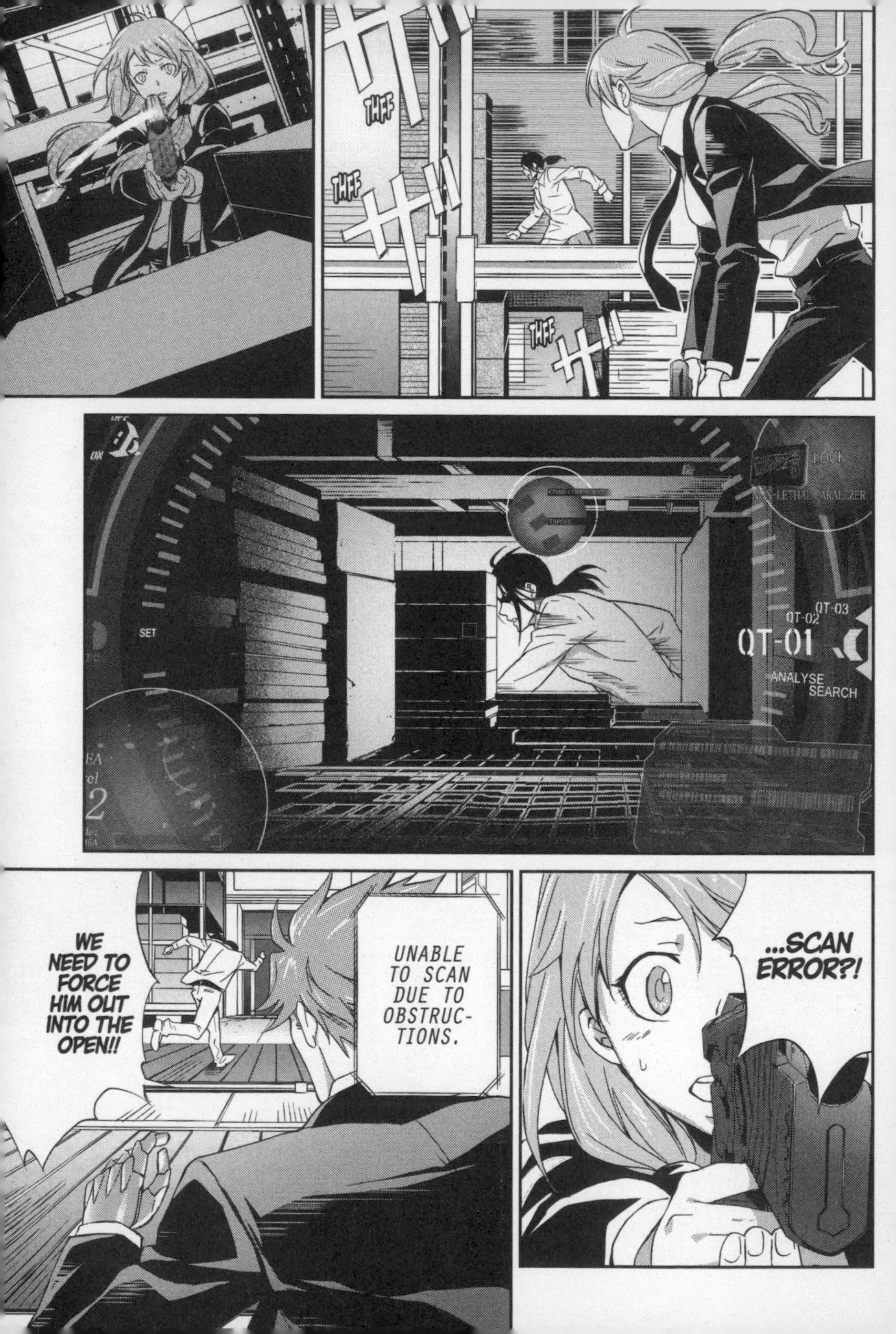
THFF
THFF
THFF
LOCK
QT-03
QT-02
QT-01
ANALYSE
SEARCH
SET
...SCAN ERROR?!
UNABLE TO SCAN DUE TO OBSTRUC- TIONS.
WE NEED TO FORCE HIM OUT INTO THE OPEN!!

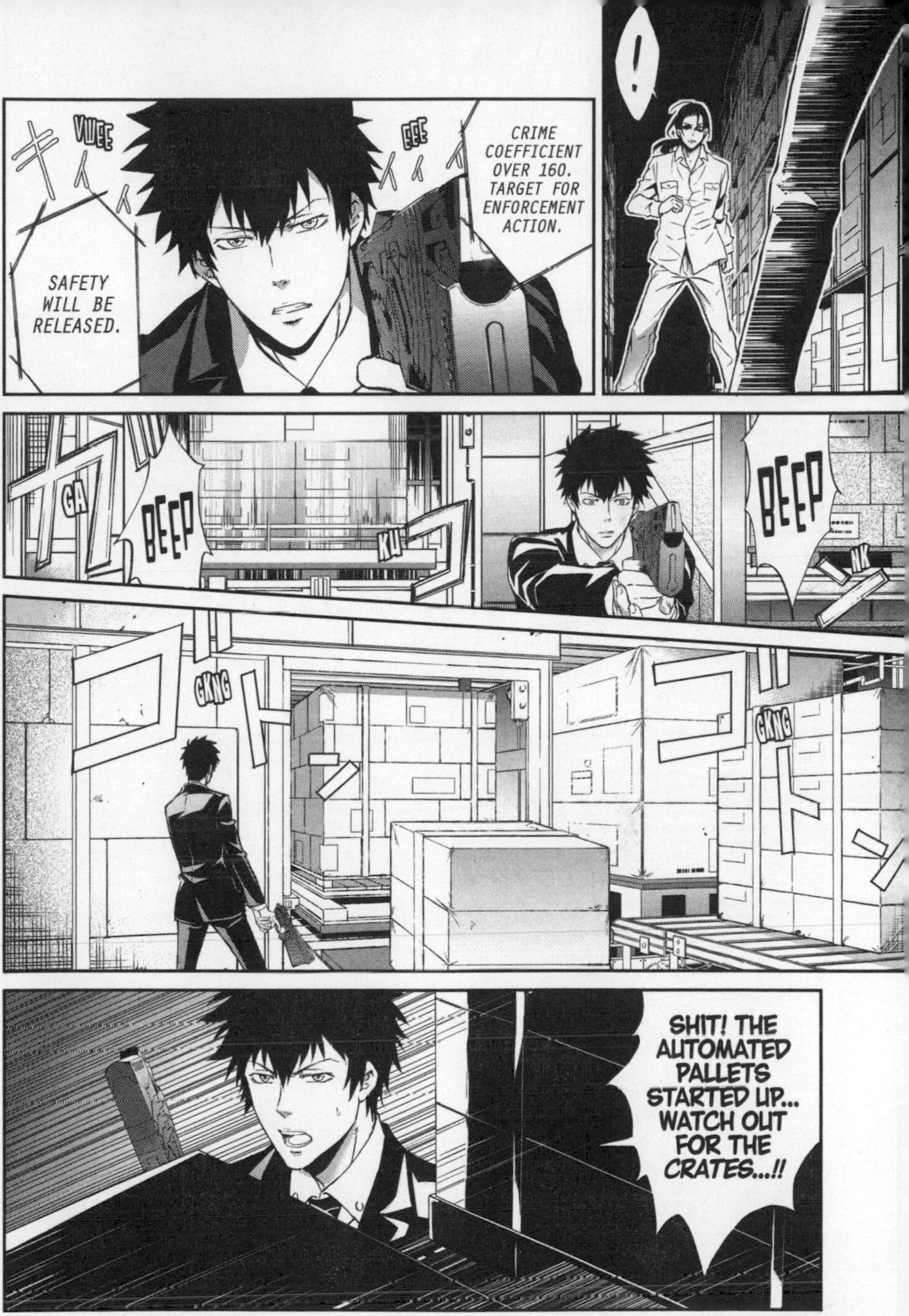
!
CRIME COEFFICIENT OVER 160. TARGET FOR ENFORCEMENT ACTION.
EEE
VWEE
SAFETY WILL BE RELEASED.
BEEP
NK
BEEP
GA
KU
GKNG
GKNG
SHIT! THE AUTOMATED PALLETS STARTED UP... WATCH OUT FOR THE CRATES...!!

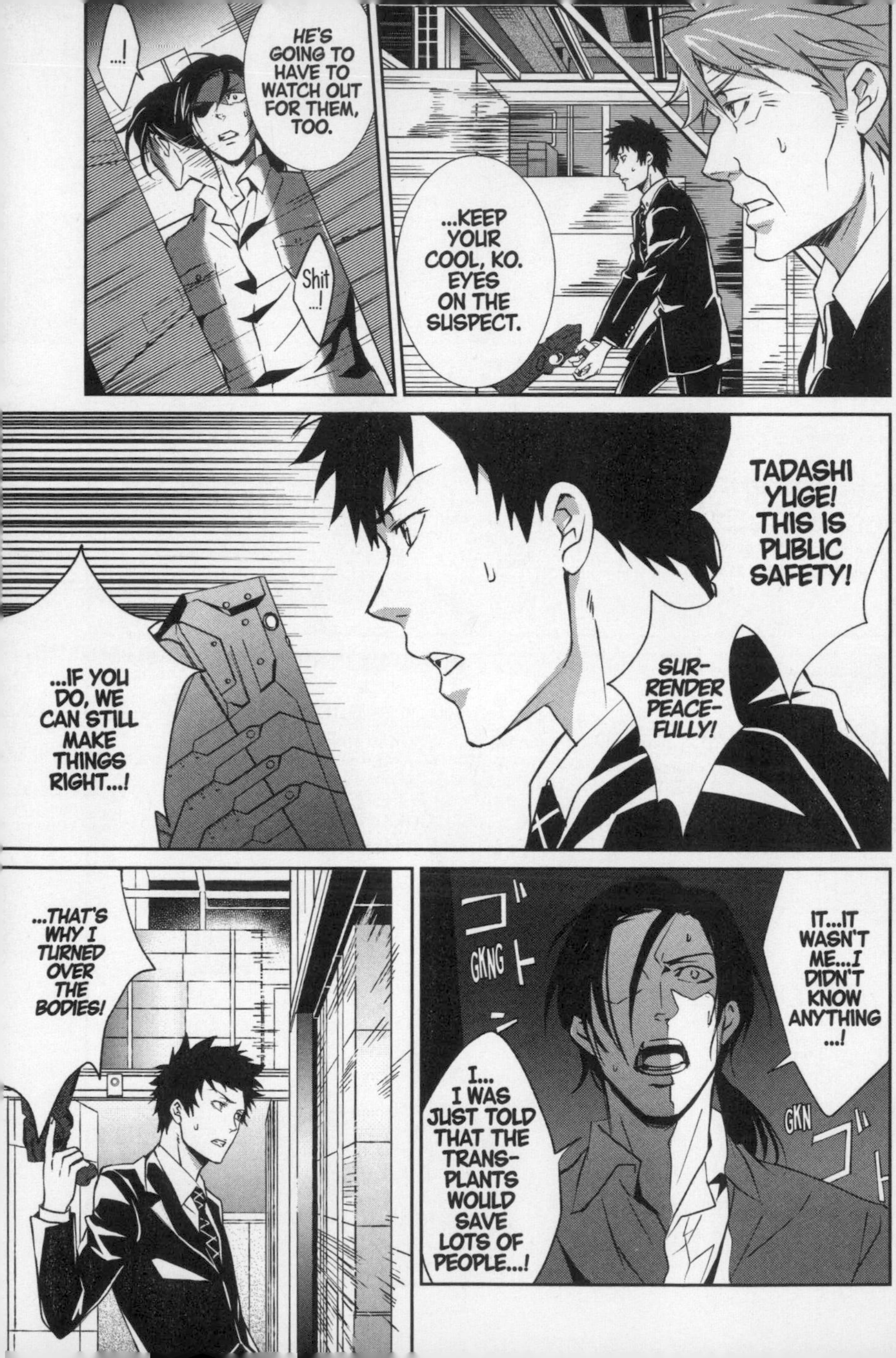
...KEEP YOUR COOL, KO. EYES ON THE SUSPECT.
HE'S GOING TO HAVE TO WATCH OUT FOR THEM, TOO.
...!
Shit ...!
TADASHI YUGE! THIS IS PUBLIC SAFETY!
SUR-RENDER PEACE-FULLY!
...IF YOU DO, WE CAN STILL MAKE THINGS RIGHT...!
IT...IT WASN'T ME...I DIDN'T KNOW ANYTHING ...!
GKNG
GKN
I... I WAS JUST TOLD THAT THE TRANS-PLANTS WOULD SAVE LOTS OF PEOPLE...!
...THAT'S WHY I TURNED OVER THE BODIES!

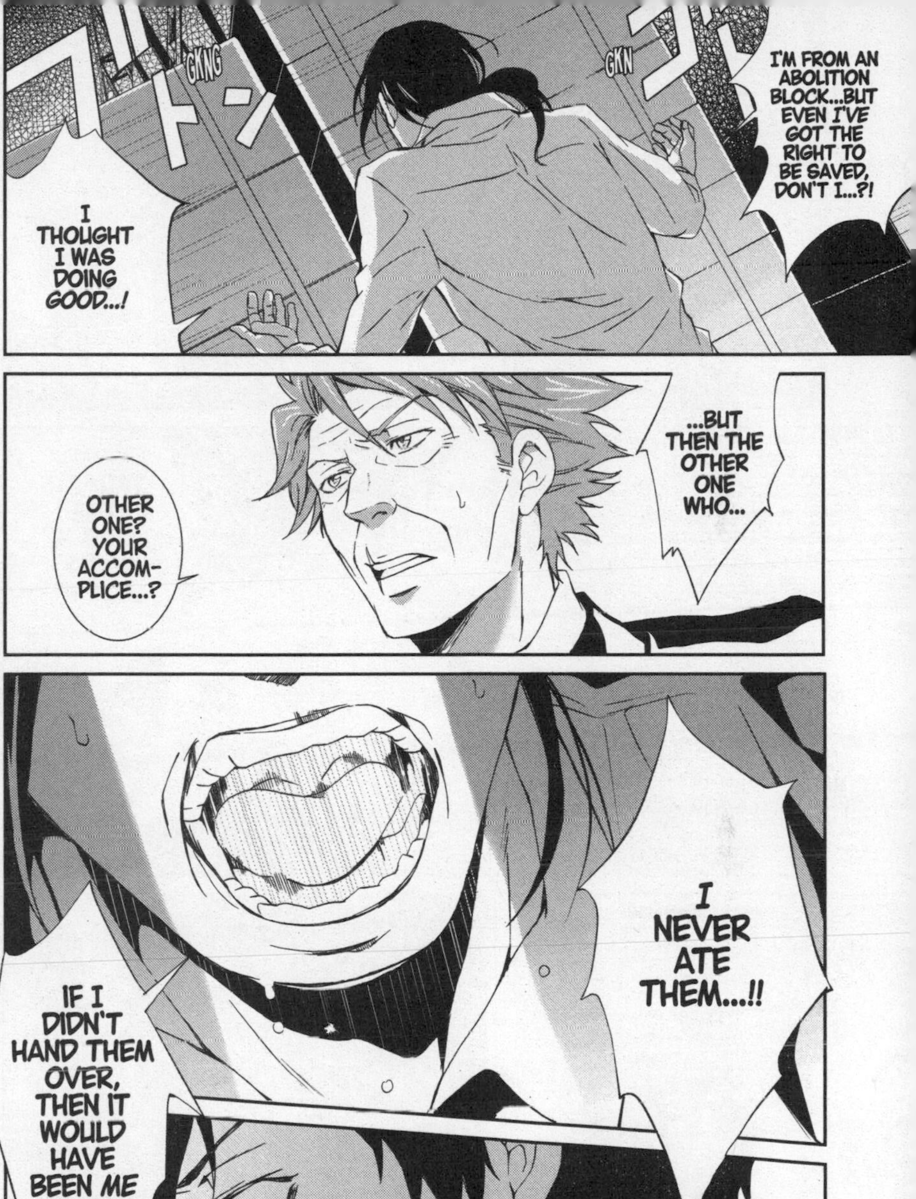
GKN
GKNG
I'M FROM AN ABOLITION BLOCK...BUT EVEN I'VE GOT THE RIGHT TO BE SAVED, DON'T I...?!
I THOUGHT I WAS DOING GOOD...!
...BUT THEN THE OTHER ONE WHO...
OTHER ONE? YOUR ACCOMPLICE...?
I NEVER ATE THEM...!!
IF I DIDN'T HAND THEM OVER, THEN IT WOULD HAVE BEEN ME INSTEAD THAT...

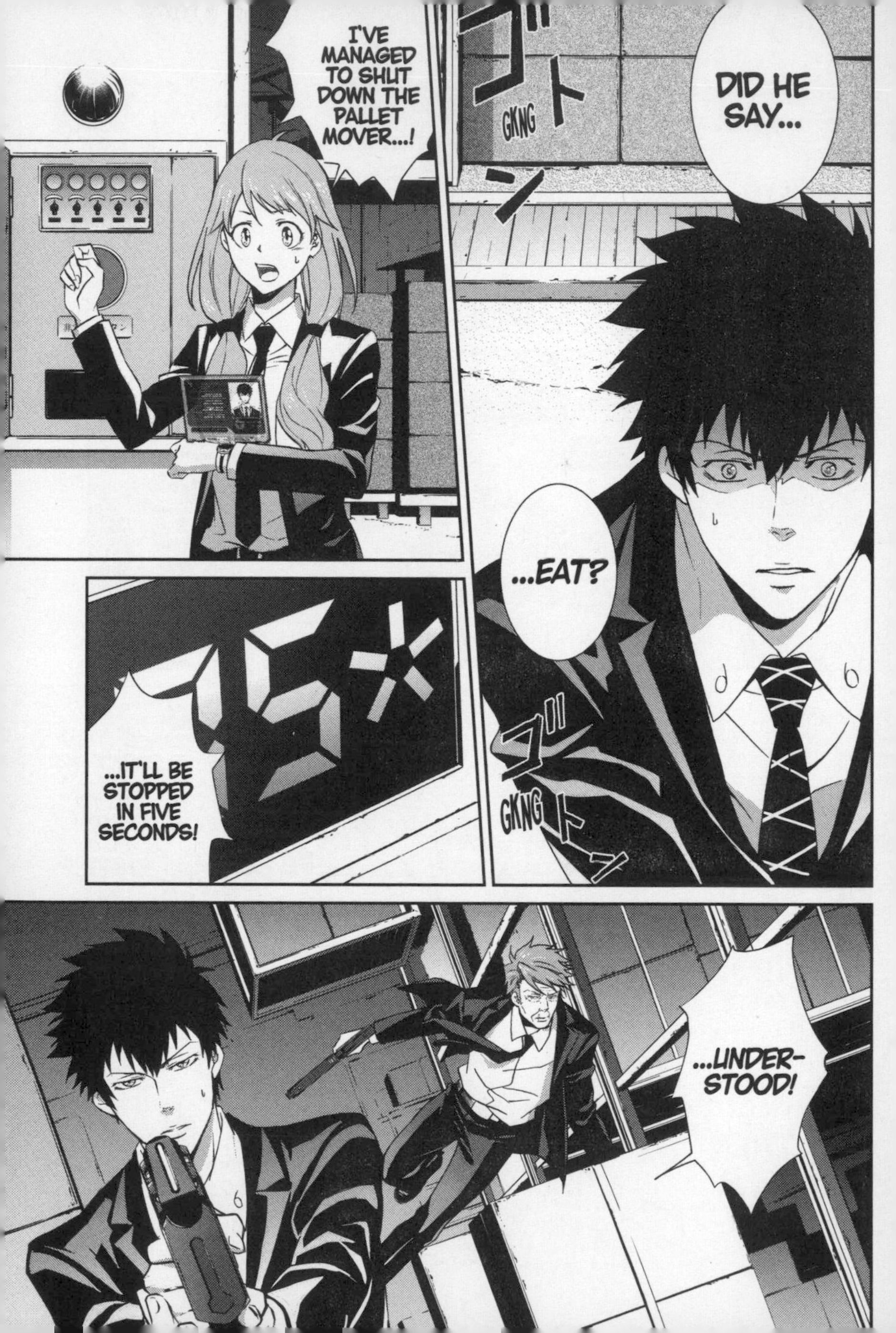
DID HE SAY...
GKNG
...EAT?
GKNG
I'VE MANAGED TO SHUT DOWN THE PALLET MOVER...!
...IT'LL BE STOPPED IN FIVE SECONDS!
...UNDER-STOOD!

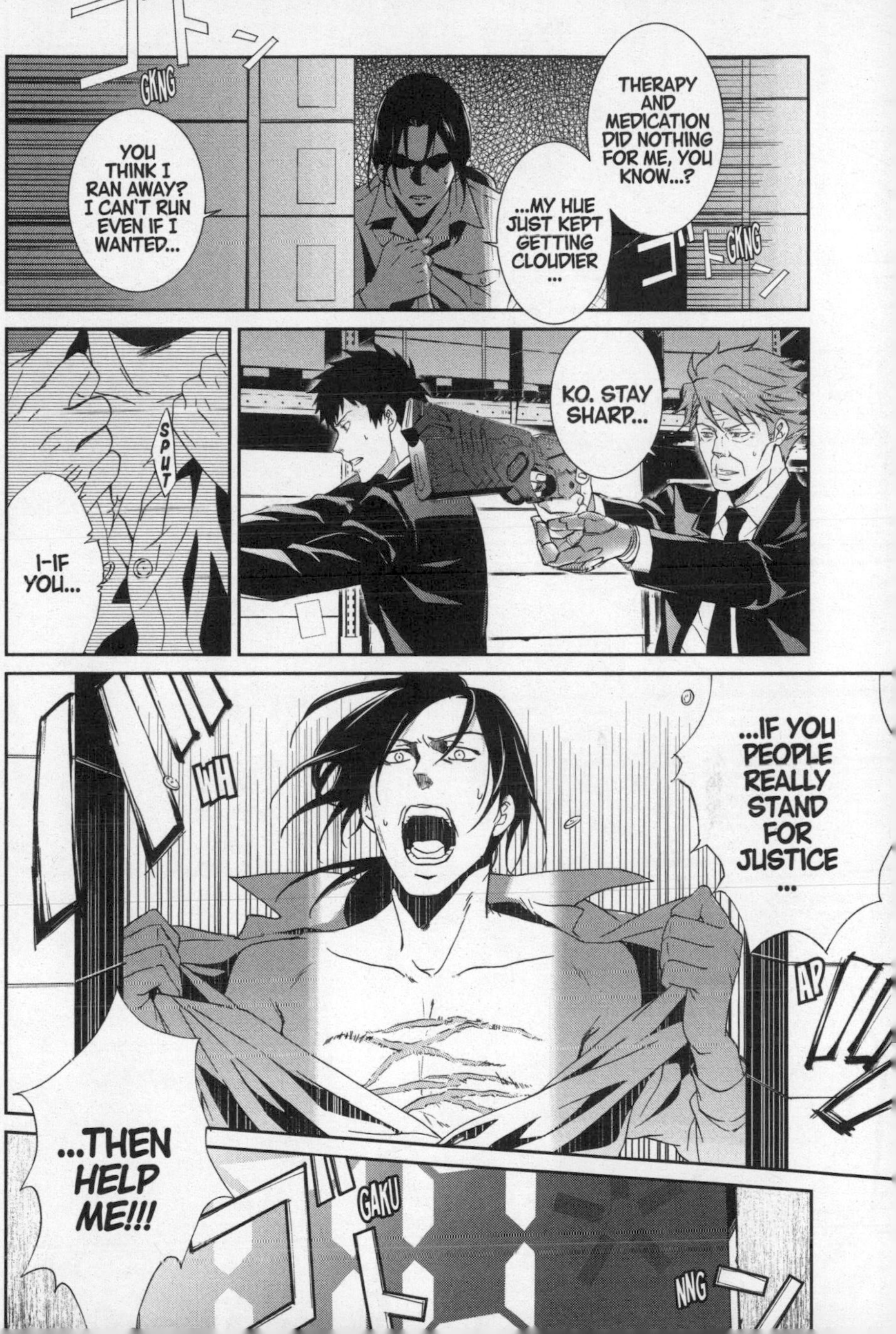
THERAPY AND MEDICATION DID NOTHING FOR ME, YOU KNOW...?
...MY HUE JUST KEPT GETTING CLOUDIER...
GKNG
YOU THINK I RAN AWAY? I CAN'T RUN EVEN IF I WANTED...
GKNG
KO. STAY SHARP...
SPUT
I-IF YOU...
...IF YOU PEOPLE REALLY STAND FOR JUSTICE...
AP
WH
...THEN HELP ME!!!
GAKU
NNG

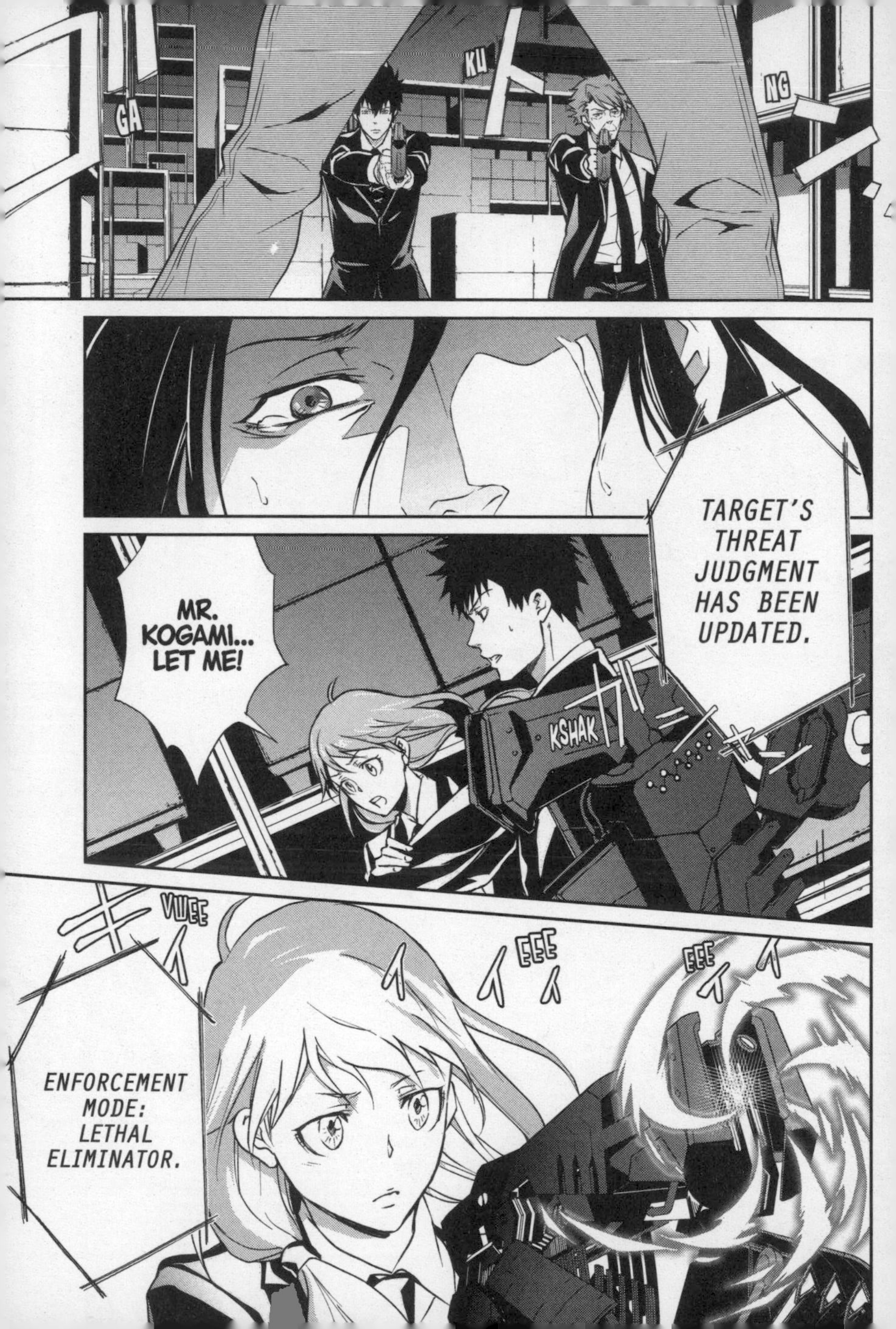
NG
KU
GA
TARGET'S THREAT JUDGMENT HAS BEEN UPDATED.
MR. KOGAMI... LET ME!
KSHAK
EEE
EEE
VWEE
ENFORCEMENT MODE: LETHAL ELIMINATOR.

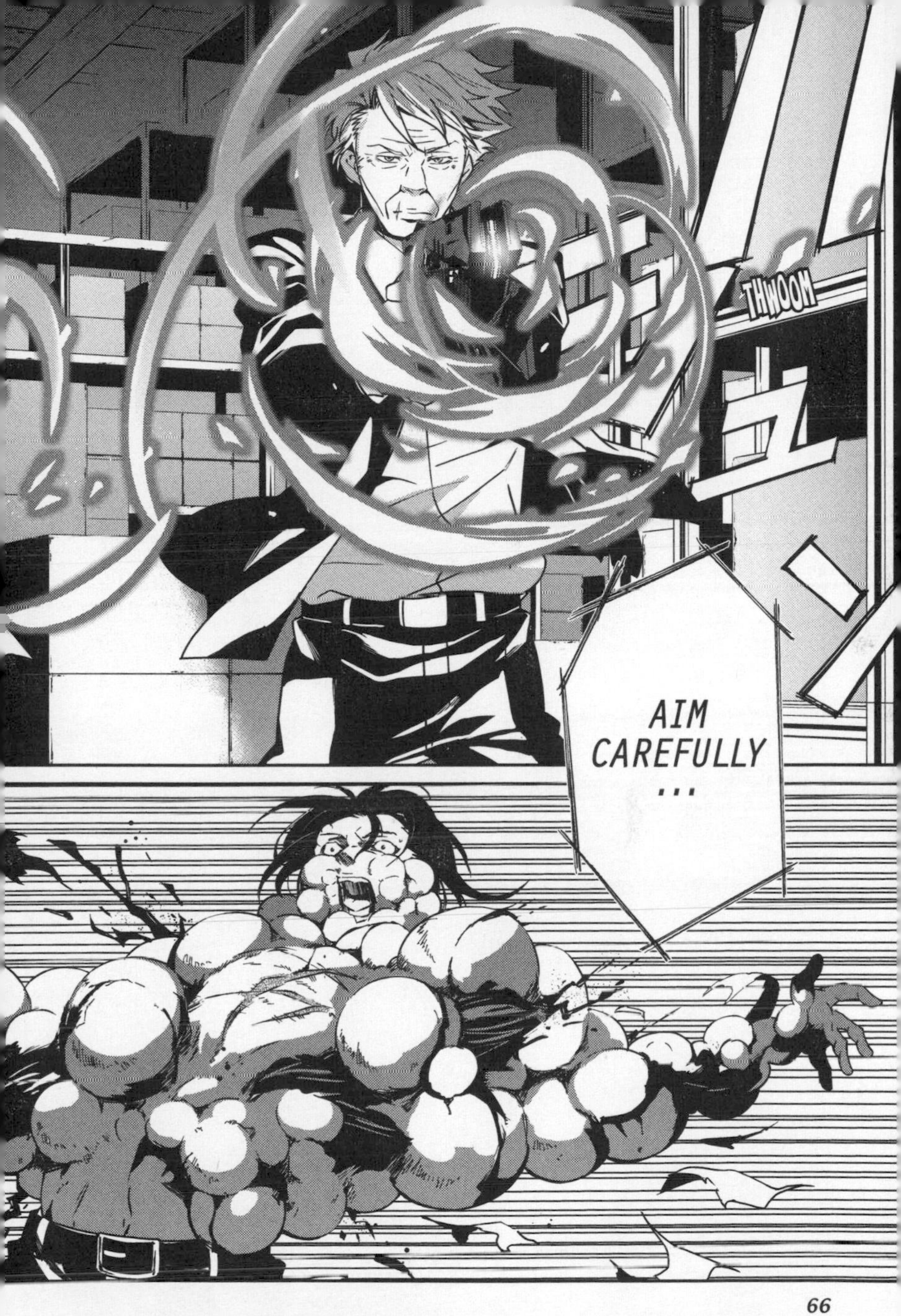
THWOOM
AIM CAREFULLY ...

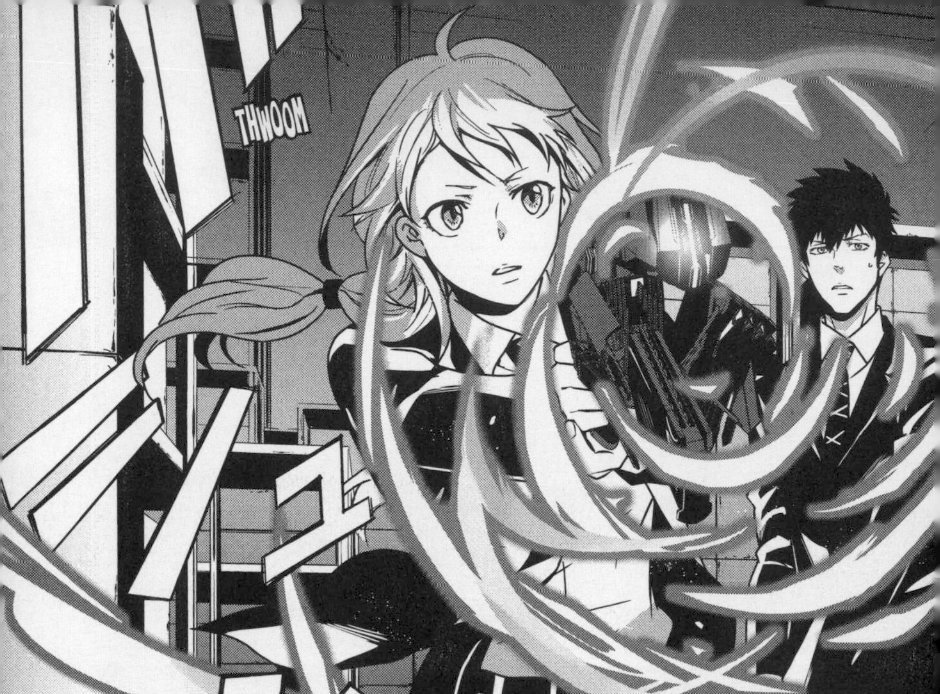
THWOOM
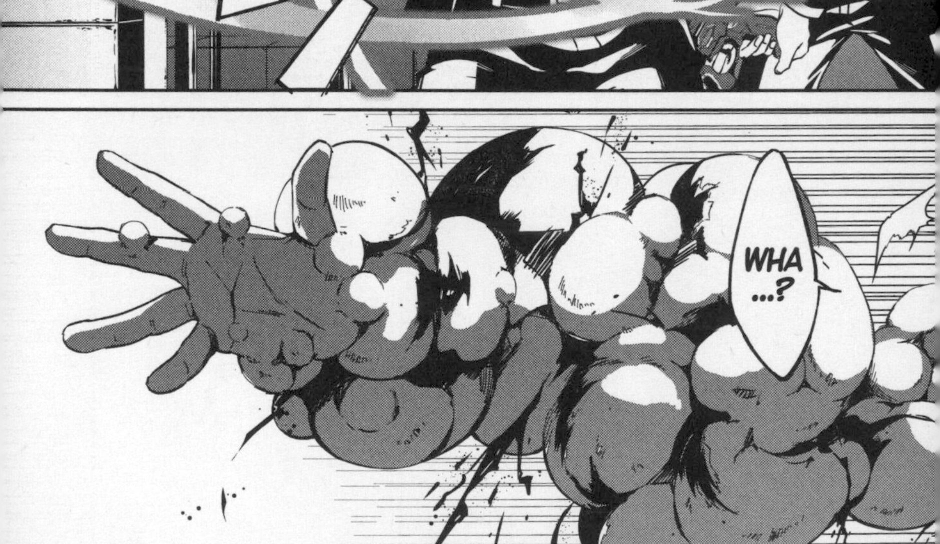
WHA ...?

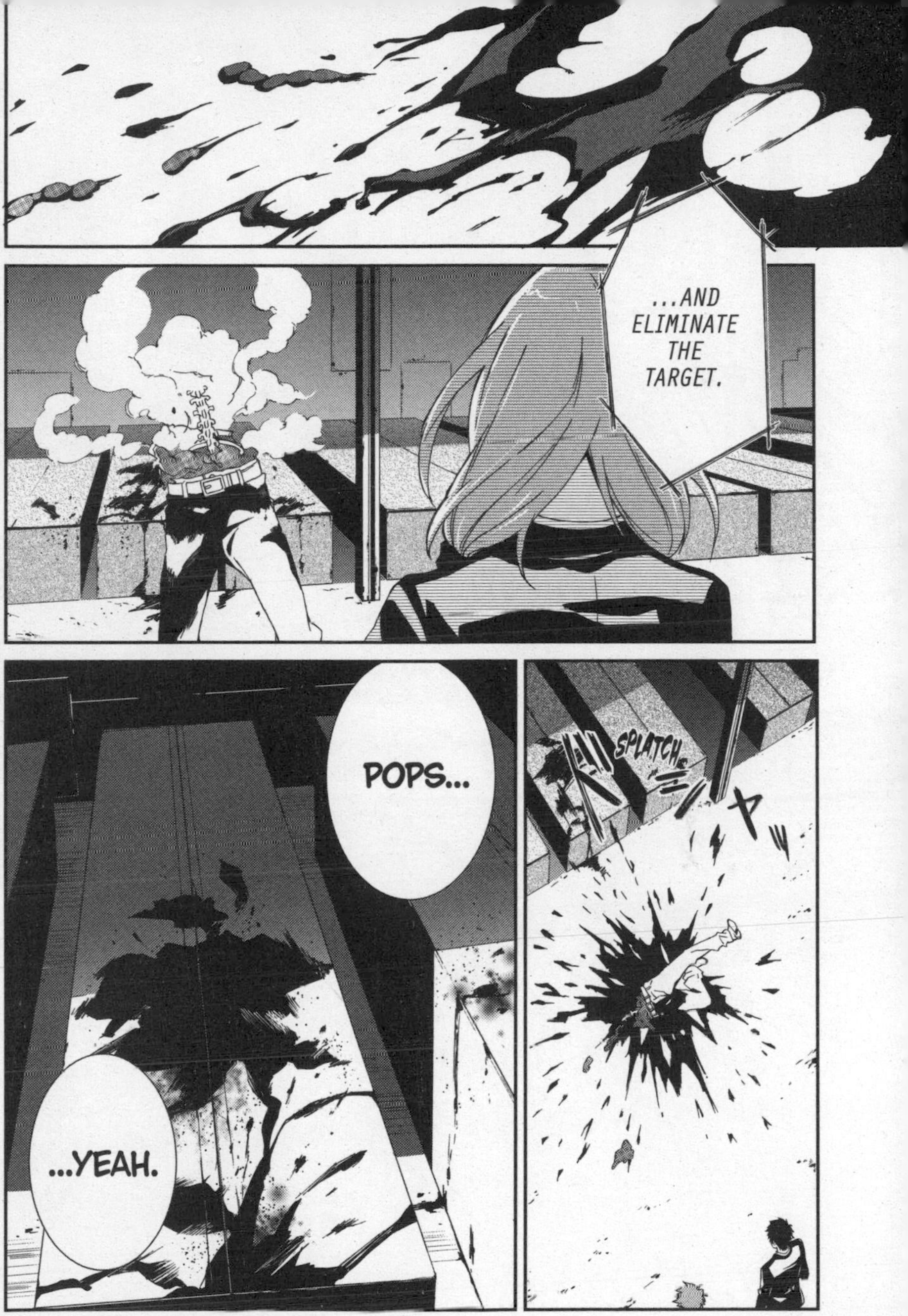
...AND ELIMINATE THE TARGET.
SPLATCH
POPS...
...YEAH.

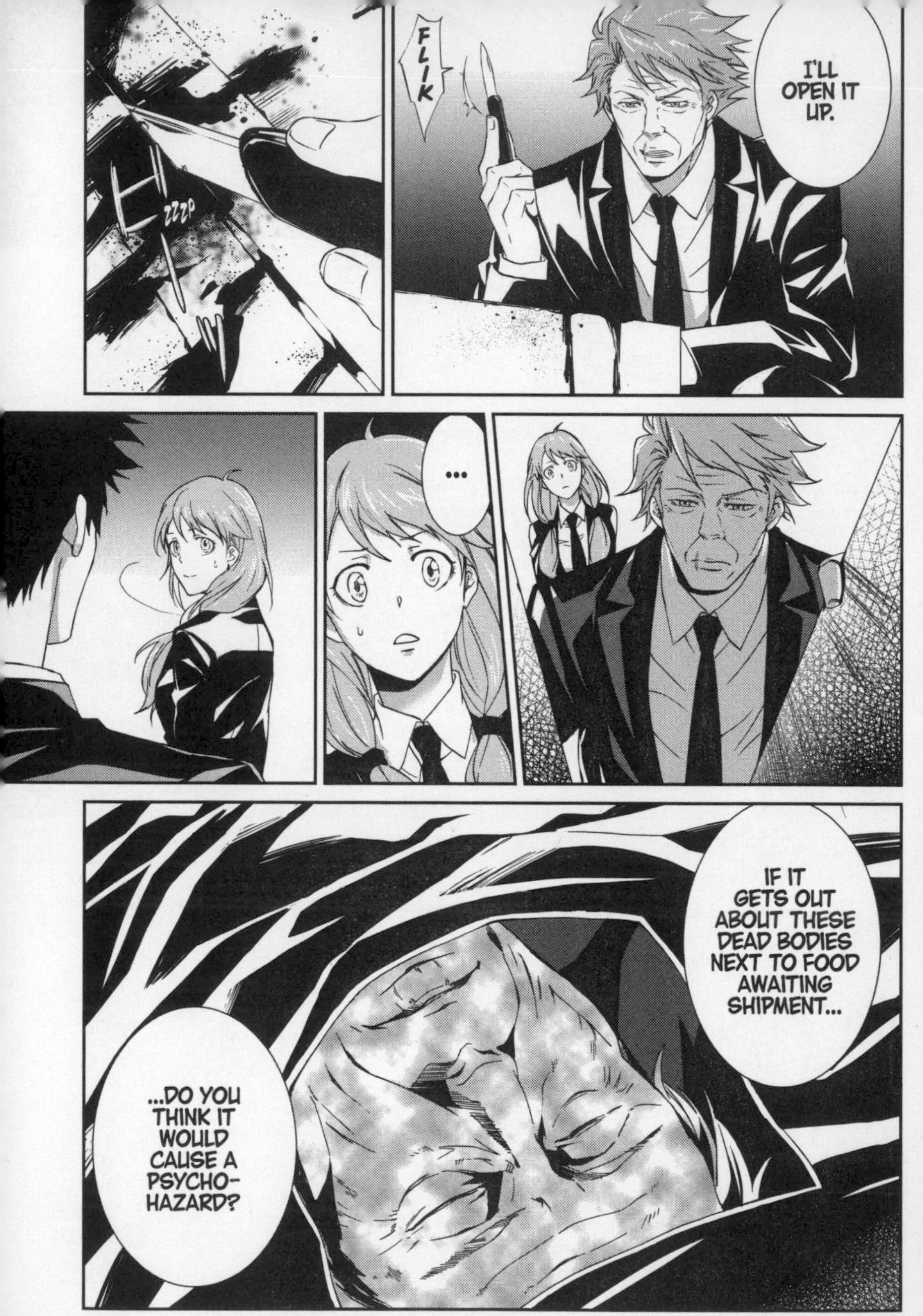
I'LL OPEN IT UP.
FLIK
ZZZP
...
IF IT GETS OUT ABOUT THESE DEAD BODIES NEXT TO FOOD AWAITING SHIPMENT...
...DO YOU THINK IT WOULD CAUSE A PSYCHO-HAZARD?

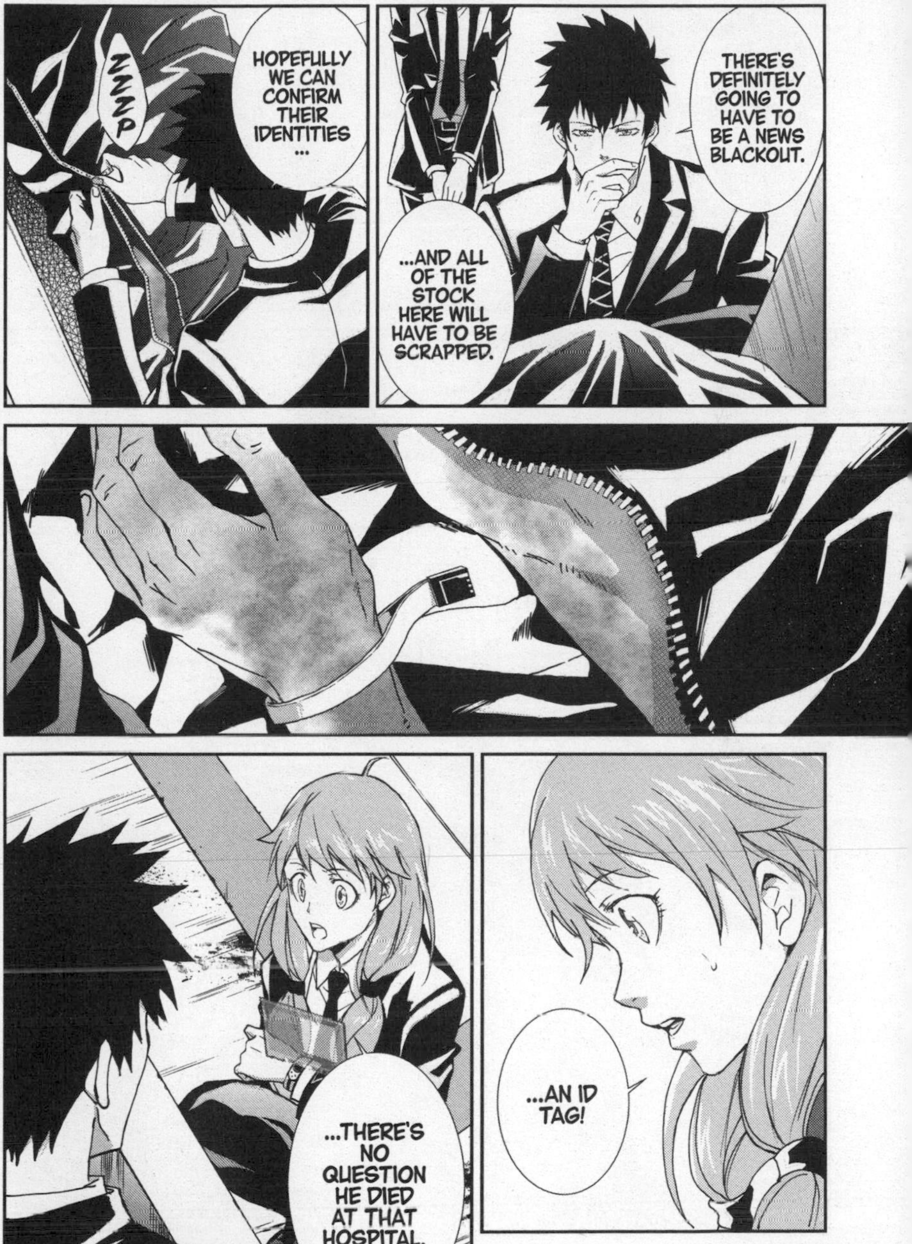
THERE'S DEFINITELY GOING TO HAVE TO BE A NEWS BLACKOUT.
...AND ALL OF THE STOCK HERE WILL HAVE TO BE SCRAPPED.
HOPEFULLY WE CAN CONFIRM THEIR IDENTITIES ...
ZZZP
...AN ID TAG!
...THERE'S NO QUESTION HE DIED AT THAT HOSPITAL.

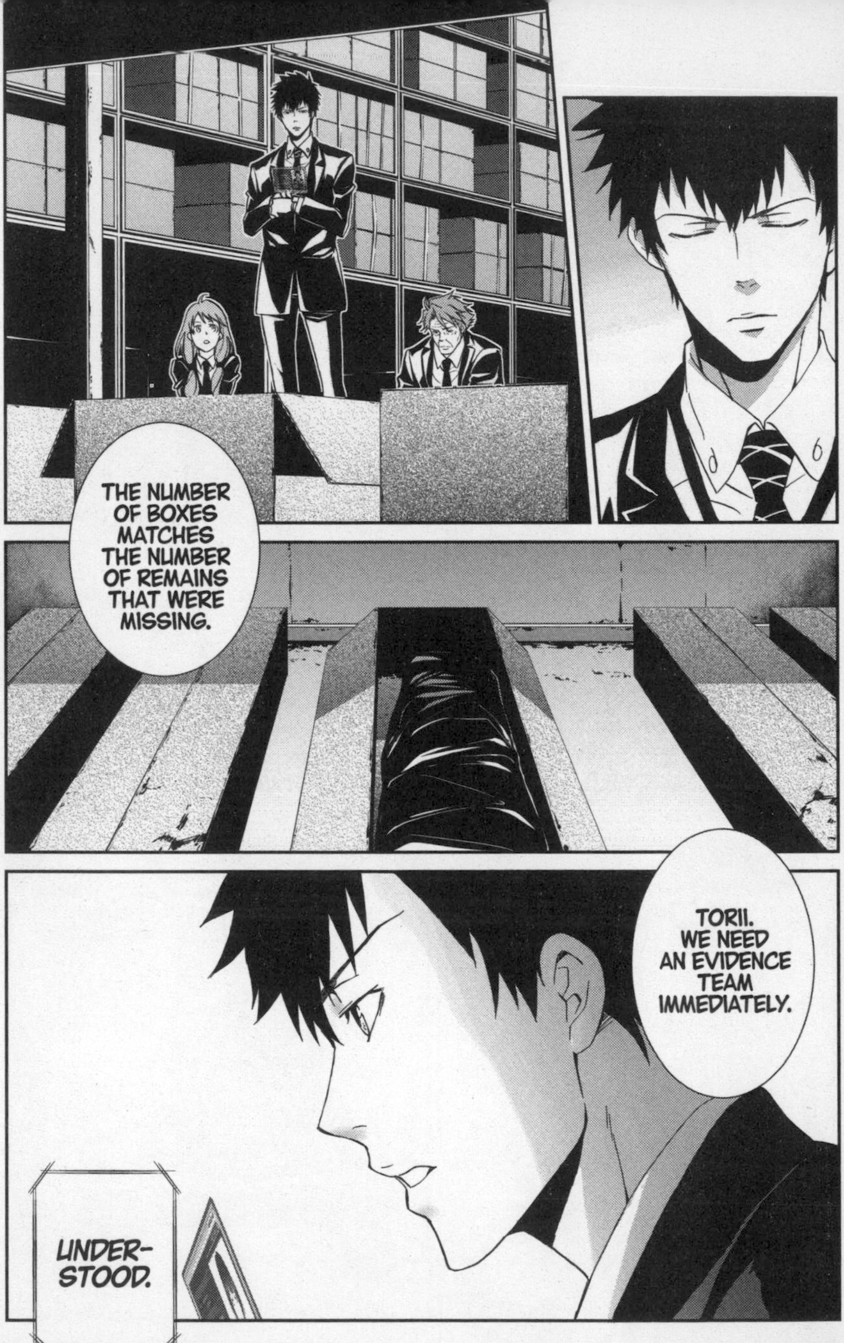
THE NUMBER OF BOXES MATCHES THE NUMBER OF REMAINS THAT WERE MISSING.
TORII. WE NEED AN EVIDENCE TEAM IMMEDIATELY.
UNDER-STOOD.

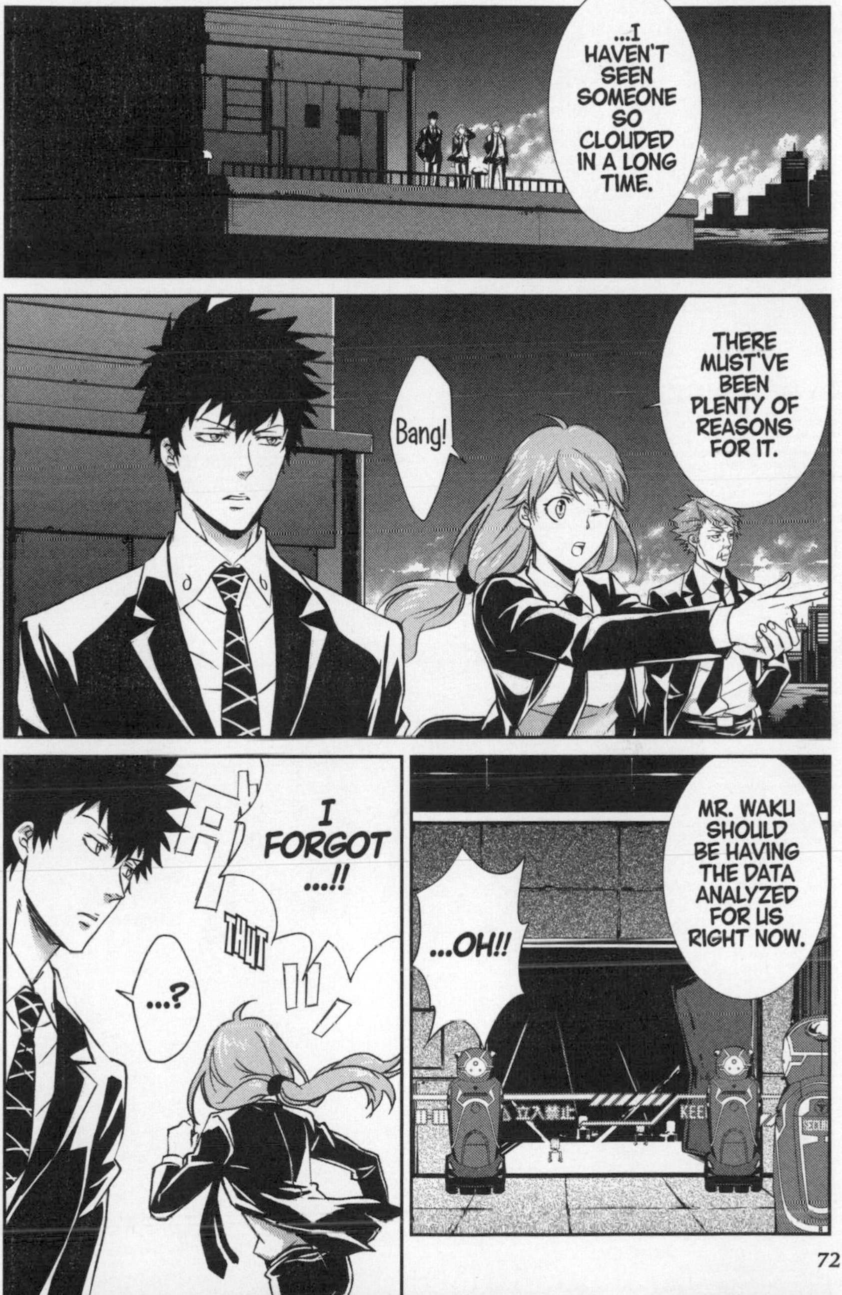
...I HAVEN'T SEEN SOMEONE SO CLOUDED IN A LONG TIME.
THERE MUST'VE BEEN PLENTY OF REASONS FOR IT.
Bang!
MR. WAKU SHOULD BE HAVING THE DATA ANALYZED FOR US RIGHT NOW.
立入禁止
...OH!!
I FORGOT ...!!
THUT
...?

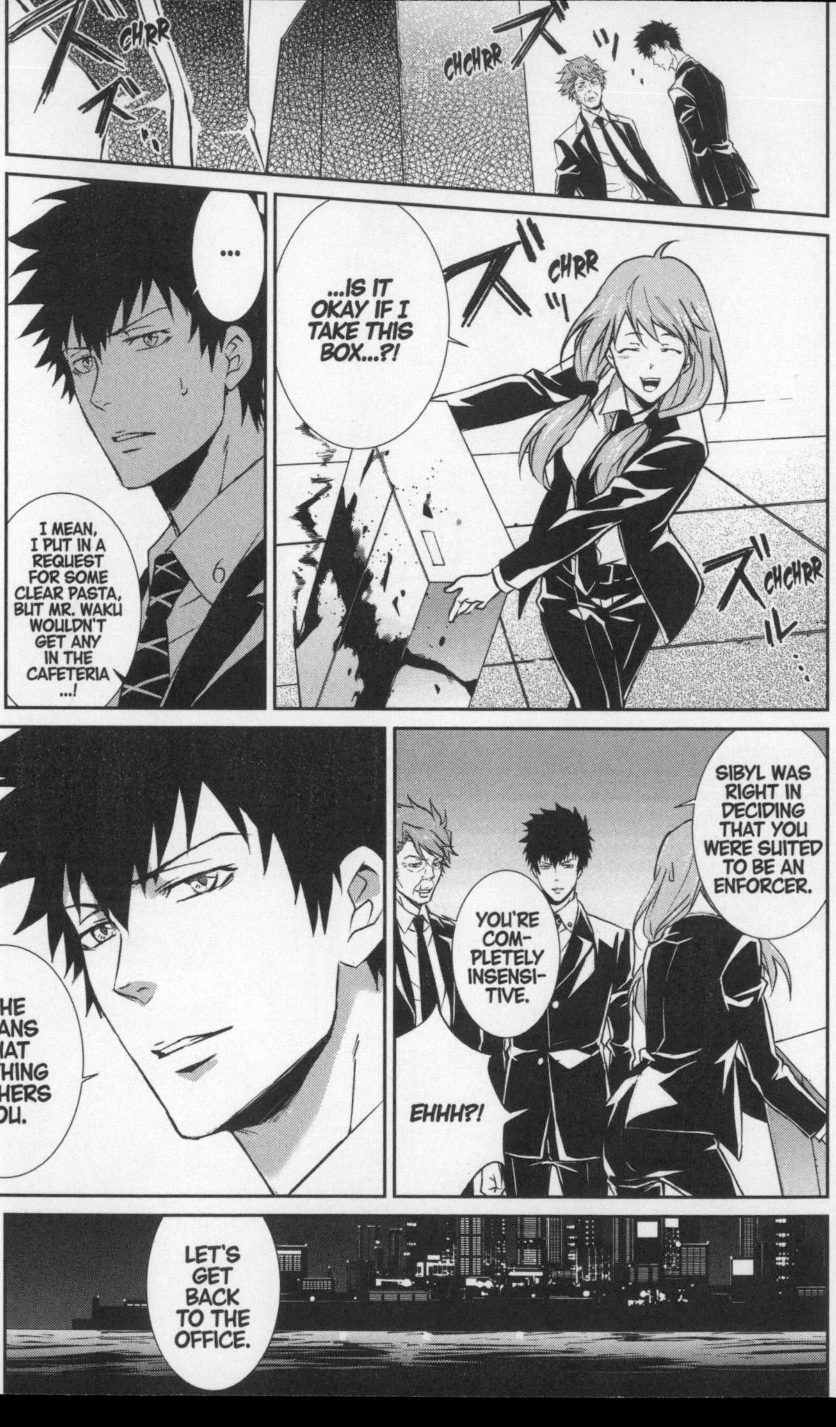
CHCHRR
CHRR
...IS IT OKAY IF I TAKE THIS BOX...?!
CHRR
CHCHRR
...
I MEAN, I PUT IN A REQUEST FOR SOME CLEAR PASTA, BUT MR. WAKU WOULDN'T GET ANY IN THE CAFETERIA ...!
SIBYL WAS RIGHT IN DECIDING THAT YOU WERE SUITED TO BE AN ENFORCER.
YOU'RE COM-PLETELY INSENSI-TIVE.
EHHH?!
...HE MEANS THAT NOTHING BOTHERS YOU.
LET'S GET BACK TO THE OFFICE.

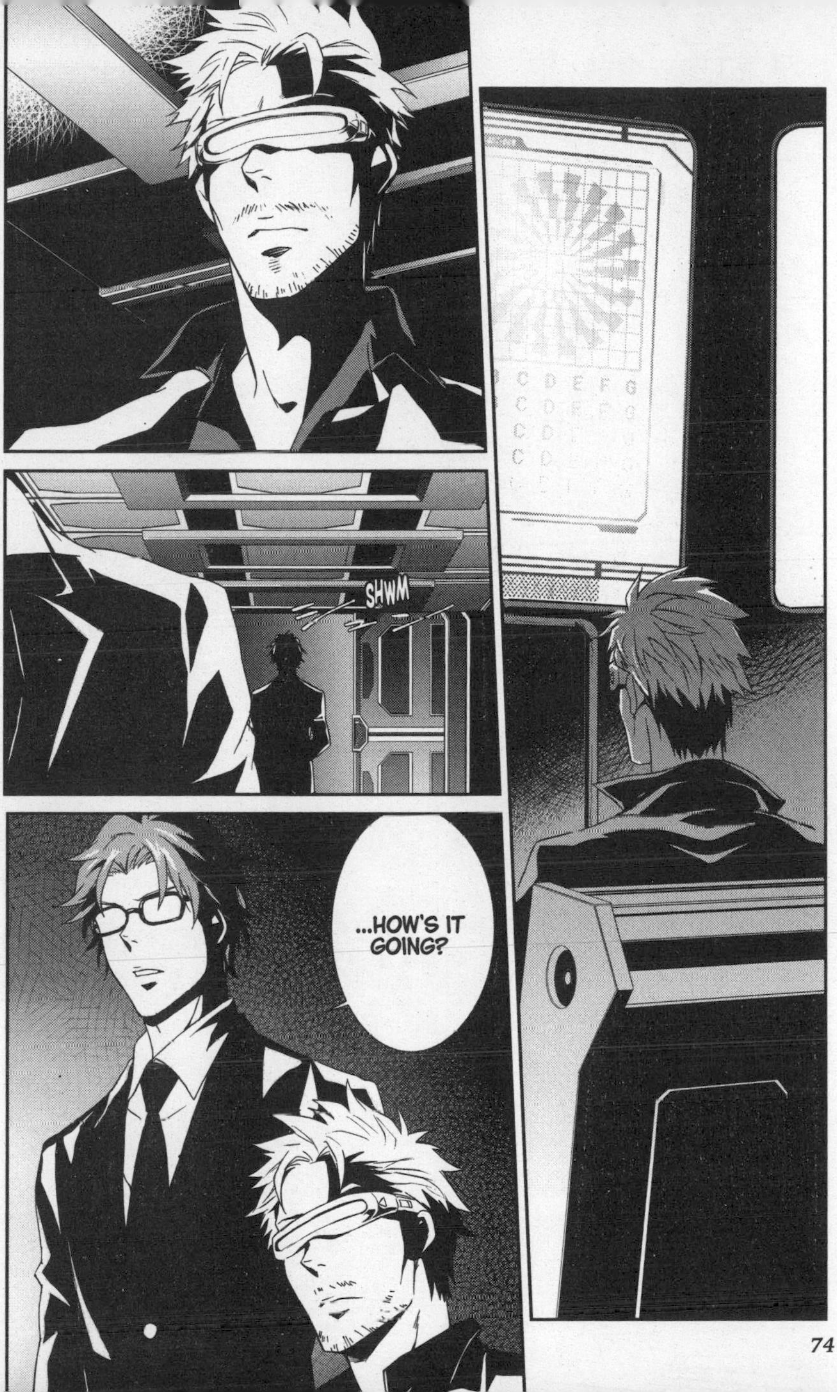
C D E F G
SHWM
...HOW'S IT GOING?

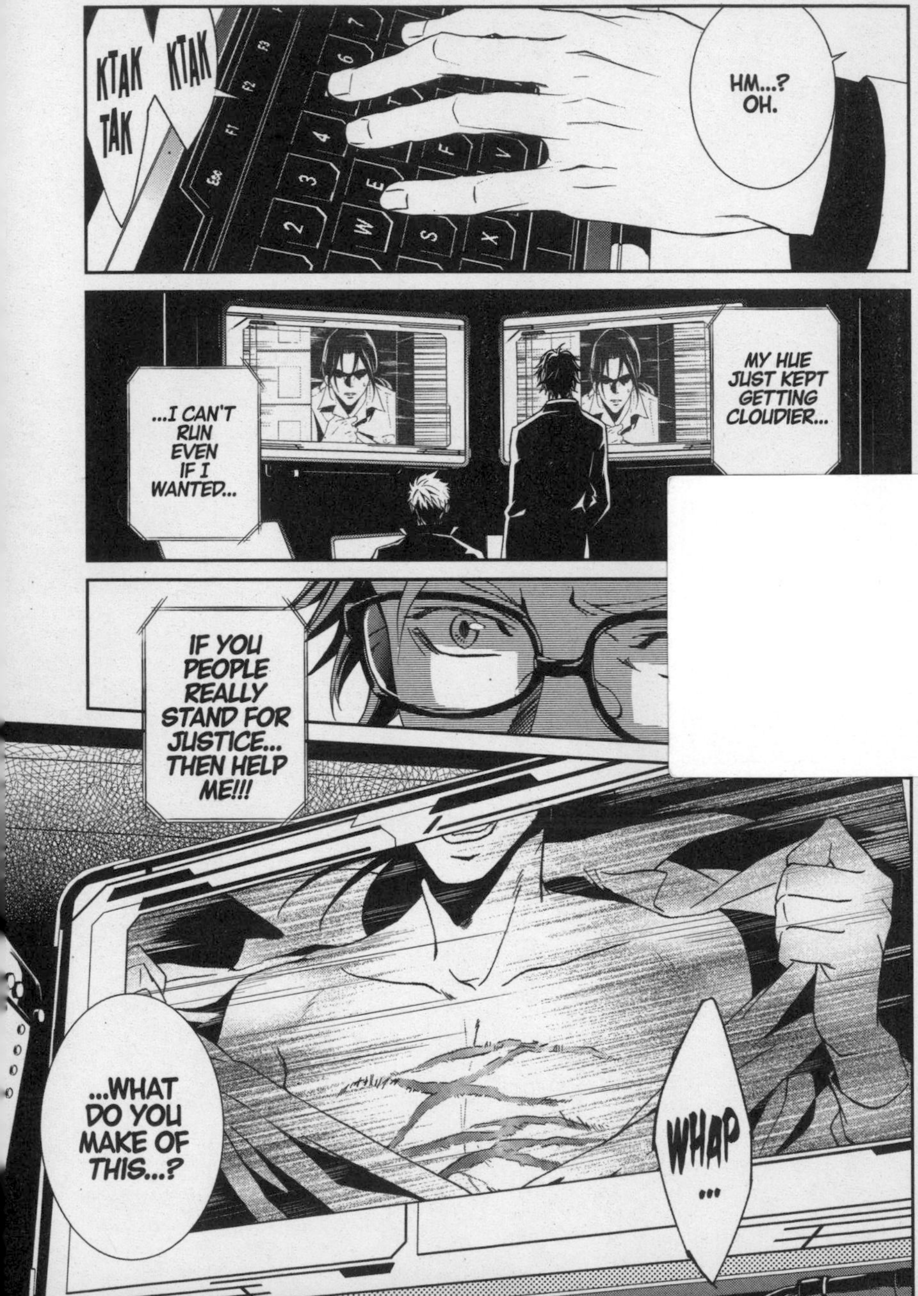
HM...? OH.
KTAK KTAK TAK
MY HUE JUST KEPT GETTING CLOUDIER...
...I CAN'T RUN EVEN IF I WANTED...
IF YOU PEOPLE REALLY STAND FOR JUSTICE... THEN HELP ME!!!
WHAP...
...WHAT DO YOU MAKE OF THIS...?

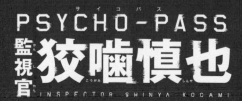

PSYCHO-PASS
サイコパス
監視官 狂噛慎也
かんしかん こうがみ しんや
INSPECTOR SHINYA KOGAMI

File No.003

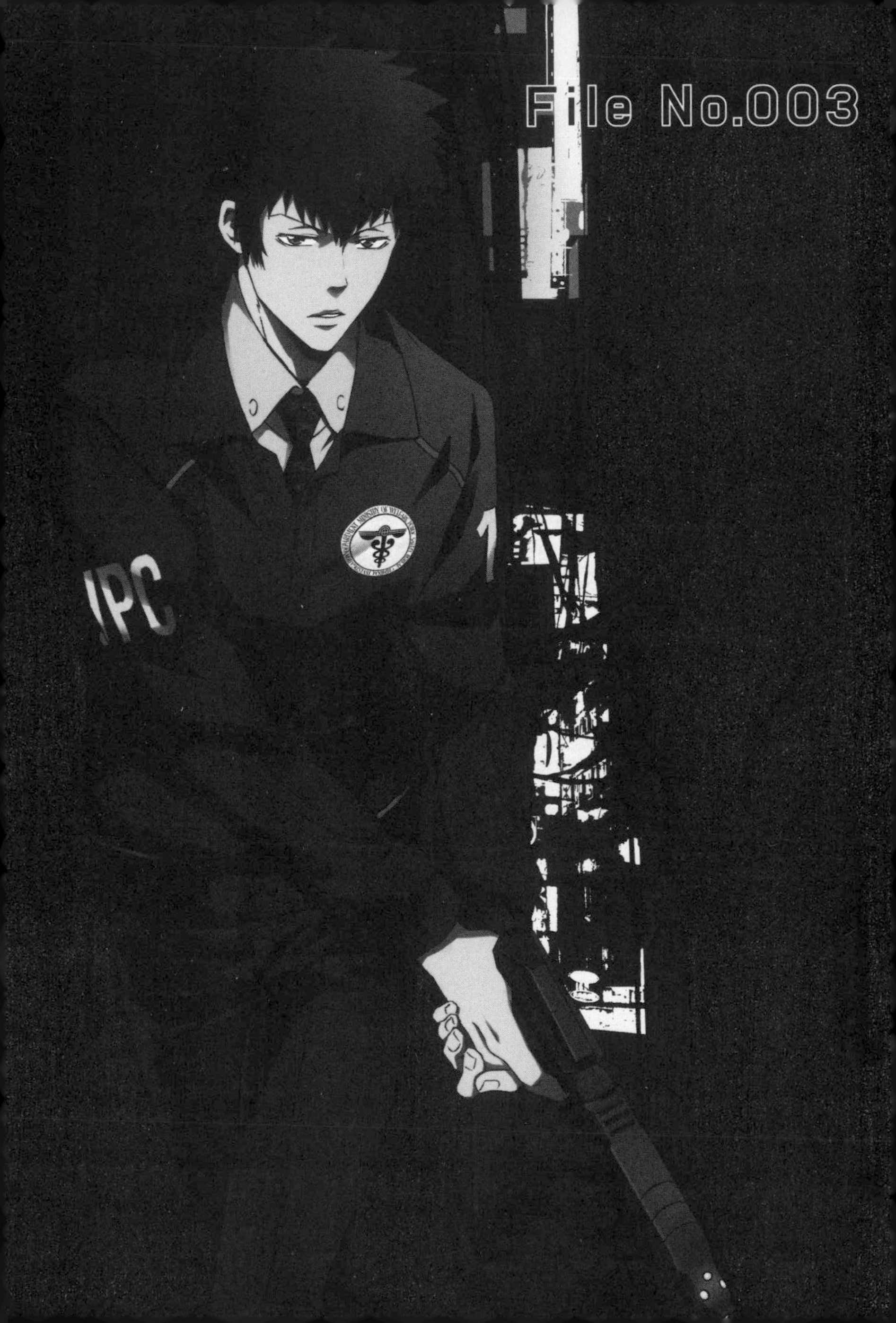

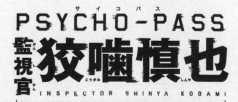

PSYCHO-PASS
監視官 狂噛慎也
INSPECTOR SHINYA KOGAMI

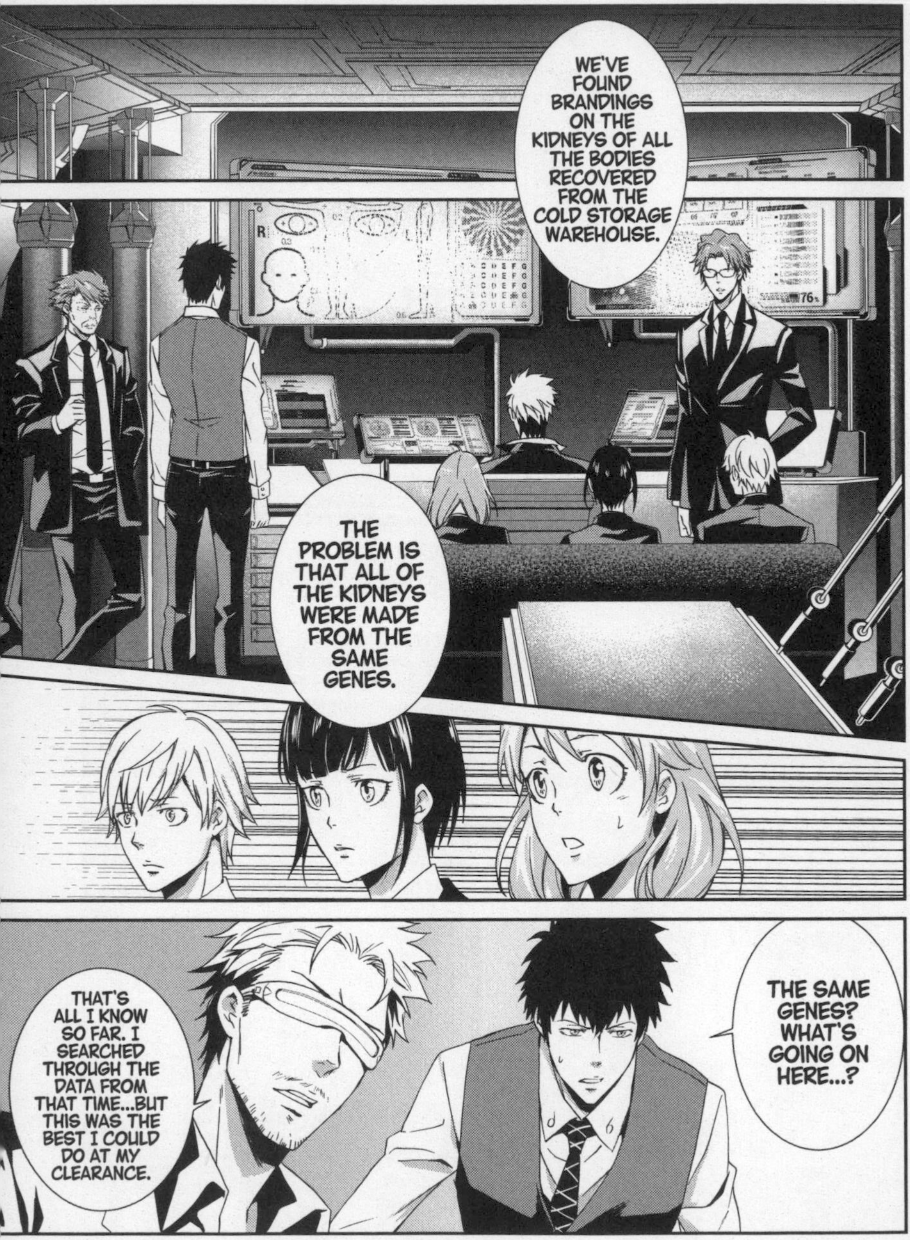
WE'VE FOUND BRANDINGS ON THE KIDNEYS OF ALL THE BODIES RECOVERED FROM THE COLD STORAGE WAREHOUSE.
THE PROBLEM IS THAT ALL OF THE KIDNEYS WERE MADE FROM THE SAME GENES.
THE SAME GENES? WHAT'S GOING ON HERE...?
THAT'S ALL I KNOW SO FAR. I SEARCHED THROUGH THE DATA FROM THAT TIME...BUT THIS WAS THE BEST I COULD DO AT MY CLEARANCE.

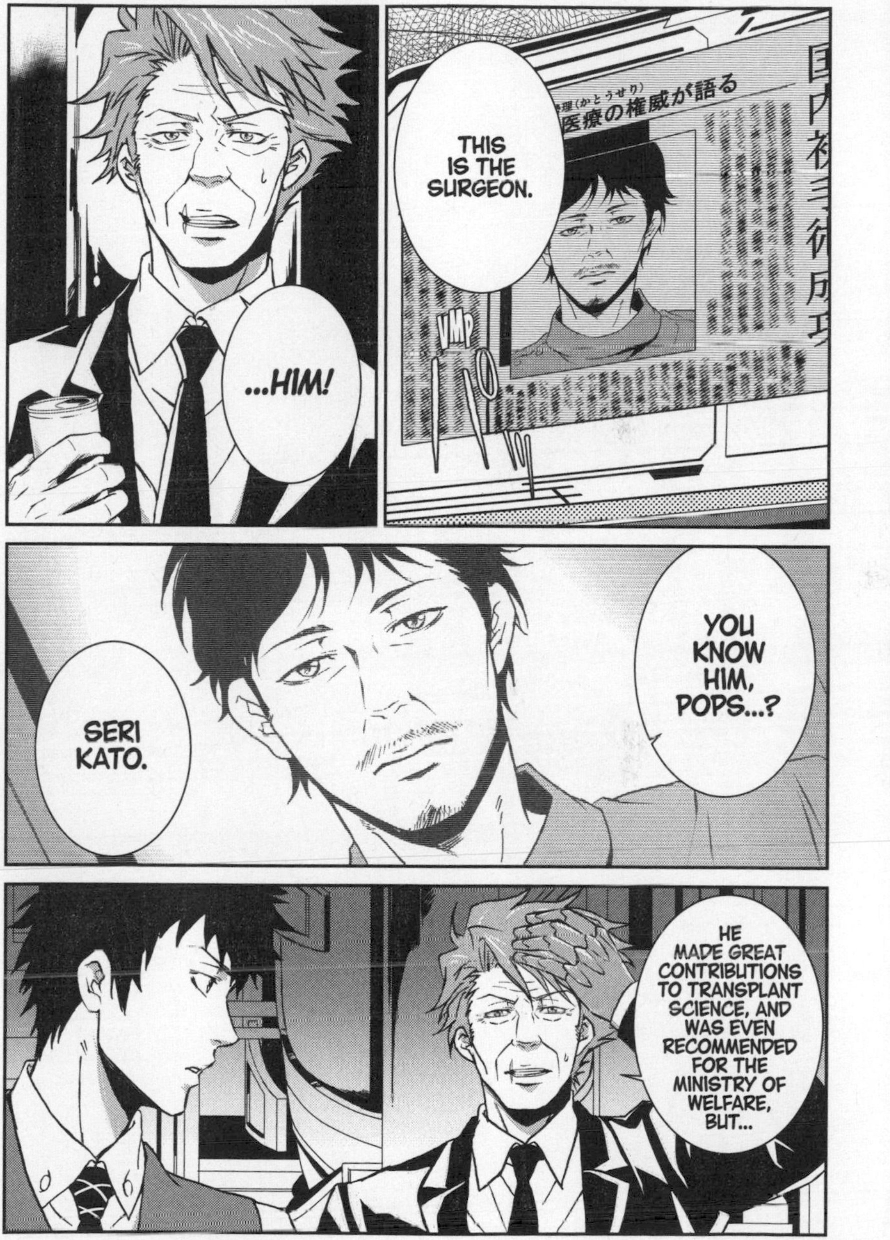
医療の権威が語る
VMP
THIS IS THE SURGEON.
...HIM!
YOU KNOW HIM, POPS...?
SERI KATO.
HE MADE GREAT CONTRIBUTIONS TO TRANSPLANT SCIENCE, AND WAS EVEN RECOMMENDED FOR THE MINISTRY OF WELFARE, BUT...

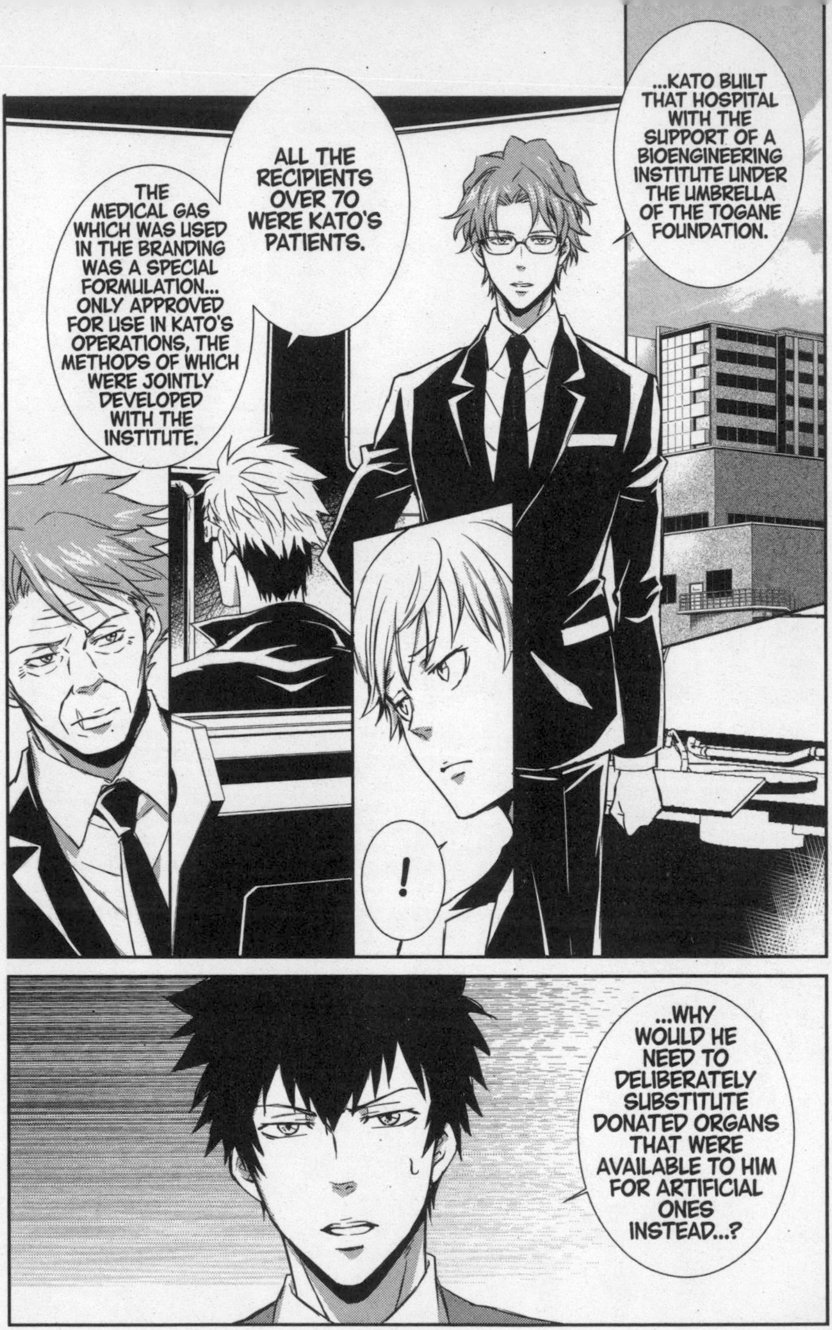
...KATO BUILT THAT HOSPITAL WITH THE SUPPORT OF A BIOENGINEERING INSTITUTE UNDER THE UMBRELLA OF THE TOGANE FOUNDATION.
ALL THE RECIPIENTS OVER 70 WERE KATO'S PATIENTS.
THE MEDICAL GAS WHICH WAS USED IN THE BRANDING WAS A SPECIAL FORMULATION... ONLY APPROVED FOR USE IN KATO'S OPERATIONS, THE METHODS OF WHICH WERE JOINTLY DEVELOPED WITH THE INSTITUTE.
!
...WHY WOULD HE NEED TO DELIBERATELY SUBSTITUTE DONATED ORGANS THAT WERE AVAILABLE TO HIM FOR ARTIFICIAL ONES INSTEAD...?

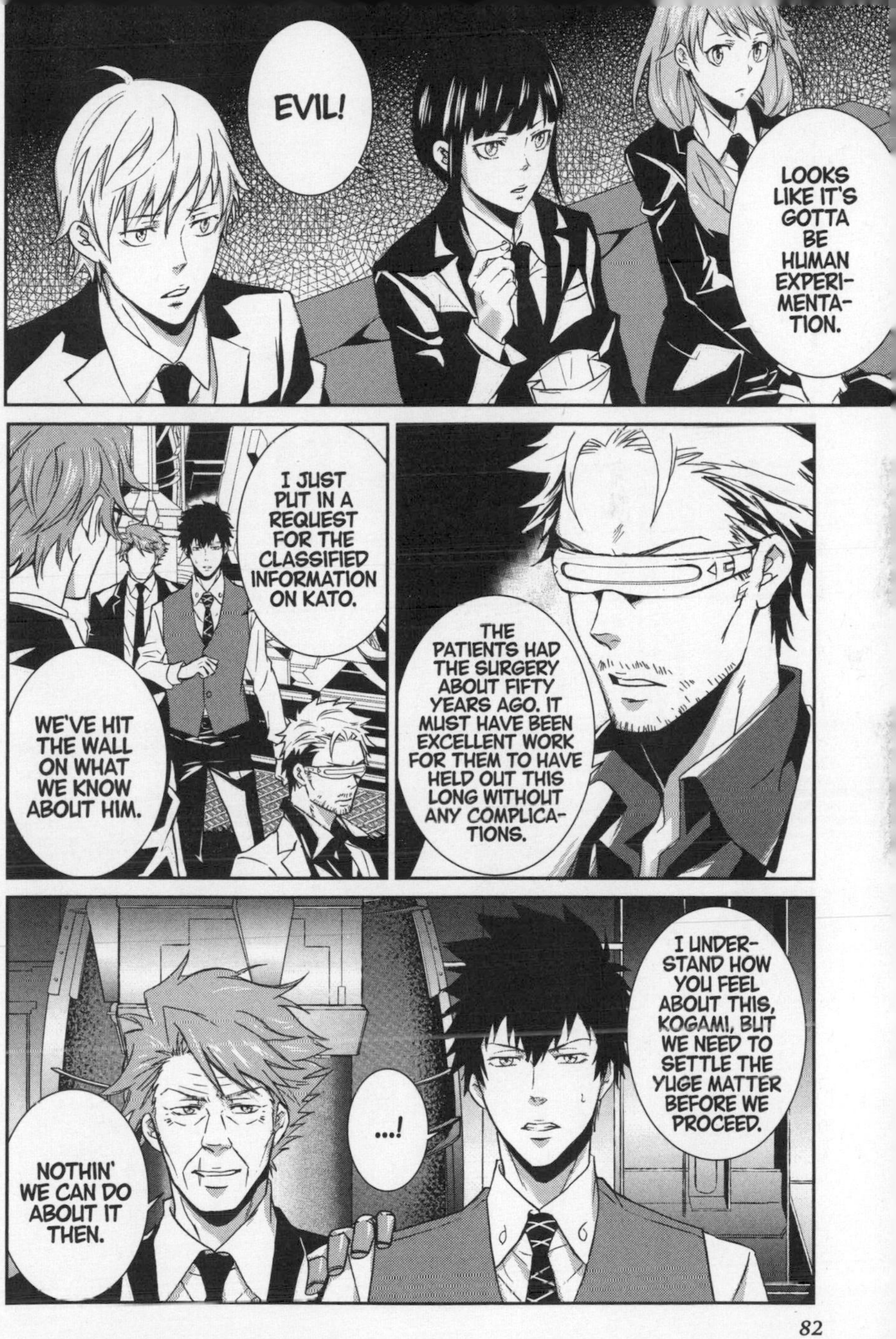
LOOKS LIKE IT'S GOTTA BE HUMAN EXPERIMENTATION.
EVIL!
THE PATIENTS HAD THE SURGERY ABOUT FIFTY YEARS AGO. IT MUST HAVE BEEN EXCELLENT WORK FOR THEM TO HAVE HELD OUT THIS LONG WITHOUT ANY COMPLICATIONS.
I JUST PUT IN A REQUEST FOR THE CLASSIFIED INFORMATION ON KATO.
WE'VE HIT THE WALL ON WHAT WE KNOW ABOUT HIM.
I UNDERSTAND HOW YOU FEEL ABOUT THIS, KOGAMI, BUT WE NEED TO SETTLE THE YUGE MATTER BEFORE WE PROCEED.
...!
NOTHIN' WE CAN DO ABOUT IT THEN.

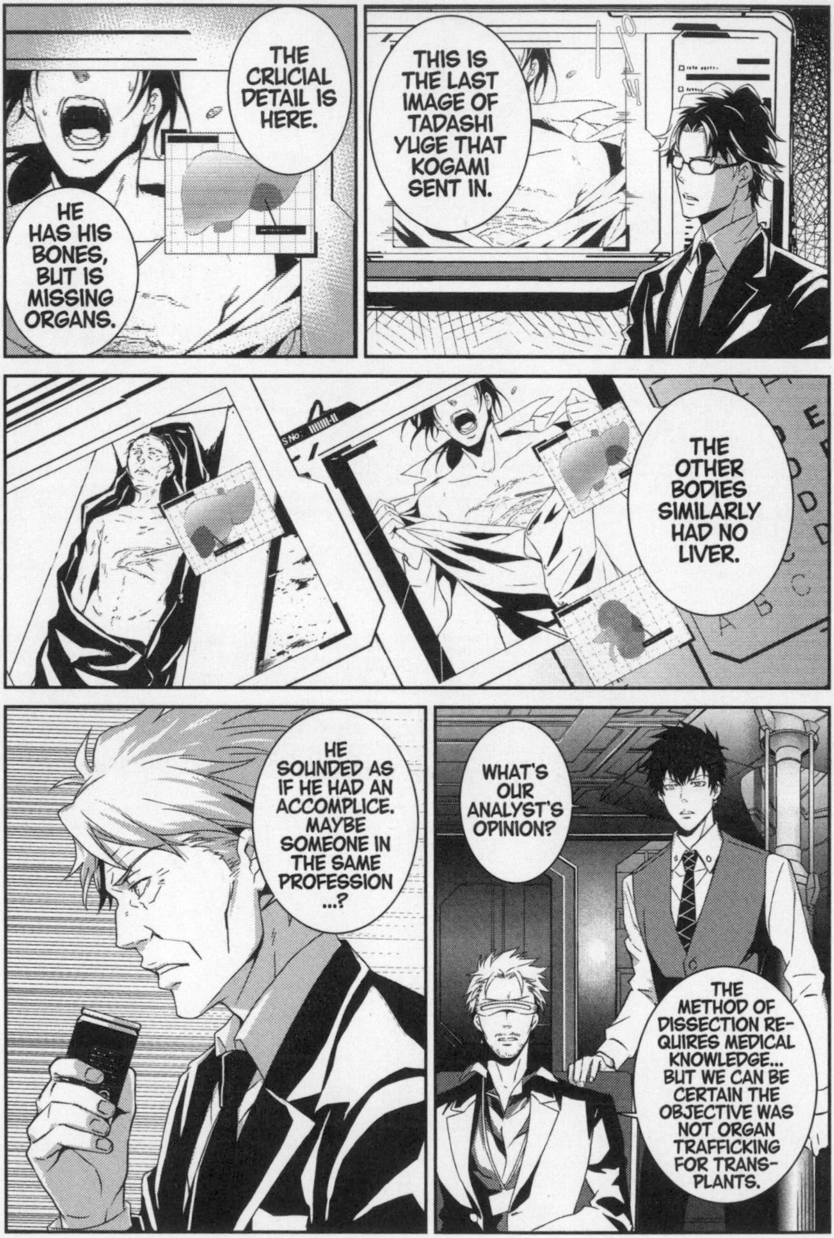
THIS IS THE LAST IMAGE OF TADASHI YUGE THAT KOGAMI SENT IN.
THE CRUCIAL DETAIL IS HERE.
HE HAS HIS BONES, BUT IS MISSING ORGANS.
THE OTHER BODIES SIMILARLY HAD NO LIVER.
WHAT'S OUR ANALYST'S OPINION?
THE METHOD OF DISSECTION REQUIRES MEDICAL KNOWLEDGE... BUT WE CAN BE CERTAIN THE OBJECTIVE WAS NOT ORGAN TRAFFICKING FOR TRANSPLANTS.
HE SOUNDED AS IF HE HAD AN ACCOMPLICE. MAYBE SOMEONE IN THE SAME PROFESSION ...?

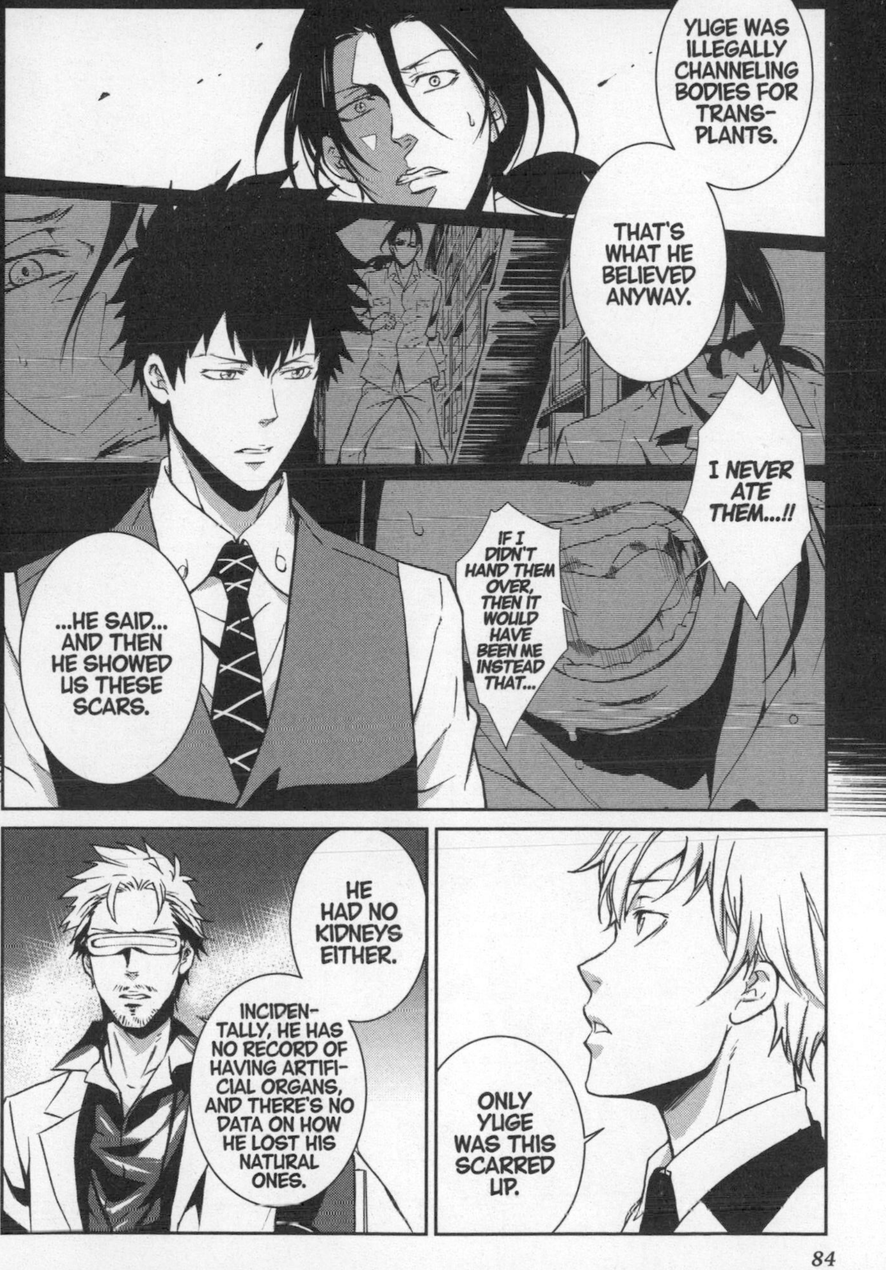
YUGE WAS ILLEGALLY CHANNELING BODIES FOR TRANS- PLANTS.
THAT'S WHAT HE BELIEVED ANYWAY.
I NEVER ATE THEM...!!
IF I DIDN'T HAND THEM OVER, THEN IT WOULD HAVE BEEN ME INSTEAD THAT...
...HE SAID... AND THEN HE SHOWED US THESE SCARS.
ONLY YUGE WAS THIS SCARRED UP.
HE HAD NO KIDNEYS EITHER.
INCIDEN- TALLY, HE HAS NO RECORD OF HAVING ARTIFI- CIAL ORGANS, AND THERE'S NO DATA ON HOW HE LOST HIS NATURAL ONES.

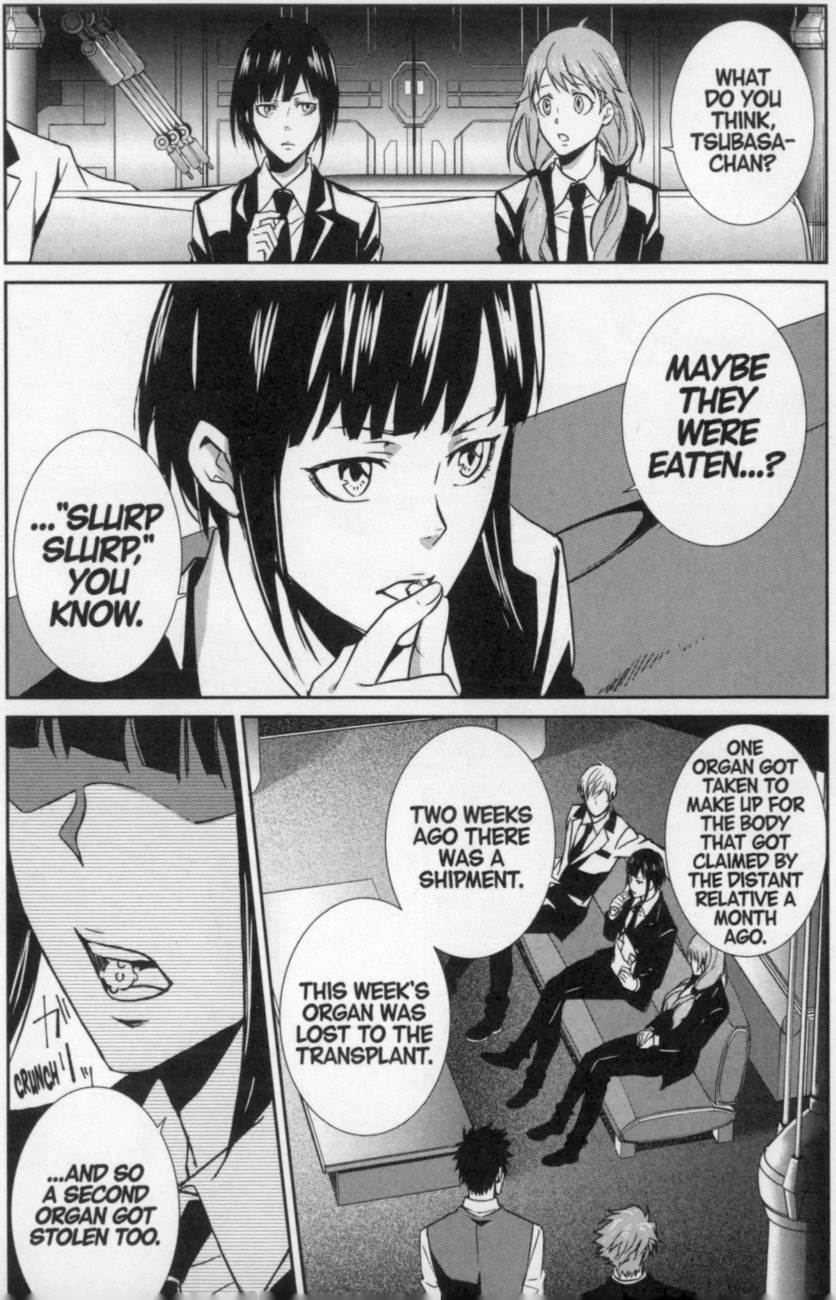
WHAT DO YOU THINK, TSUBASA-CHAN?
MAYBE THEY WERE EATEN...?
..."SLURP SLURP," YOU KNOW.
ONE ORGAN GOT TAKEN TO MAKE UP FOR THE BODY THAT GOT CLAIMED BY THE DISTANT RELATIVE A MONTH AGO.
TWO WEEKS AGO THERE WAS A SHIPMENT.
THIS WEEK'S ORGAN WAS LOST TO THE TRANSPLANT.
CRUNCH
...AND SO A SECOND ORGAN GOT STOLEN TOO.

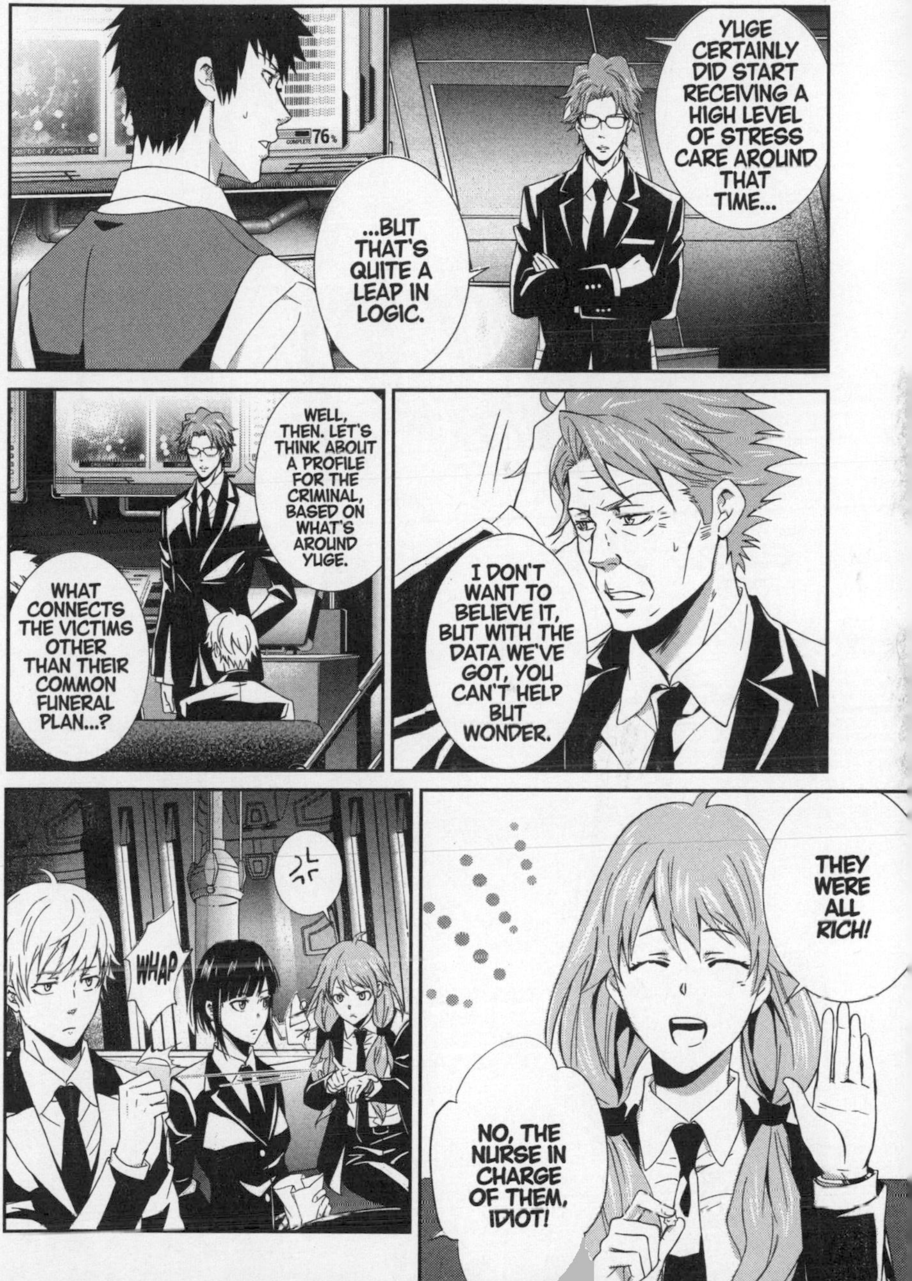
YUGE CERTAINLY DID START RECEIVING A HIGH LEVEL OF STRESS CARE AROUND THAT TIME...
...BUT THAT'S QUITE A LEAP IN LOGIC.
COMPLETE 76%
I DON'T WANT TO BELIEVE IT, BUT WITH THE DATA WE'VE GOT, YOU CAN'T HELP BUT WONDER.
WELL, THEN. LET'S THINK ABOUT A PROFILE FOR THE CRIMINAL, BASED ON WHAT'S AROUND YUGE.
WHAT CONNECTS THE VICTIMS OTHER THAN THEIR COMMON FUNERAL PLAN...?
THEY WERE ALL RICH!
NO, THE NURSE IN CHARGE OF THEM, IDIOT!
WHAP

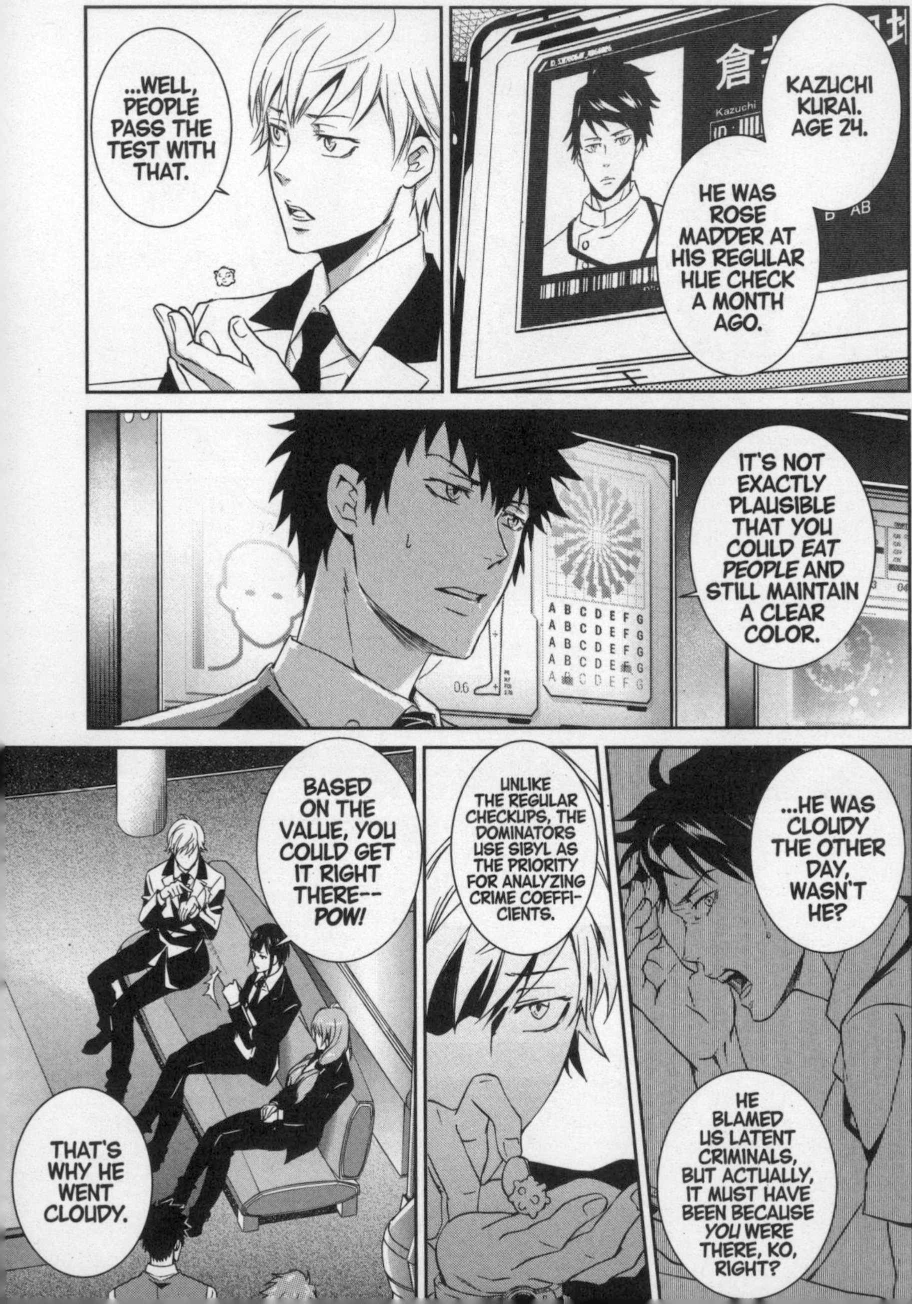
KAZUCHI KURAI. AGE 24.
HE WAS ROSE MADDER AT HIS REGULAR HUE CHECK A MONTH AGO.
...WELL, PEOPLE PASS THE TEST WITH THAT.
IT'S NOT EXACTLY PLAUSIBLE THAT YOU COULD EAT *PEOPLE* AND STILL MAINTAIN A CLEAR COLOR.
...HE WAS CLOUDY THE OTHER DAY, WASN'T HE?
HE BLAMED US LATENT CRIMINALS, BUT ACTUALLY, IT MUST HAVE BEEN BECAUSE *YOU* WERE THERE, KO, RIGHT?
UNLIKE THE REGULAR CHECKUPS, THE DOMINATORS USE SIBYL AS THE PRIORITY FOR ANALYZING CRIME COEFFI-CIENTS.
BASED ON THE VALUE, YOU COULD GET IT RIGHT THERE-- *POW!*
THAT'S WHY HE WENT CLOUDY.

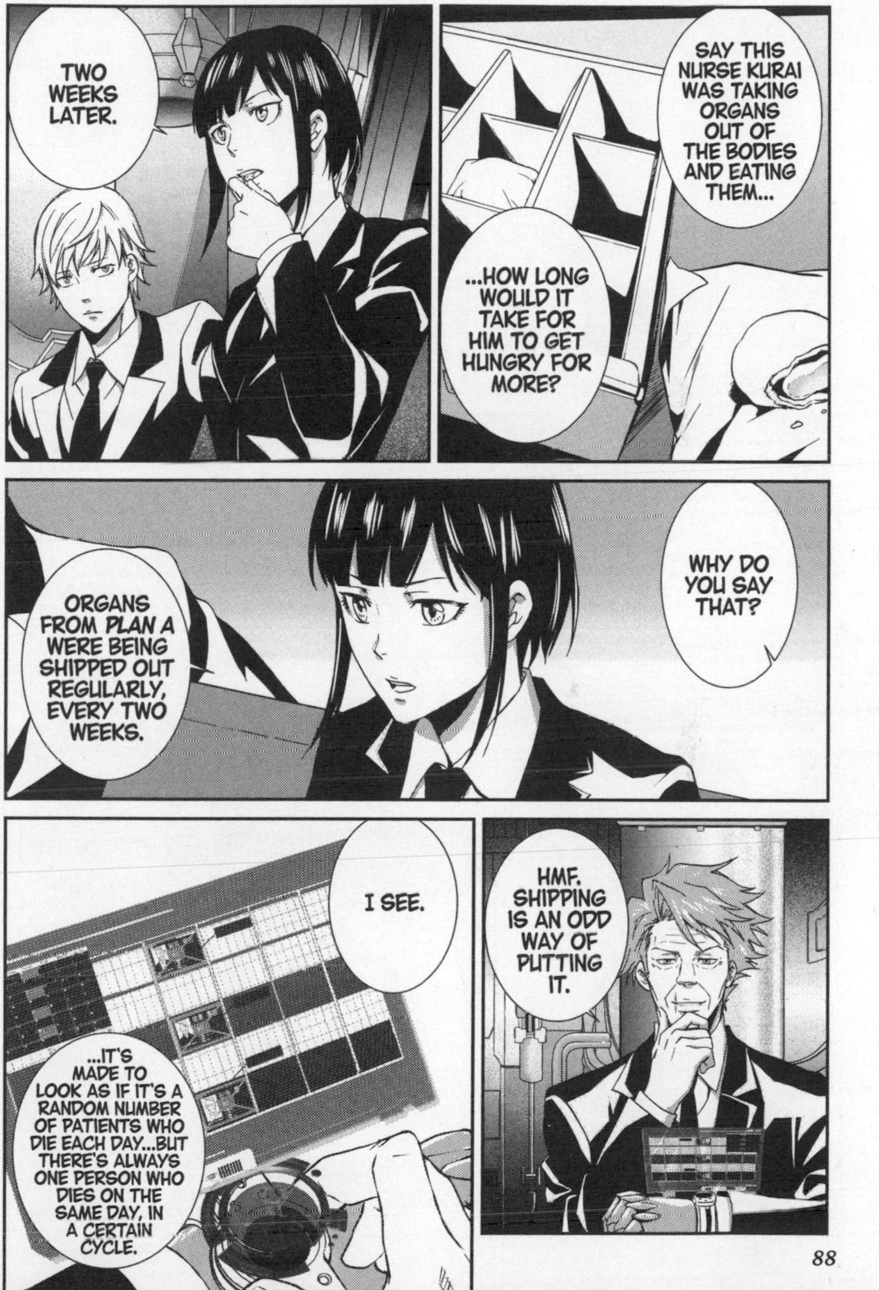
SAY THIS NURSE KURAI WAS TAKING ORGANS OUT OF THE BODIES AND EATING THEM...
...HOW LONG WOULD IT TAKE FOR HIM TO GET HUNGRY FOR MORE?
TWO WEEKS LATER.
WHY DO YOU SAY THAT?
ORGANS FROM PLAN A WERE BEING SHIPPED OUT REGULARLY, EVERY TWO WEEKS.
HMF. SHIPPING IS AN ODD WAY OF PUTTING IT.
I SEE.
...IT'S MADE TO LOOK AS IF IT'S A RANDOM NUMBER OF PATIENTS WHO DIE EACH DAY...BUT THERE'S ALWAYS ONE PERSON WHO DIES ON THE SAME DAY, IN A CERTAIN CYCLE.

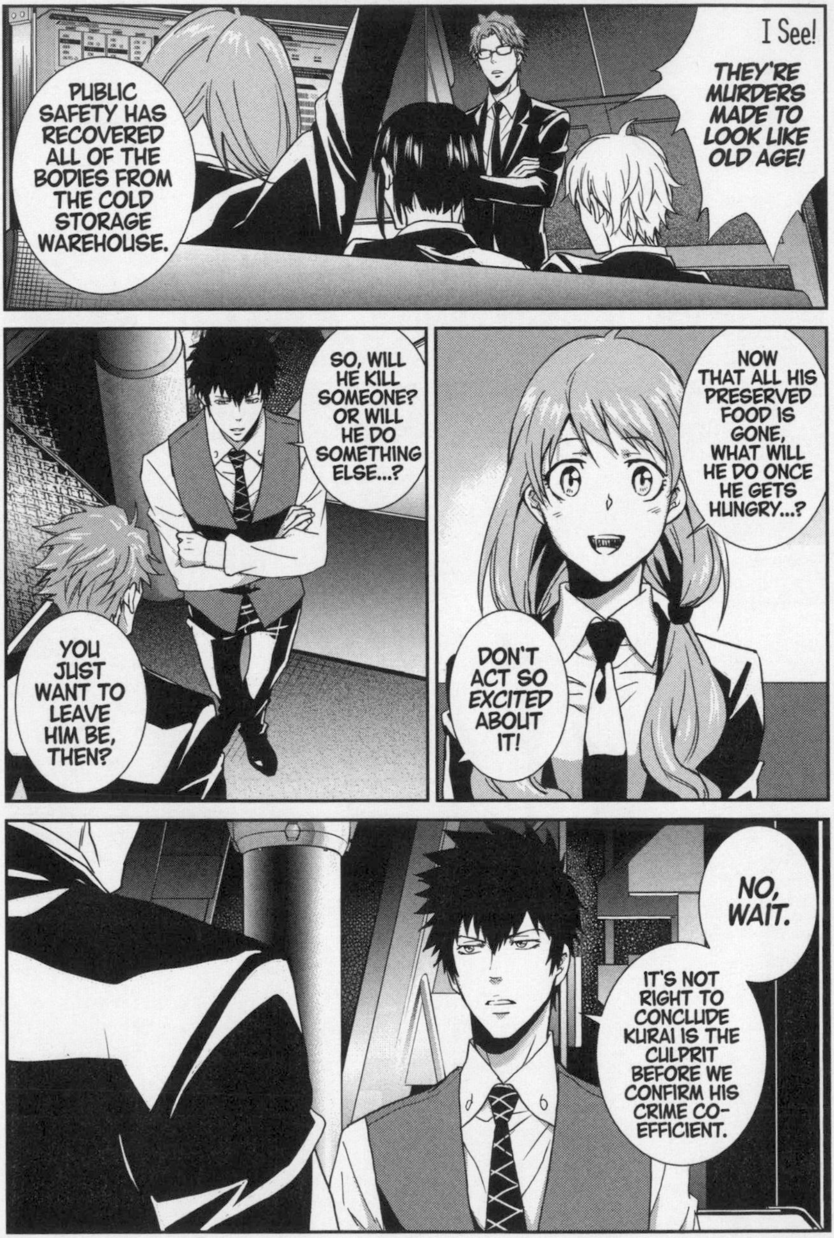
I See!
THEY'RE MURDERS MADE TO LOOK LIKE OLD AGE!
PUBLIC SAFETY HAS RECOVERED ALL OF THE BODIES FROM THE COLD STORAGE WAREHOUSE.
NOW THAT ALL HIS PRESERVED FOOD IS GONE, WHAT WILL HE DO ONCE HE GETS HUNGRY...?
DON'T ACT SO EXCITED ABOUT IT!
SO, WILL HE KILL SOMEONE? OR WILL HE DO SOMETHING ELSE...?
YOU JUST WANT TO LEAVE HIM BE, THEN?
NO, WAIT.
IT'S NOT RIGHT TO CONCLUDE KURAI IS THE CULPRIT BEFORE WE CONFIRM HIS CRIME CO-EFFICIENT.

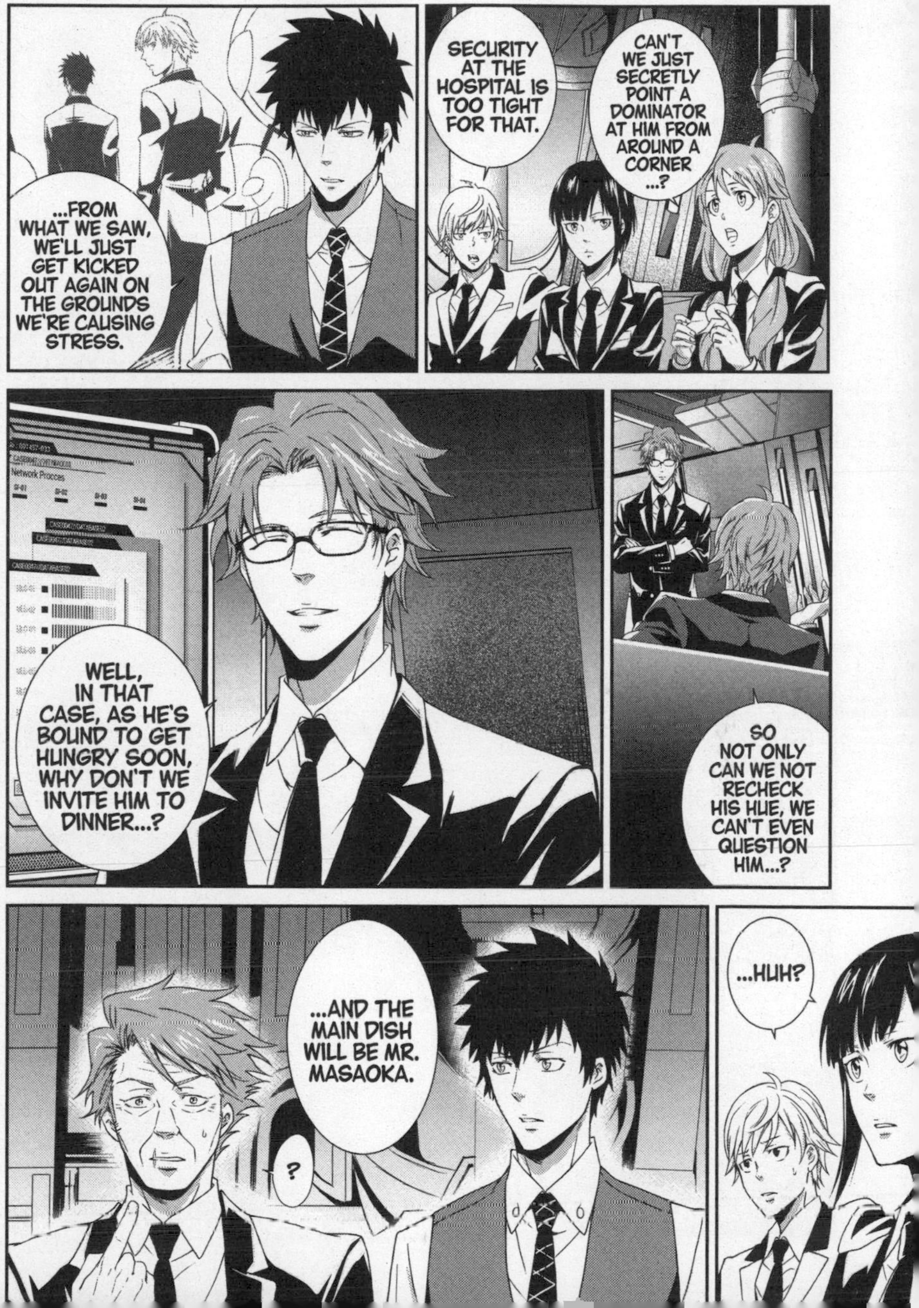
CAN'T WE JUST SECRETLY POINT A DOMINATOR AT HIM FROM AROUND A CORNER ...?
SECURITY AT THE HOSPITAL IS TOO TIGHT FOR THAT.
...FROM WHAT WE SAW, WE'LL JUST GET KICKED OUT AGAIN ON THE GROUNDS WE'RE CAUSING STRESS.
SO NOT ONLY CAN WE NOT RECHECK HIS HUE, WE CAN'T EVEN QUESTION HIM...?
WELL, IN THAT CASE, AS HE'S BOUND TO GET HUNGRY SOON, WHY DON'T WE INVITE HIM TO DINNER...?
...HUH?
...AND THE MAIN DISH WILL BE MR. MASAOKA.
?

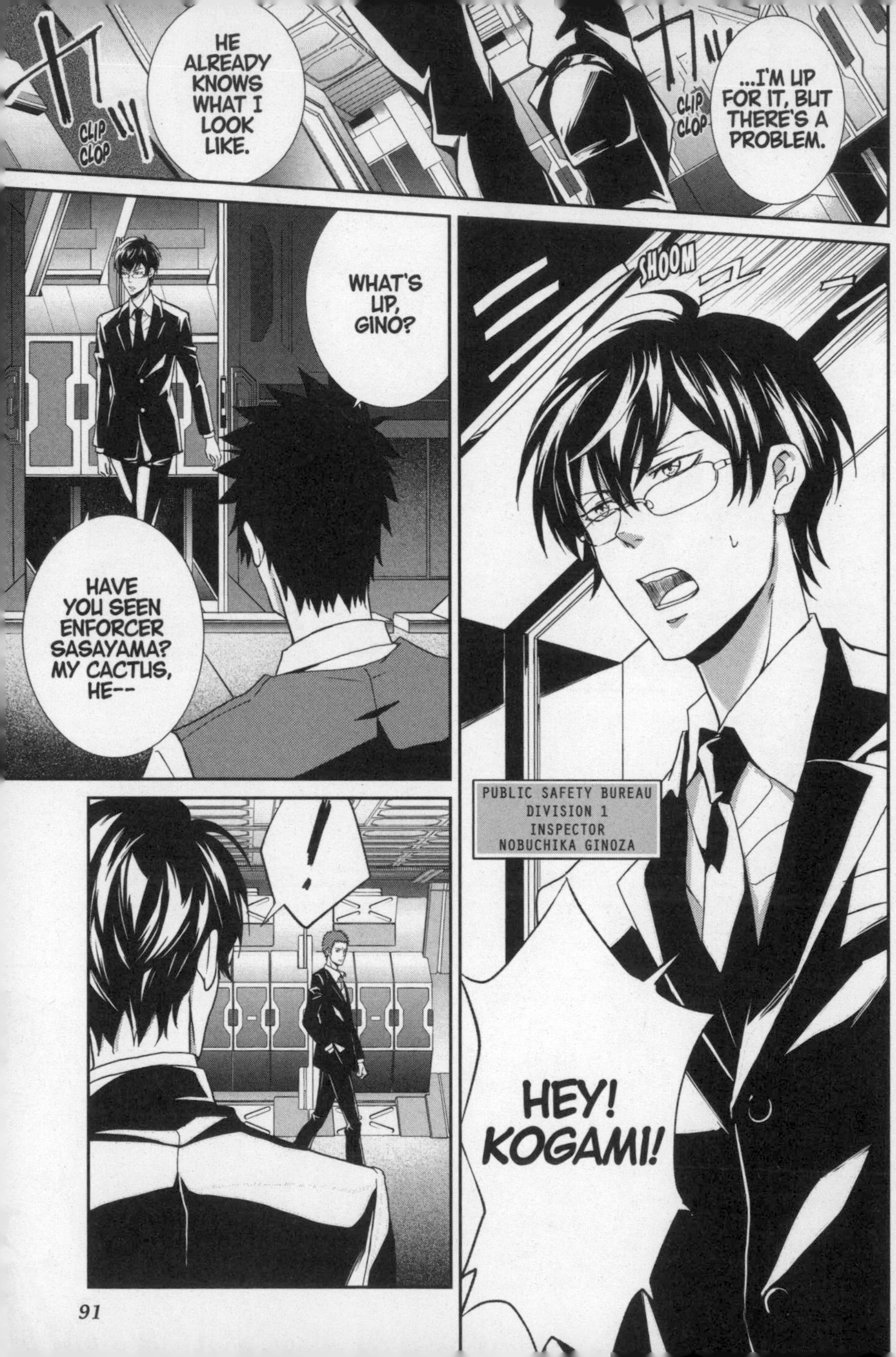

CLIP CLOP
...I'M UP FOR IT, BUT THERE'S A PROBLEM.
HE ALREADY KNOWS WHAT I LOOK LIKE.
CLIP CLOP
SHOOM
PUBLIC SAFETY BUREAU DIVISION 1 INSPECTOR NOBUCHIKA GINOZA
HEY! KOGAMI!
WHAT'S UP, GINO?
HAVE YOU SEEN ENFORCER SASAYAMA? MY CACTUS, HE--
!

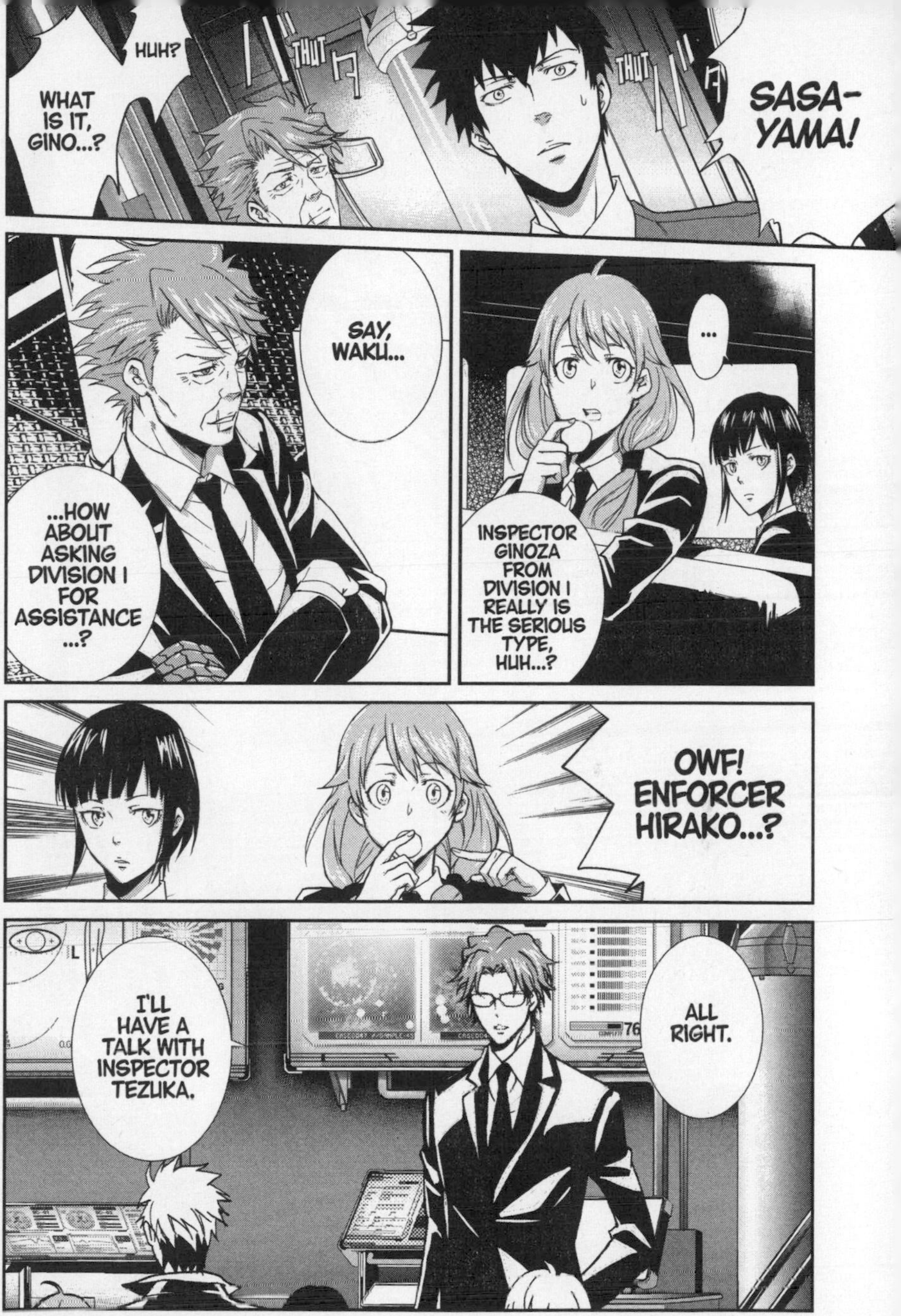
SASA-YAMA!
THUT
THUT
HUH?
WHAT IS IT, GINO...?
...
INSPECTOR GINOZA FROM DIVISION I REALLY IS THE SERIOUS TYPE, HUH...?
SAY, WAKU...
...HOW ABOUT ASKING DIVISION I FOR ASSISTANCE ...?
OWF! ENFORCER HIRAKO...?
ALL RIGHT.
I'LL HAVE A TALK WITH INSPECTOR TEZUKA.

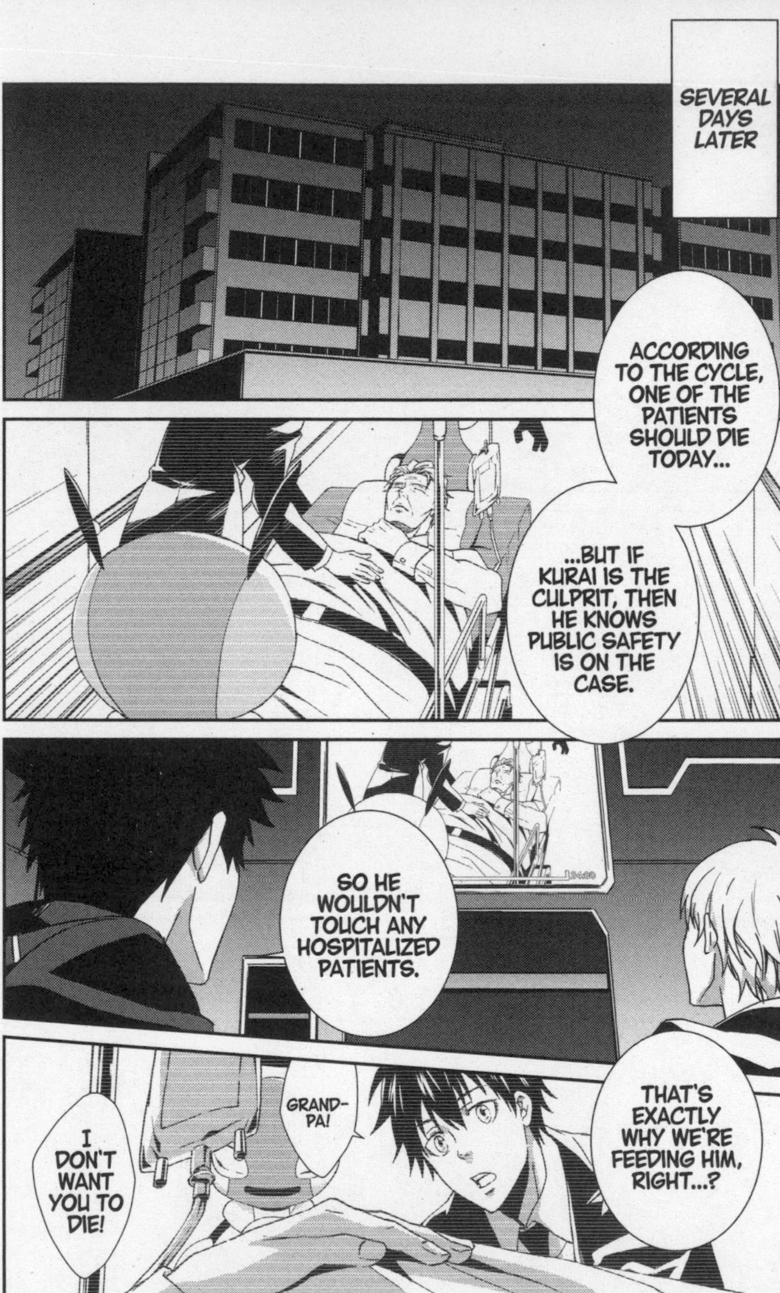
SEVERAL DAYS LATER
ACCORDING TO THE CYCLE, ONE OF THE PATIENTS SHOULD DIE TODAY...
...BUT IF KURAI IS THE CULPRIT, THEN HE KNOWS PUBLIC SAFETY IS ON THE CASE.
SO HE WOULDN'T TOUCH ANY HOSPITALIZED PATIENTS.
THAT'S EXACTLY WHY WE'RE FEEDING HIM, RIGHT...?
GRAND-PA!
I DON'T WANT YOU TO DIE!

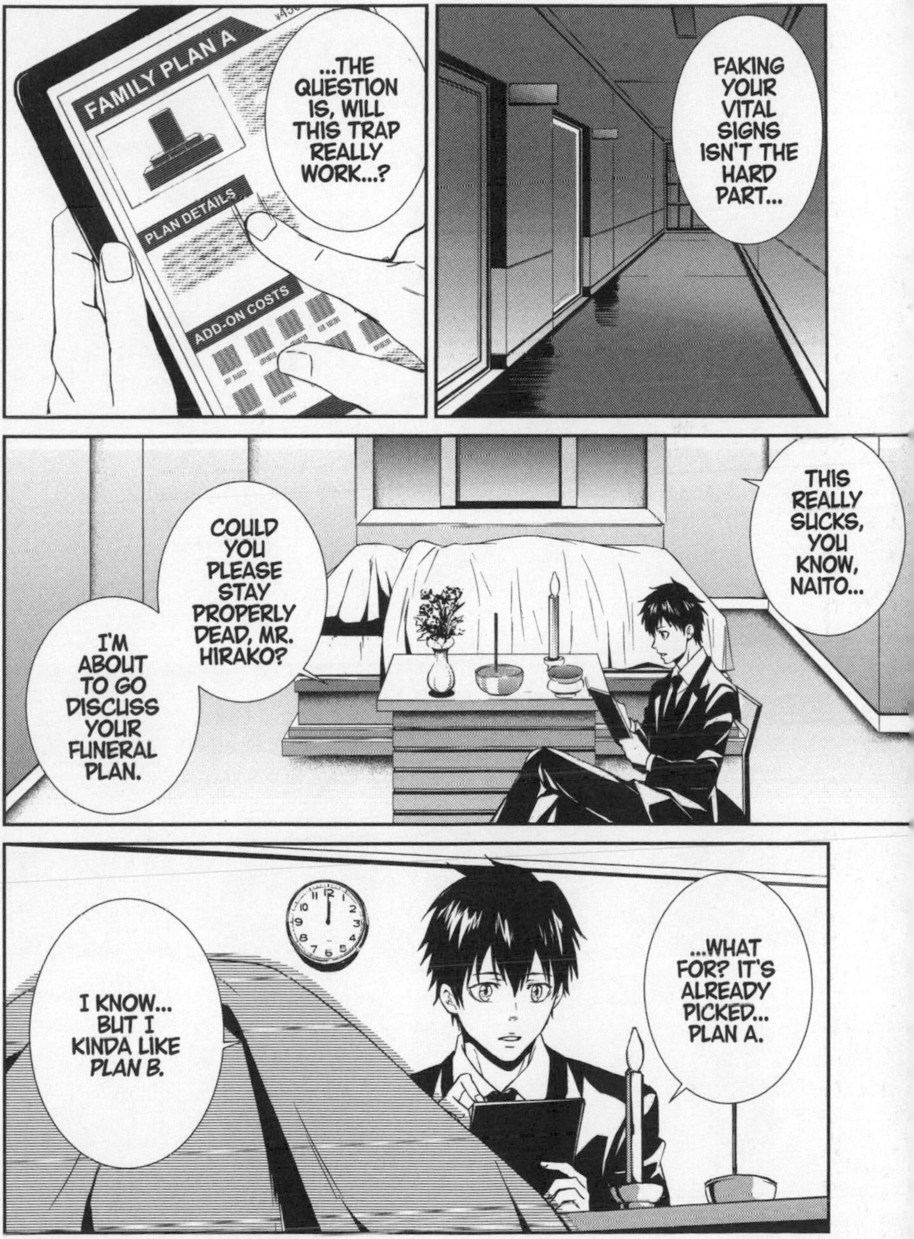
FAKING YOUR VITAL SIGNS ISN'T THE HARD PART...
FAMILY PLAN A
PLAN DETAILS
ADD-ON COSTS
...THE QUESTION IS, WILL THIS TRAP REALLY WORK...?
THIS REALLY SUCKS, YOU KNOW, NAITO...
COULD YOU PLEASE STAY PROPERLY DEAD, MR. HIRAKO?
I'M ABOUT TO GO DISCUSS YOUR FUNERAL PLAN.
...WHAT FOR? IT'S ALREADY PICKED... PLAN A.
I KNOW... BUT I KINDA LIKE PLAN B.

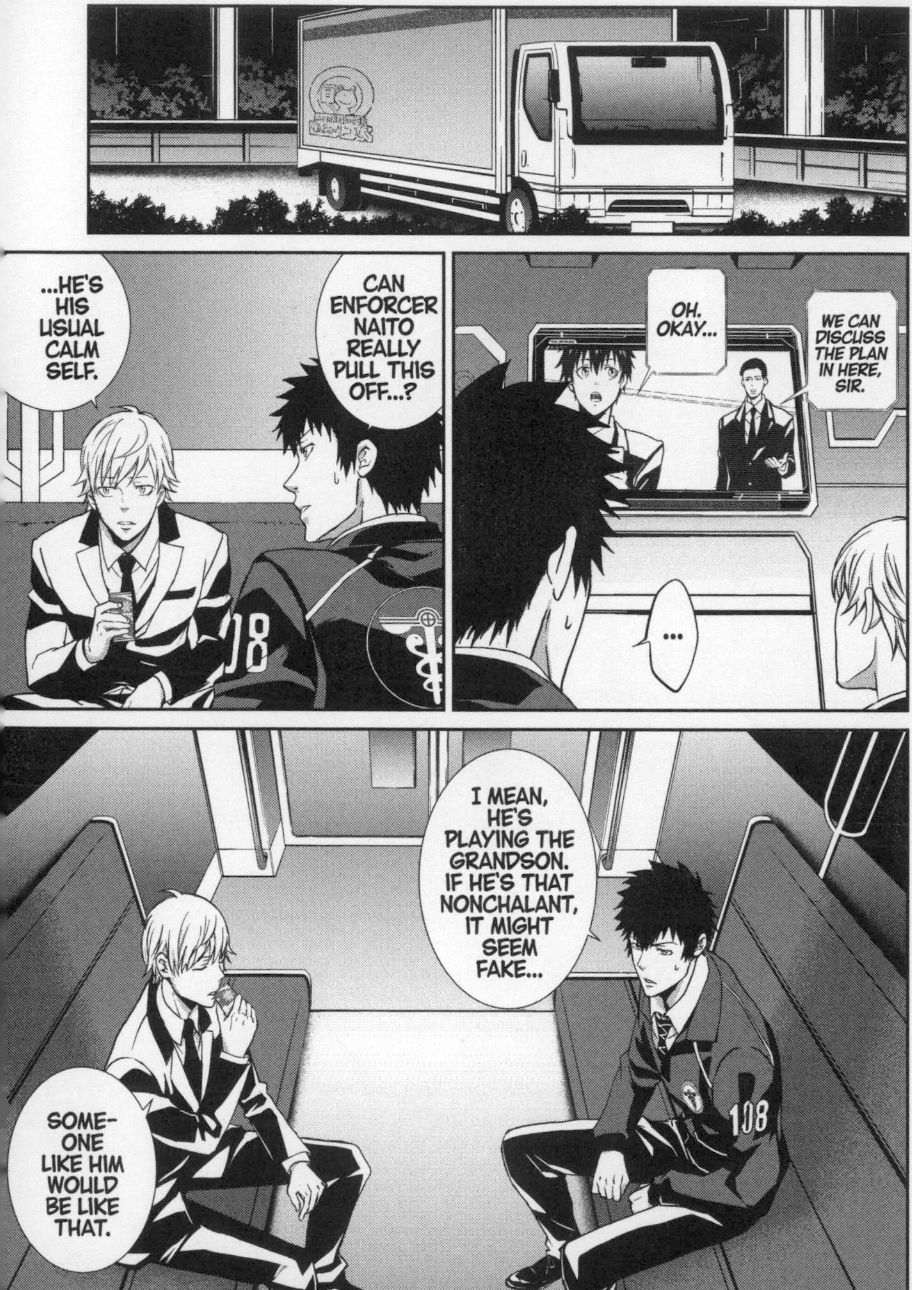

WE CAN DISCUSS THE PLAN IN HERE, SIR.
OH. OKAY...
...
CAN ENFORCER NAITO REALLY PULL THIS OFF...?
...HE'S HIS USUAL CALM SELF.
I MEAN, HE'S PLAYING THE GRANDSON. IF HE'S THAT NONCHALANT, IT MIGHT SEEM FAKE...
SOMEONE LIKE HIM WOULD BE LIKE THAT.

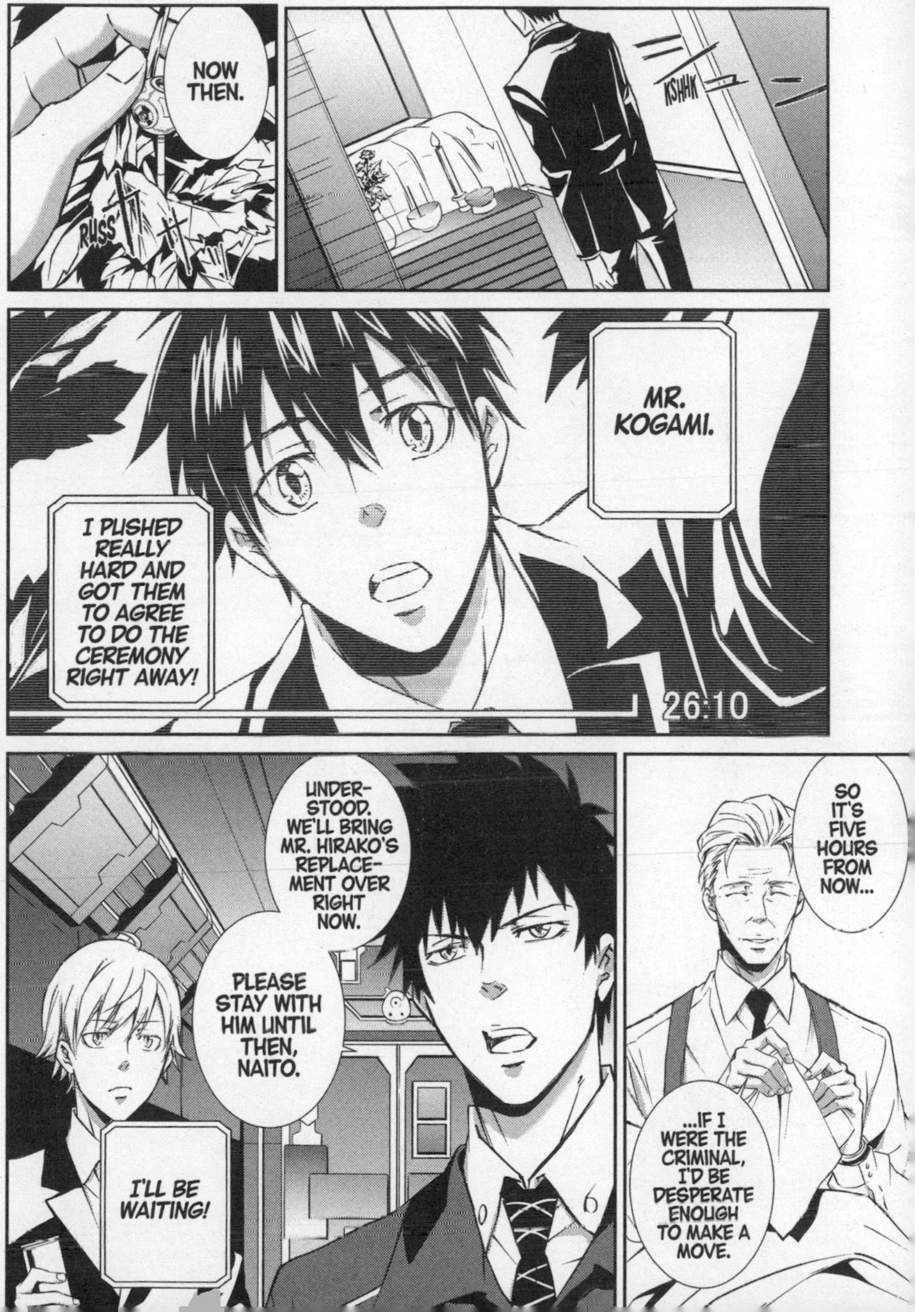
KSHHK
NOW THEN.
RUSS'
MR. KOGAMI.
I PUSHED REALLY HARD AND GOT THEM TO AGREE TO DO THE CEREMONY RIGHT AWAY!
26:10
SO IT'S FIVE HOURS FROM NOW...
...IF I WERE THE CRIMINAL, I'D BE DESPERATE ENOUGH TO MAKE A MOVE.
UNDERSTOOD. WE'LL BRING MR. HIRAKO'S REPLACEMENT OVER RIGHT NOW.
PLEASE STAY WITH HIM UNTIL THEN, NAITO.
I'LL BE WAITING!

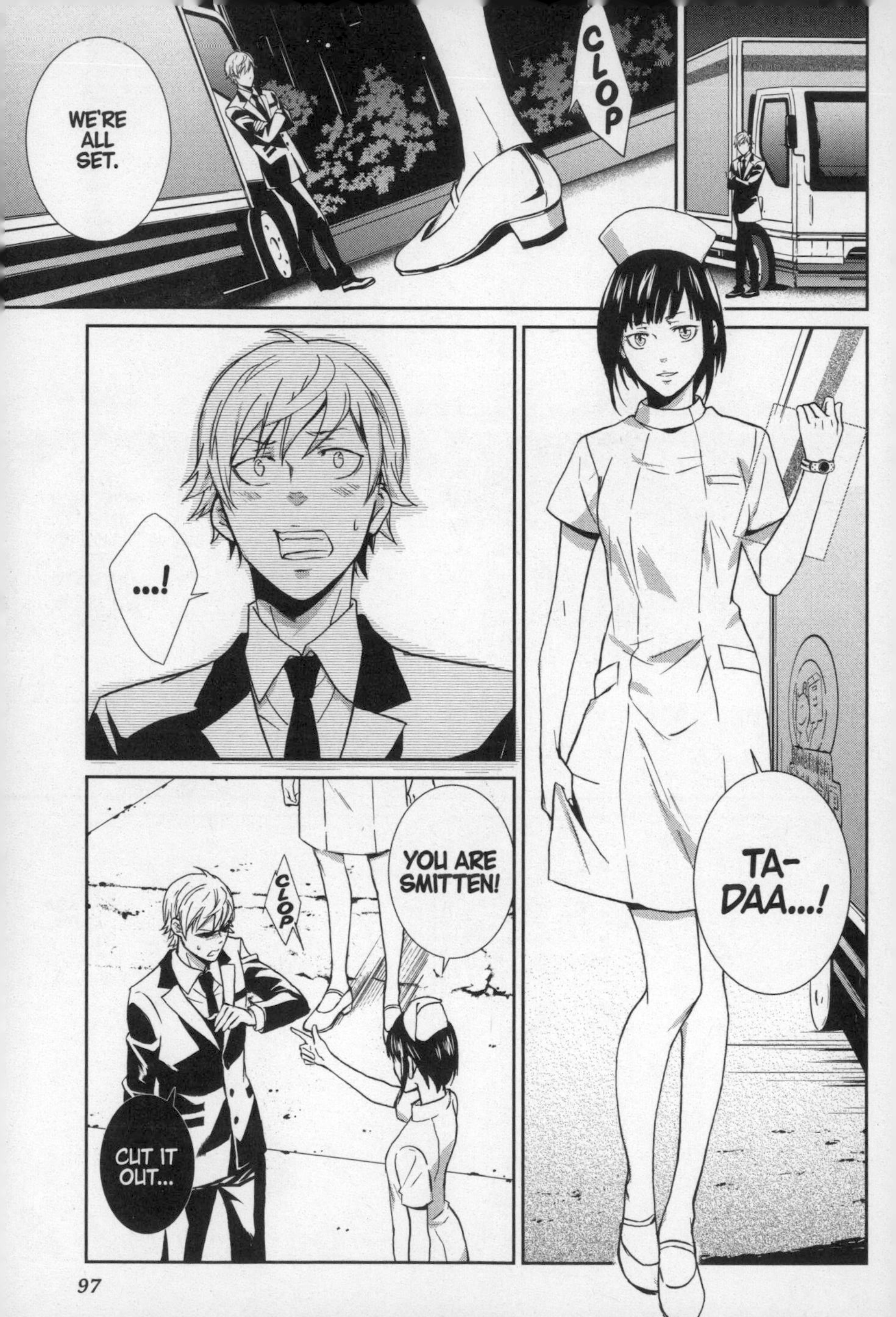
CLOP
WE'RE ALL SET.
TA-DAA...!
...!
YOU ARE SMITTEN!
CLOP
CUT IT OUT...

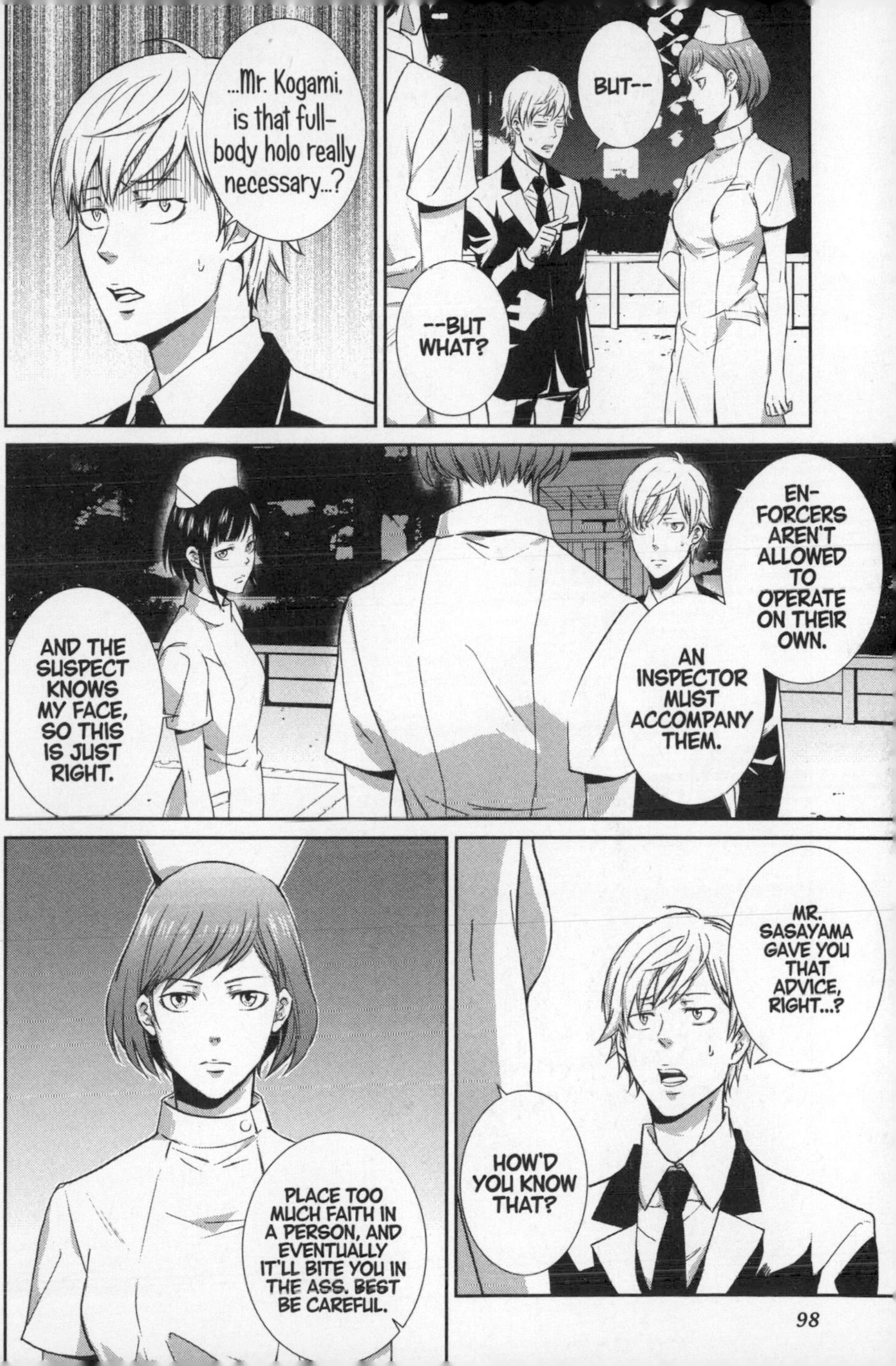
BUT--
--BUT WHAT?
...Mr. Kogami, is that full-body holo really necessary...?
EN-FORCERS AREN'T ALLOWED TO OPERATE ON THEIR OWN.
AN INSPECTOR MUST ACCOMPANY THEM.
AND THE SUSPECT KNOWS MY FACE, SO THIS IS JUST RIGHT.
MR. SASAYAMA GAVE YOU THAT ADVICE, RIGHT...?
HOW'D YOU KNOW THAT?
PLACE TOO MUCH FAITH IN A PERSON, AND EVENTUALLY IT'LL BITE YOU IN THE ASS. BEST BE CAREFUL.

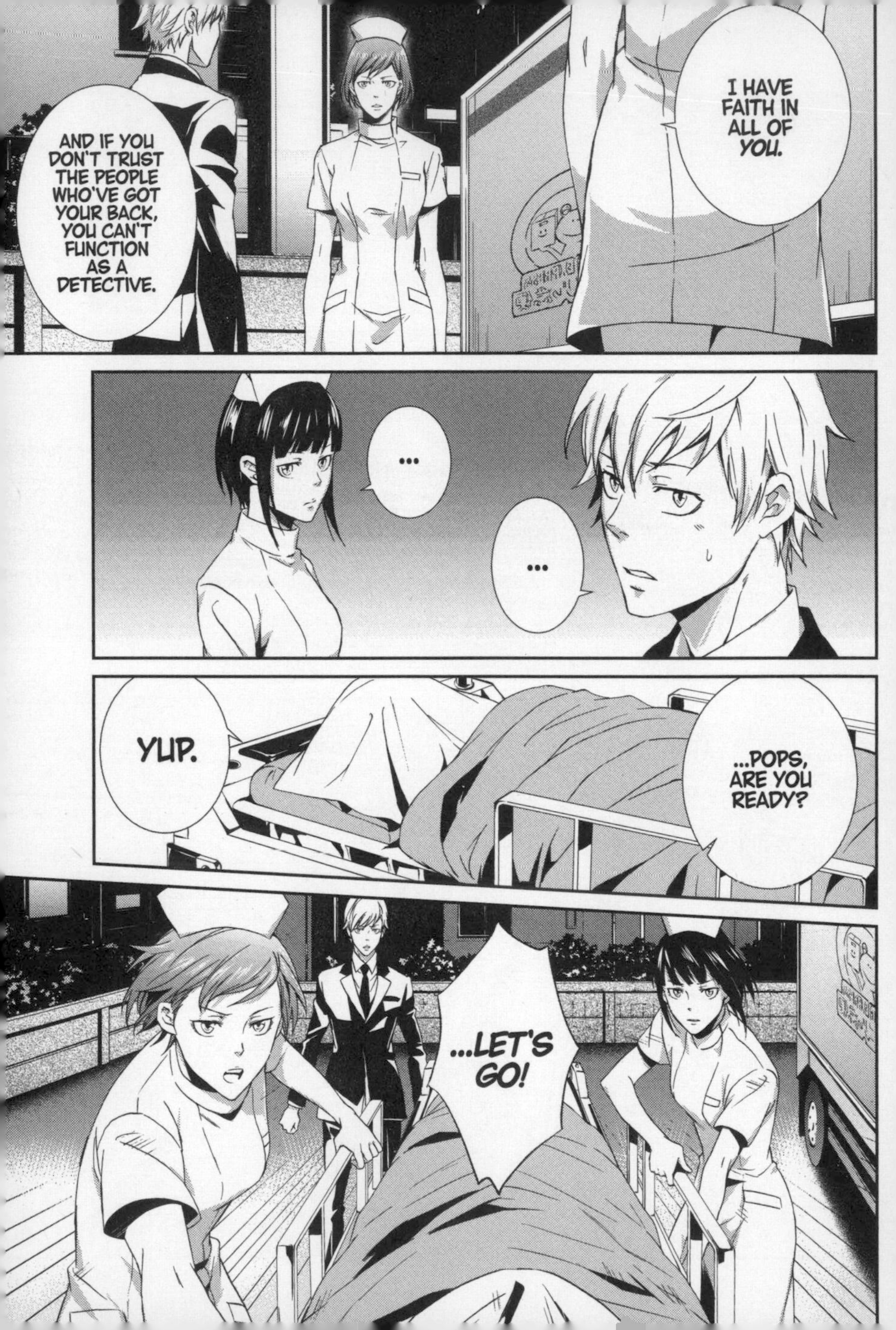
I HAVE FAITH IN ALL OF YOU.
AND IF YOU DON'T TRUST THE PEOPLE WHO'VE GOT YOUR BACK, YOU CAN'T FUNCTION AS A DETECTIVE.
...
...
...POPS, ARE YOU READY?
YUP.
...LET'S GO!

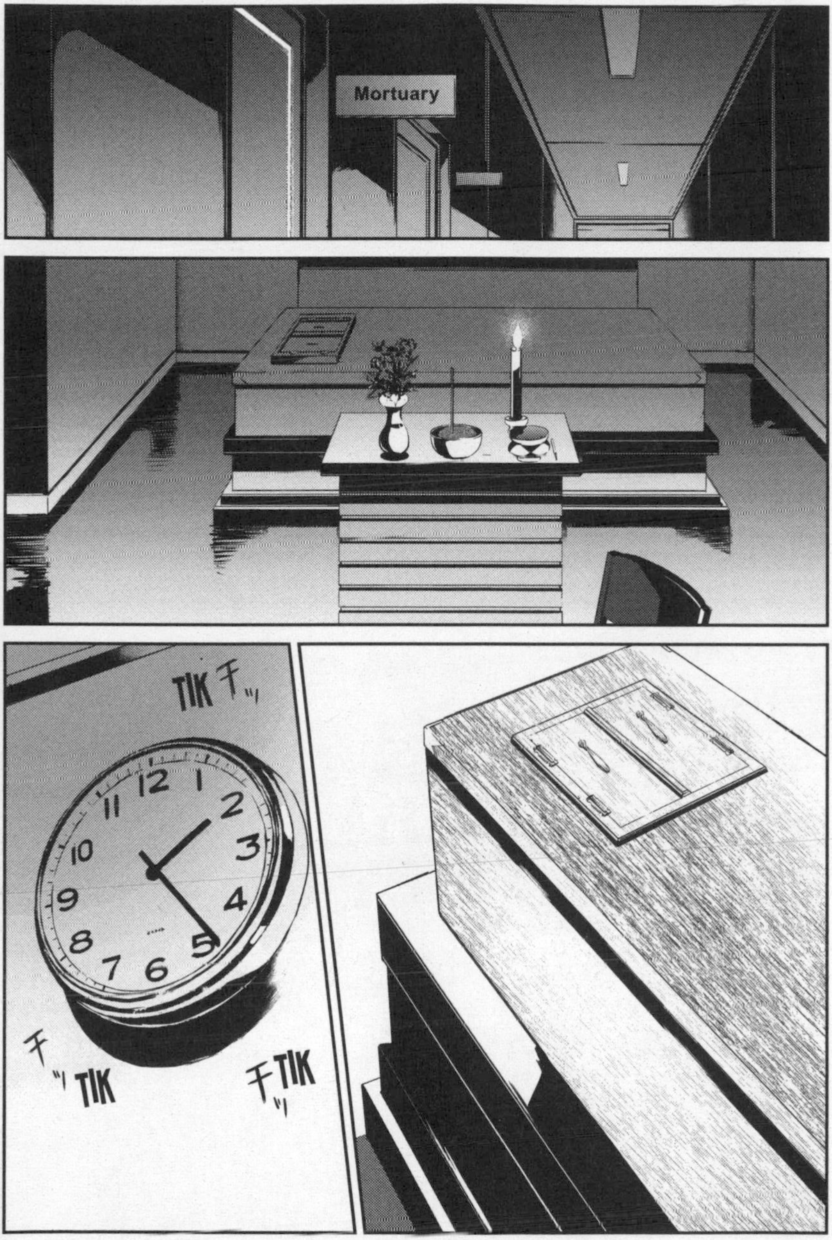
Mortuary
TIK チッ
チッ TIK
チッ TIK

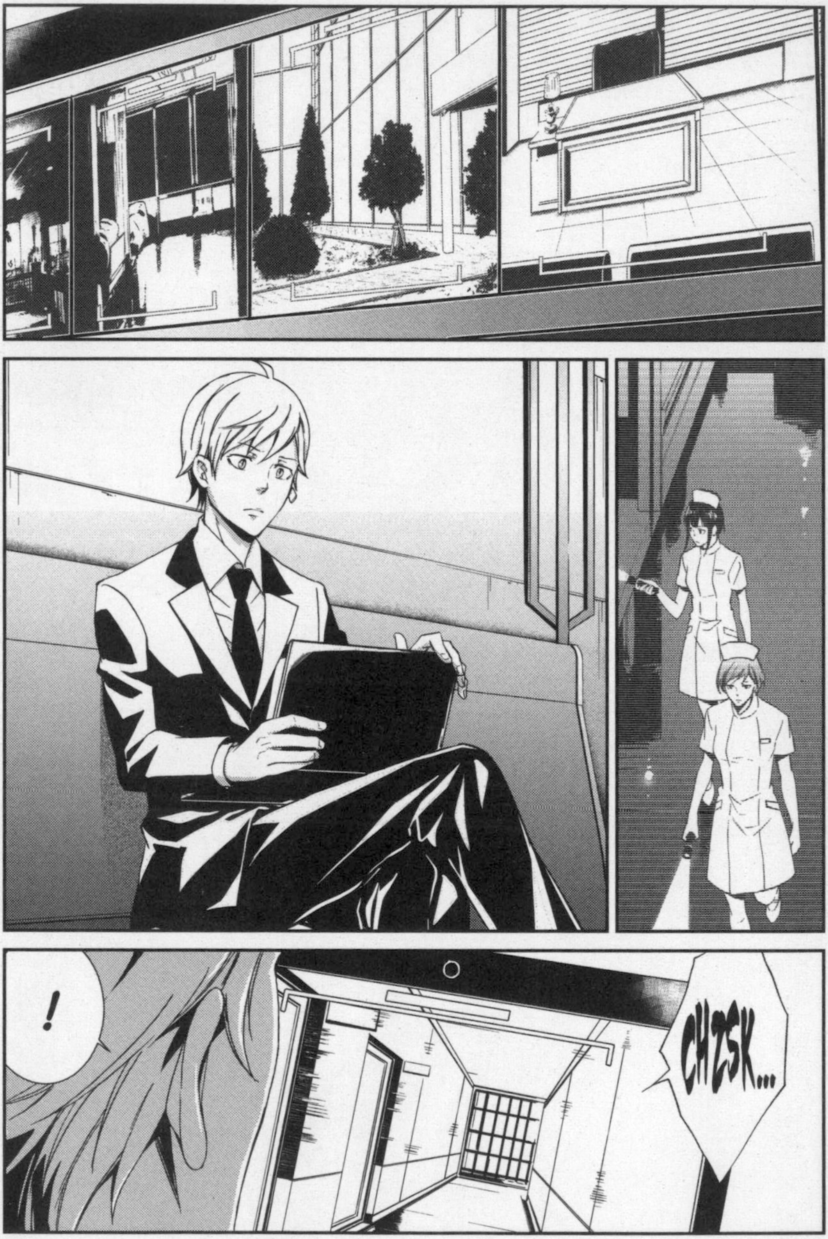
CHZSK...
!

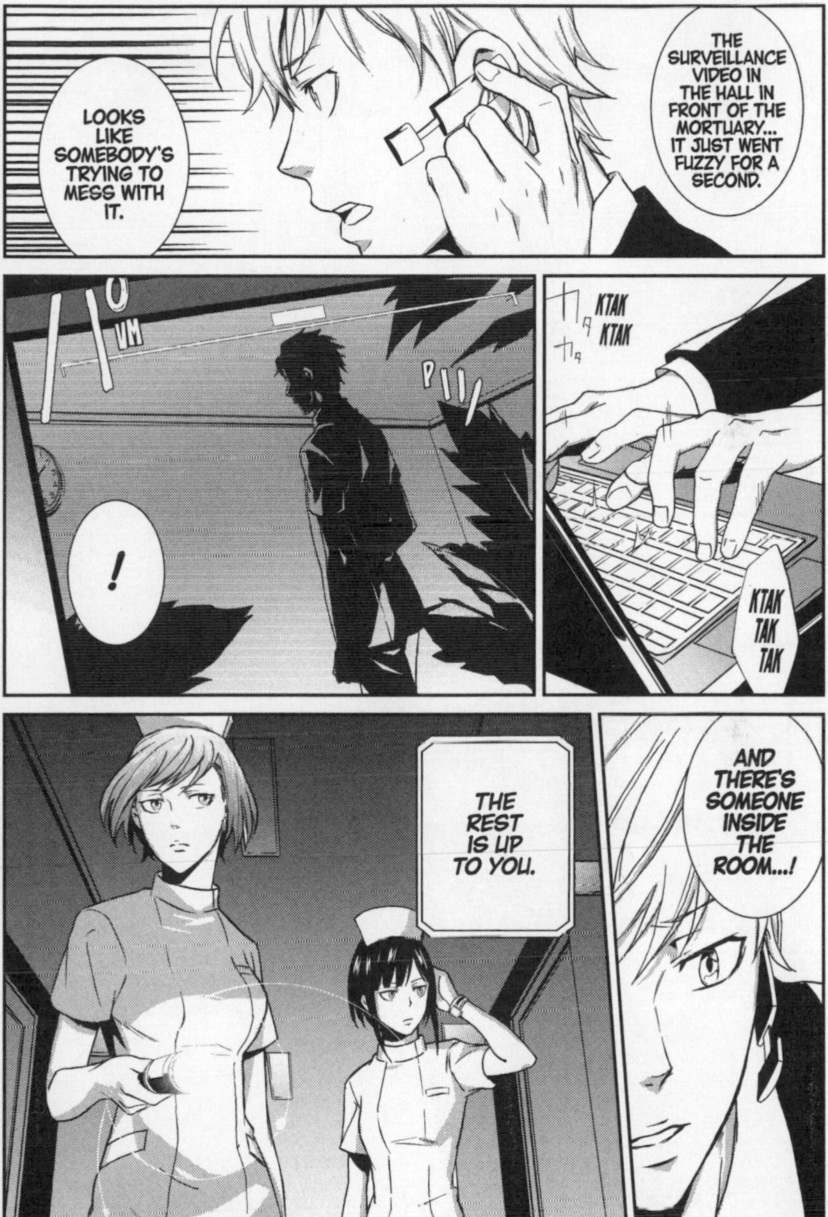
THE SURVEILLANCE VIDEO IN THE HALL IN FRONT OF THE MORTUARY... IT JUST WENT FUZZY FOR A SECOND.
LOOKS LIKE SOMEBODY'S TRYING TO MESS WITH IT.
KTAK KTAK
KTAK TAK TAK
VM
!
AND THERE'S SOMEONE INSIDE THE ROOM...!
THE REST IS UP TO YOU.

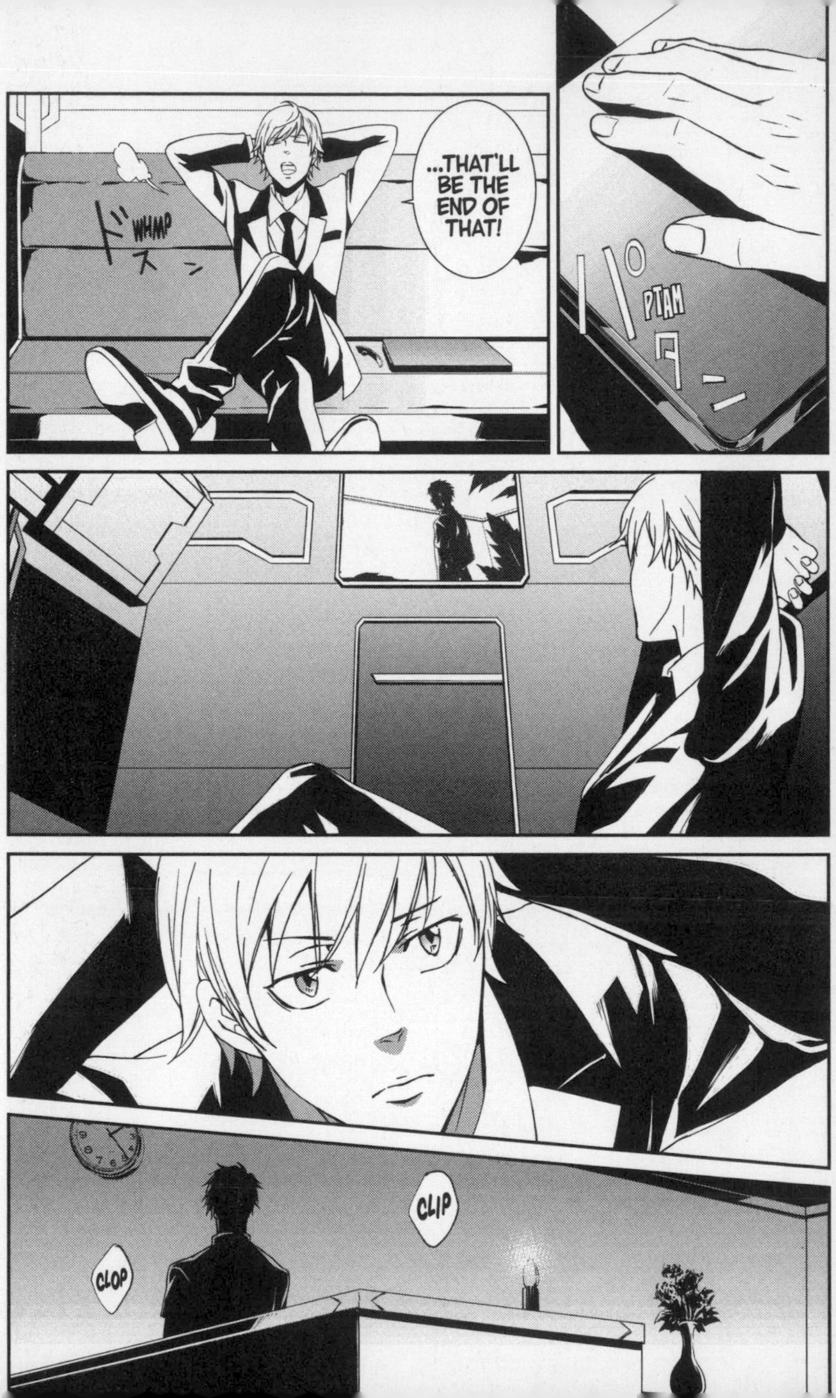
PTAM
パ
...THAT'LL BE THE END OF THAT!
WHMP
ドスン
CLIP
CLOP

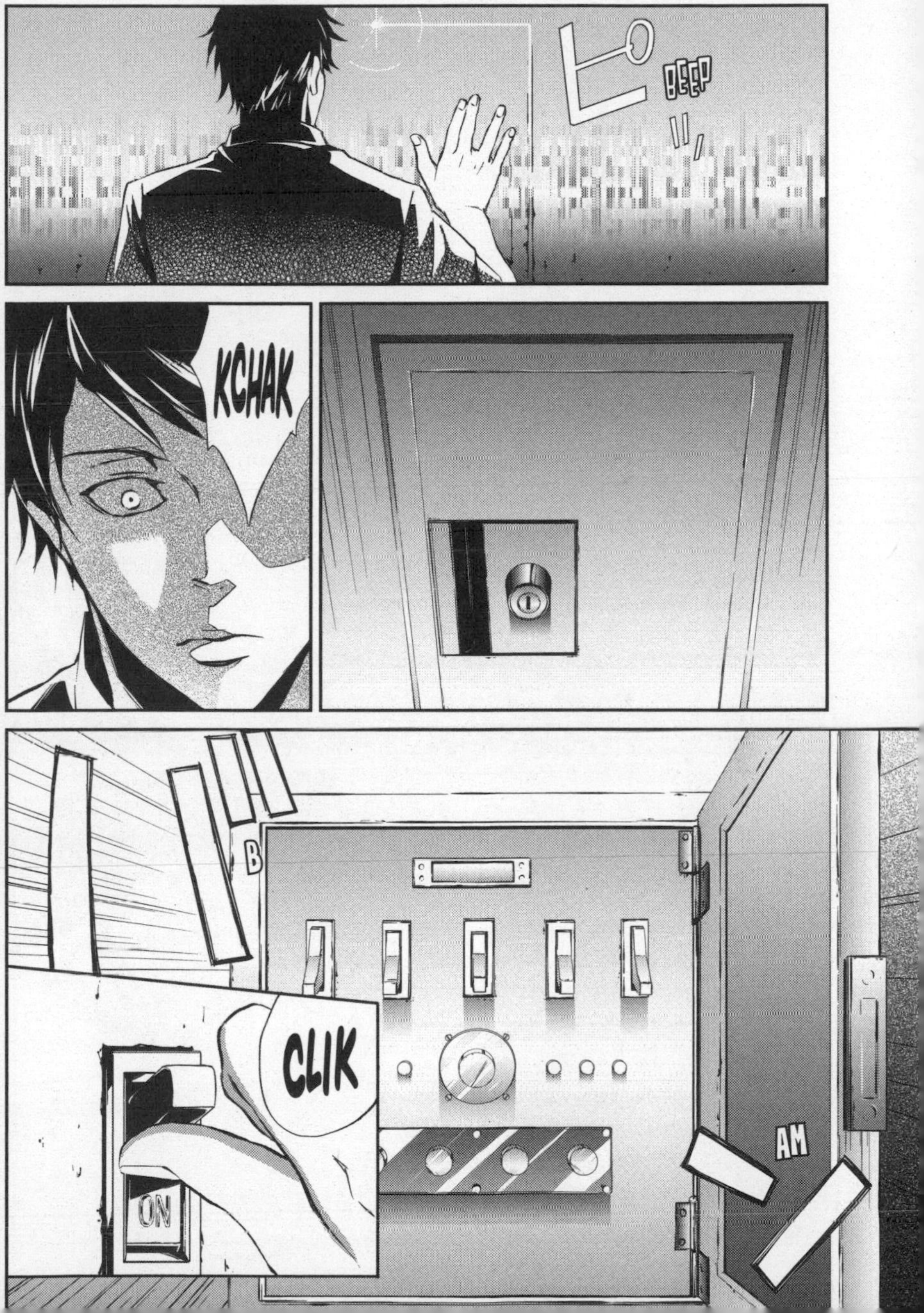
ピ
BEEP
KCHAK
B
AM
CLIK
ON

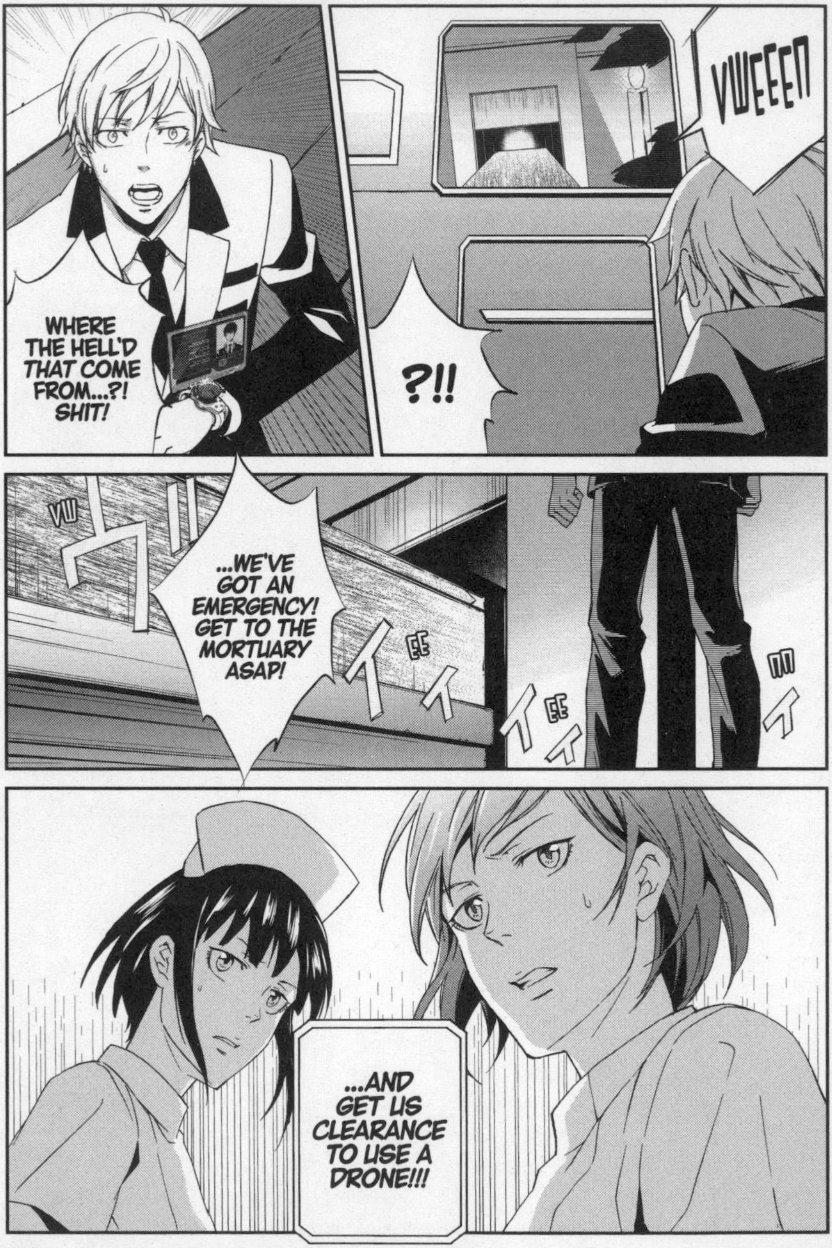
VWEEEN
?!!
WHERE THE HELL'D THAT COME FROM...?! SHIT!
EE
EE
...WE'VE GOT AN EMERGENCY! GET TO THE MORTUARY ASAP!
EE
VU
...AND GET US CLEARANCE TO USE A DRONE!!!

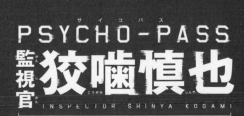

PSYCHO-PASS

監視官 狡噛慎也

INSPECTOR SHINYA KOGAMI

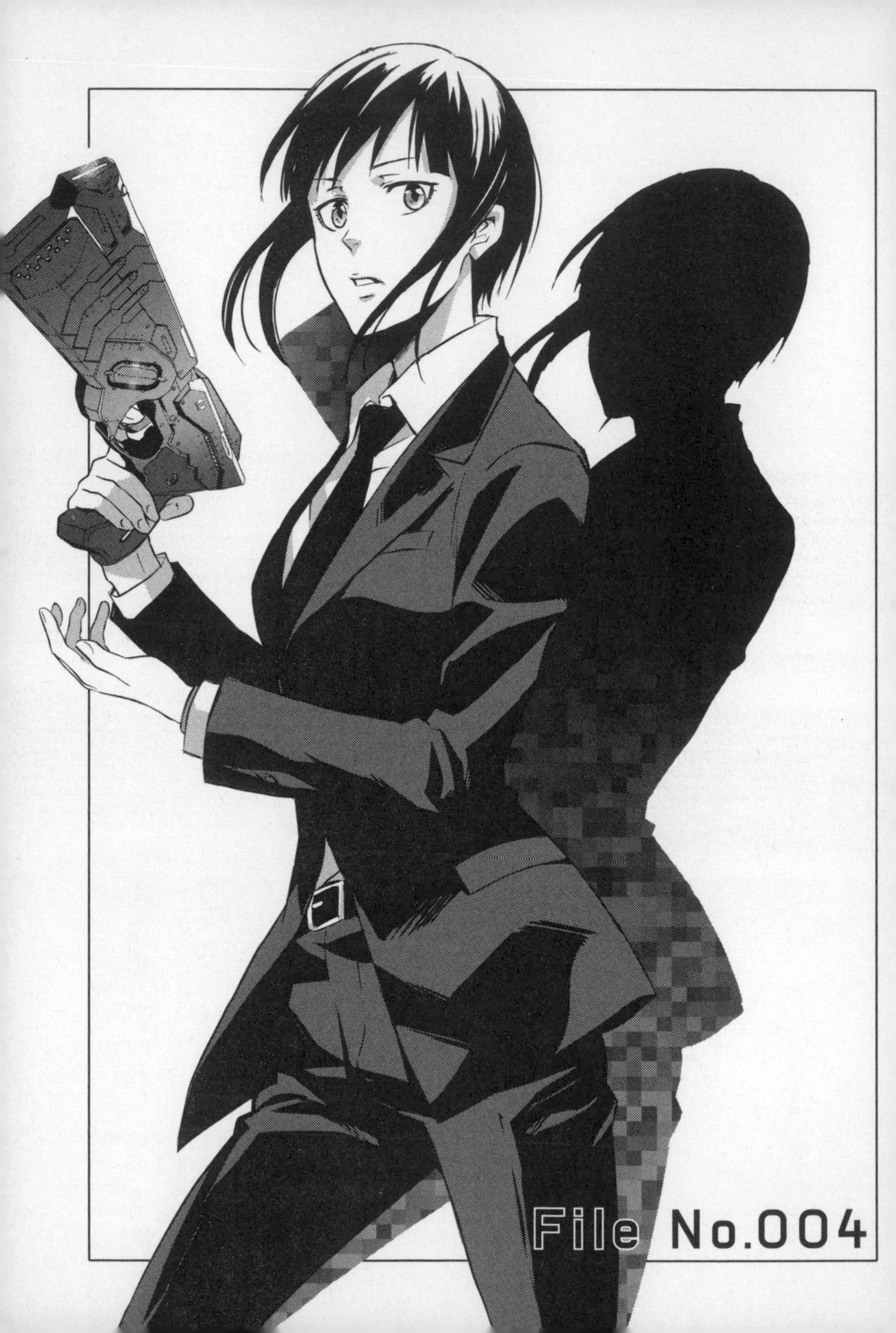
File No.004

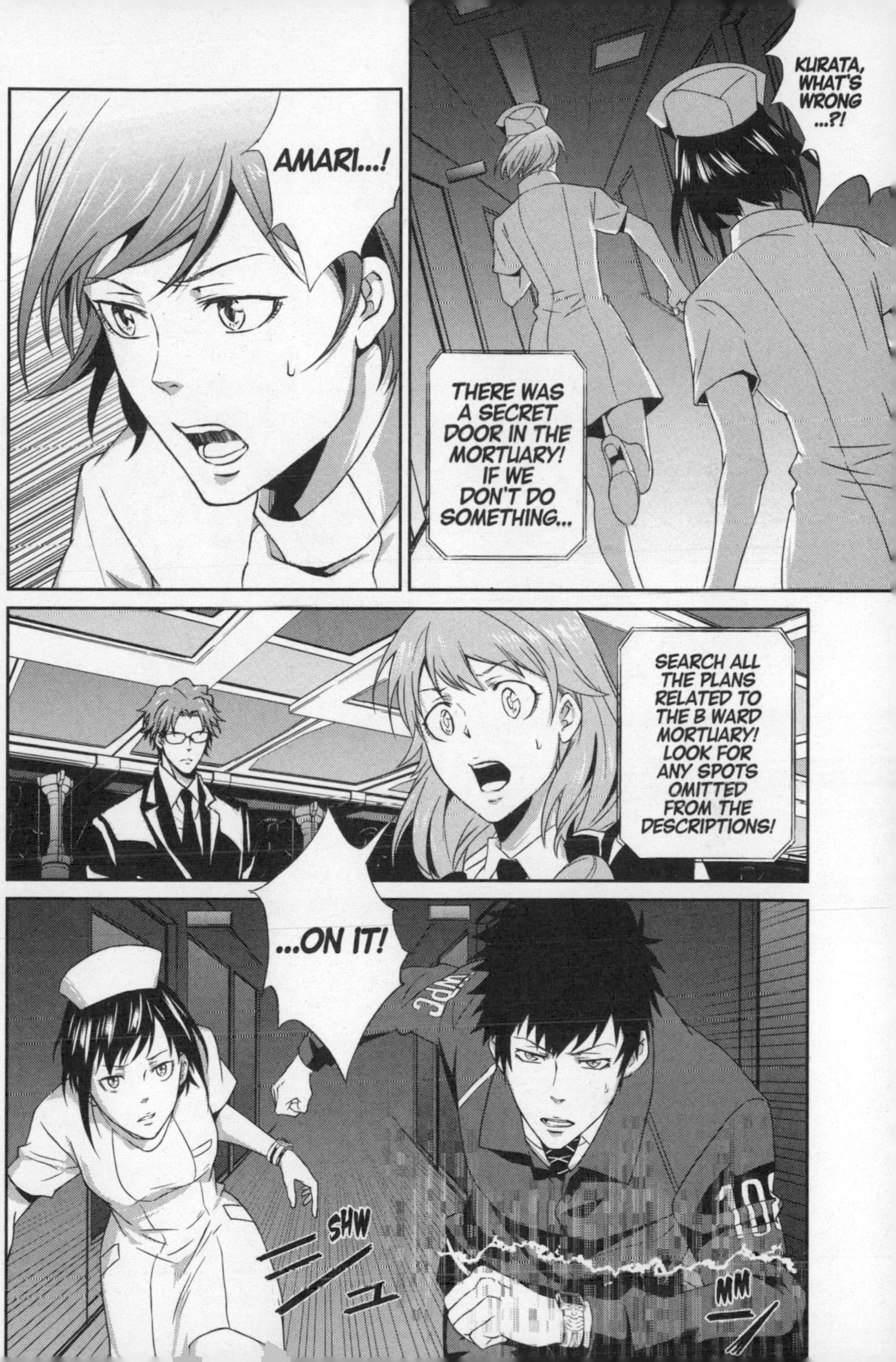
KURATA, WHAT'S WRONG ...?!
THERE WAS A SECRET DOOR IN THE MORTUARY! IF WE DON'T DO SOMETHING...
AMARI...!
SEARCH ALL THE PLANS RELATED TO THE B WARD MORTUARY! LOOK FOR ANY SPOTS OMITTED FROM THE DESCRIPTIONS!
...ON IT!
SHW
MM

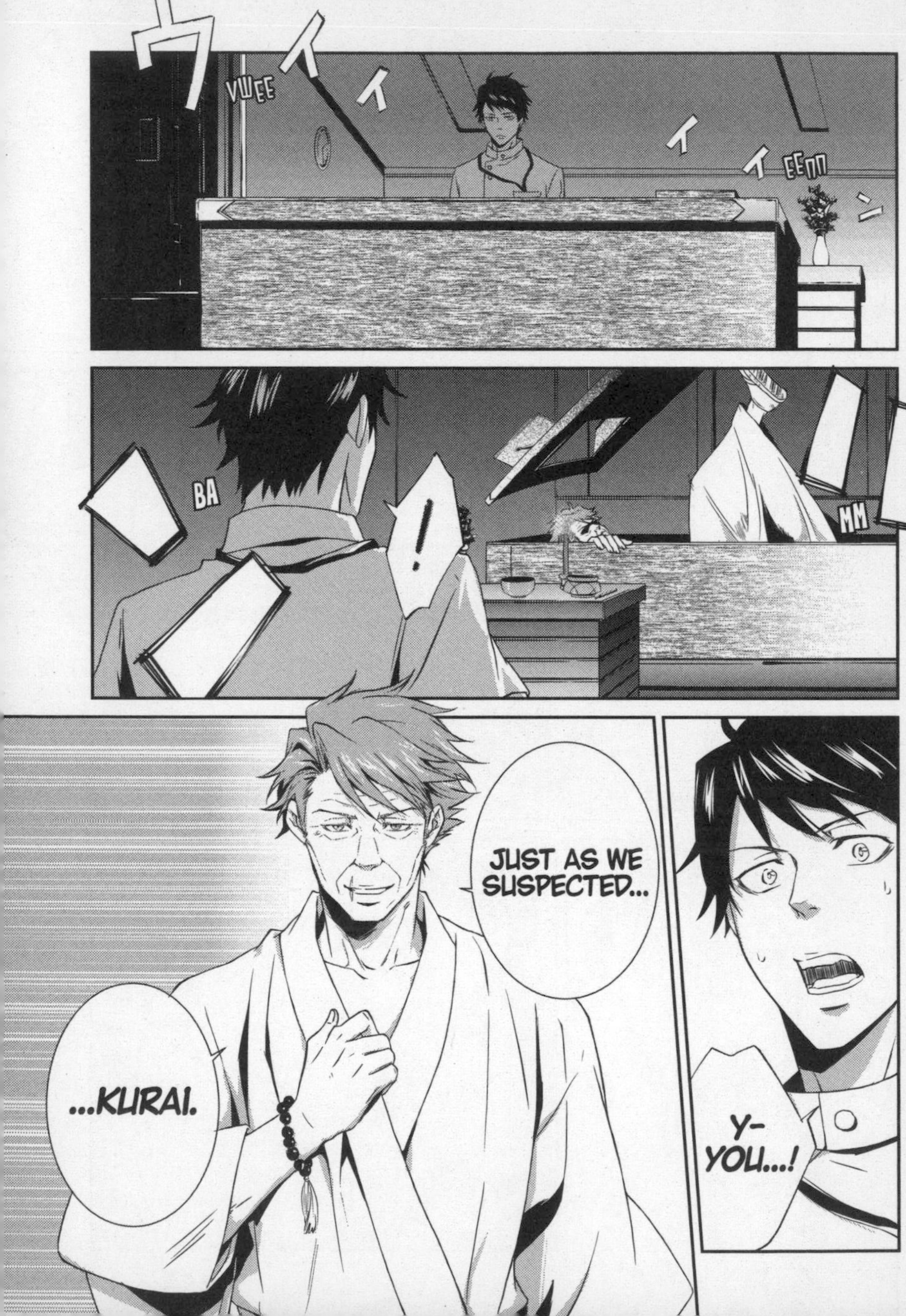
VWEE
EENN
BA
!
MM
Y-
YOU...!
JUST AS WE SUSPECTED...
...KURAI.

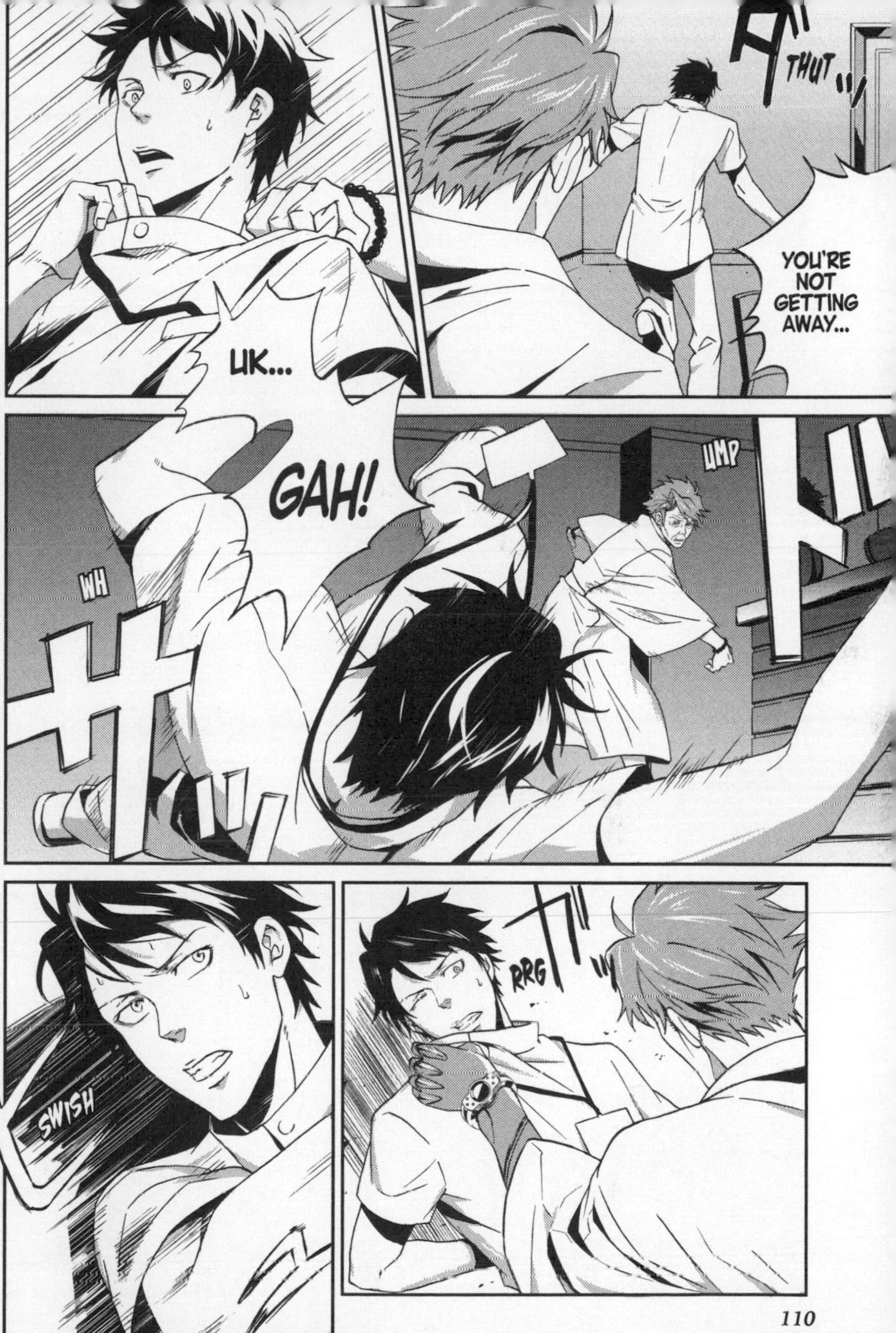
THUT
YOU'RE NOT GETTING AWAY...
UK...
UMP
GAH!
WH
RRG
SWISH

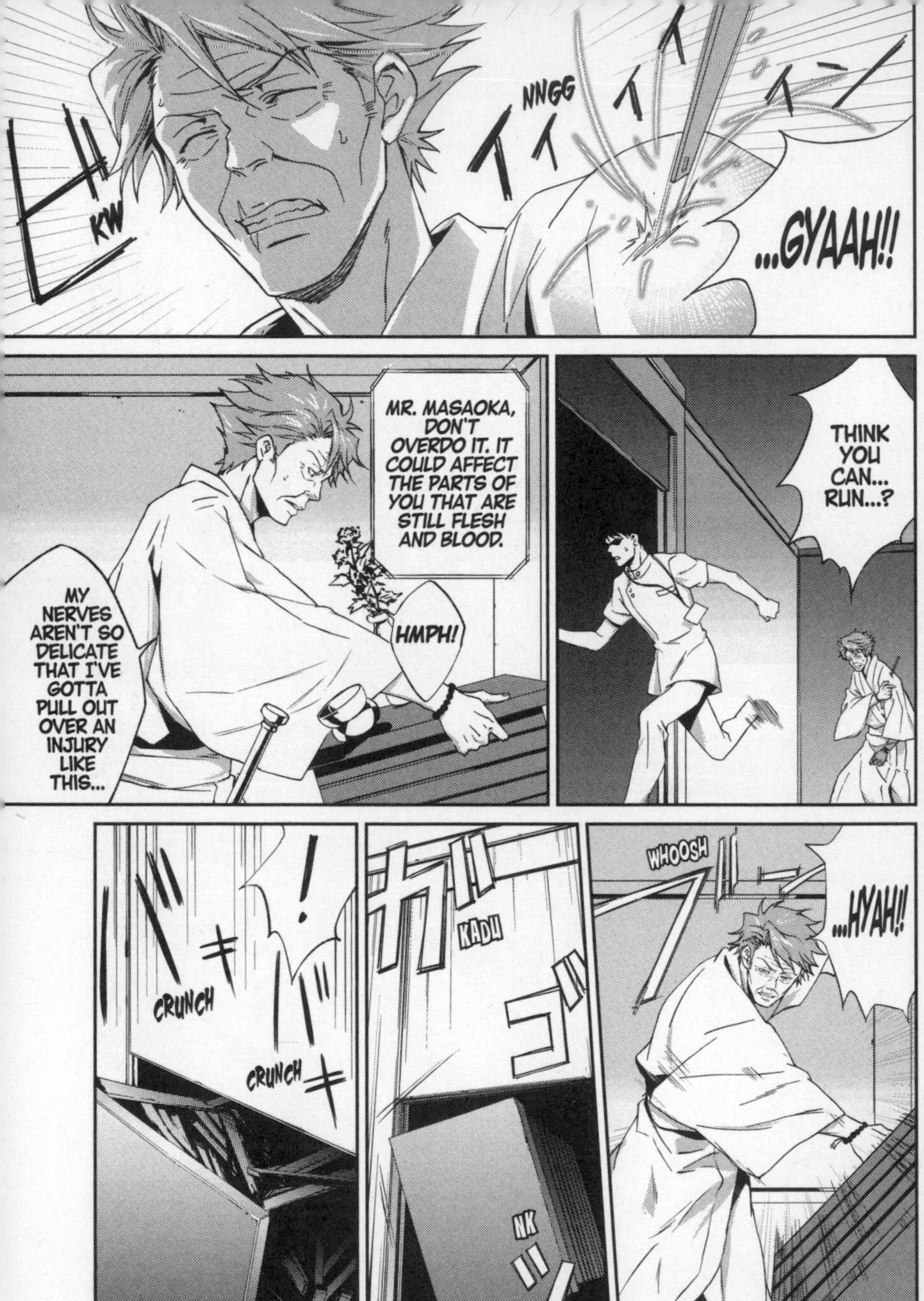
...GYAAH!!
NNGG
KW
THINK YOU CAN... RUN...?
MR. MASAOKA, DON'T OVERDO IT. IT COULD AFFECT THE PARTS OF YOU THAT ARE STILL FLESH AND BLOOD.
HMPH!
MY NERVES AREN'T SO DELICATE THAT I'VE GOTTA PULL OUT OVER AN INJURY LIKE THIS...
WHOOSH
...HYAH!!
KADU
NK
!
CRUNCH
CRUNCH

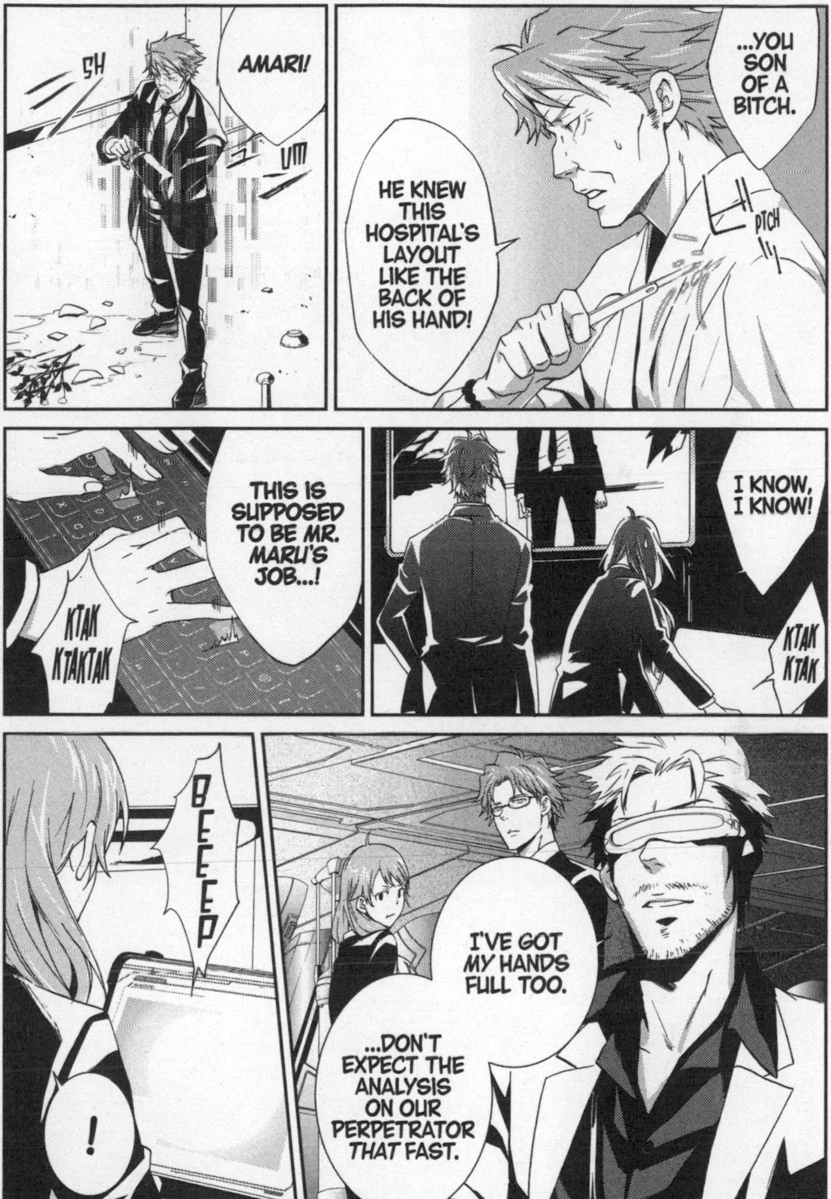
...YOU SON OF A BITCH.
HE KNEW THIS HOSPITAL'S LAYOUT LIKE THE BACK OF HIS HAND!
PTCH
AMARI!
SH
UM
I KNOW, I KNOW!
KTAK KTAK
THIS IS SUPPOSED TO BE MR. MARU'S JOB...!
KTAK KTAKTAK
I'VE GOT MY HANDS FULL TOO.
...DON'T EXPECT THE ANALYSIS ON OUR PERPETRATOR *THAT* FAST.
BEEEP
!

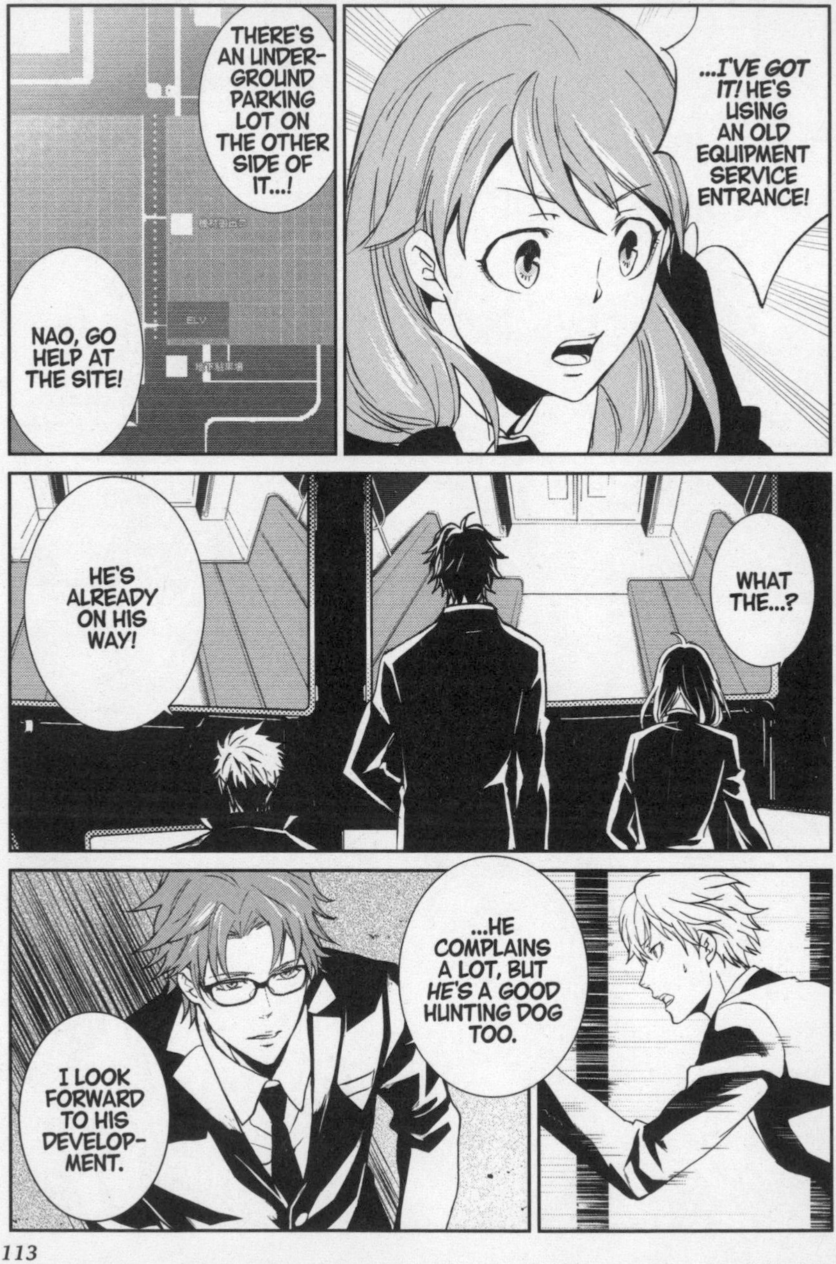
...I'VE GOT IT! HE'S USING AN OLD EQUIPMENT SERVICE ENTRANCE!
THERE'S AN UNDER-GROUND PARKING LOT ON THE OTHER SIDE OF IT...!
NAO, GO HELP AT THE SITE!
ELV
WHAT THE...?
HE'S ALREADY ON HIS WAY!
...HE COMPLAINS A LOT, BUT HE'S A GOOD HUNTING DOG TOO.
I LOOK FORWARD TO HIS DEVELOP-MENT.

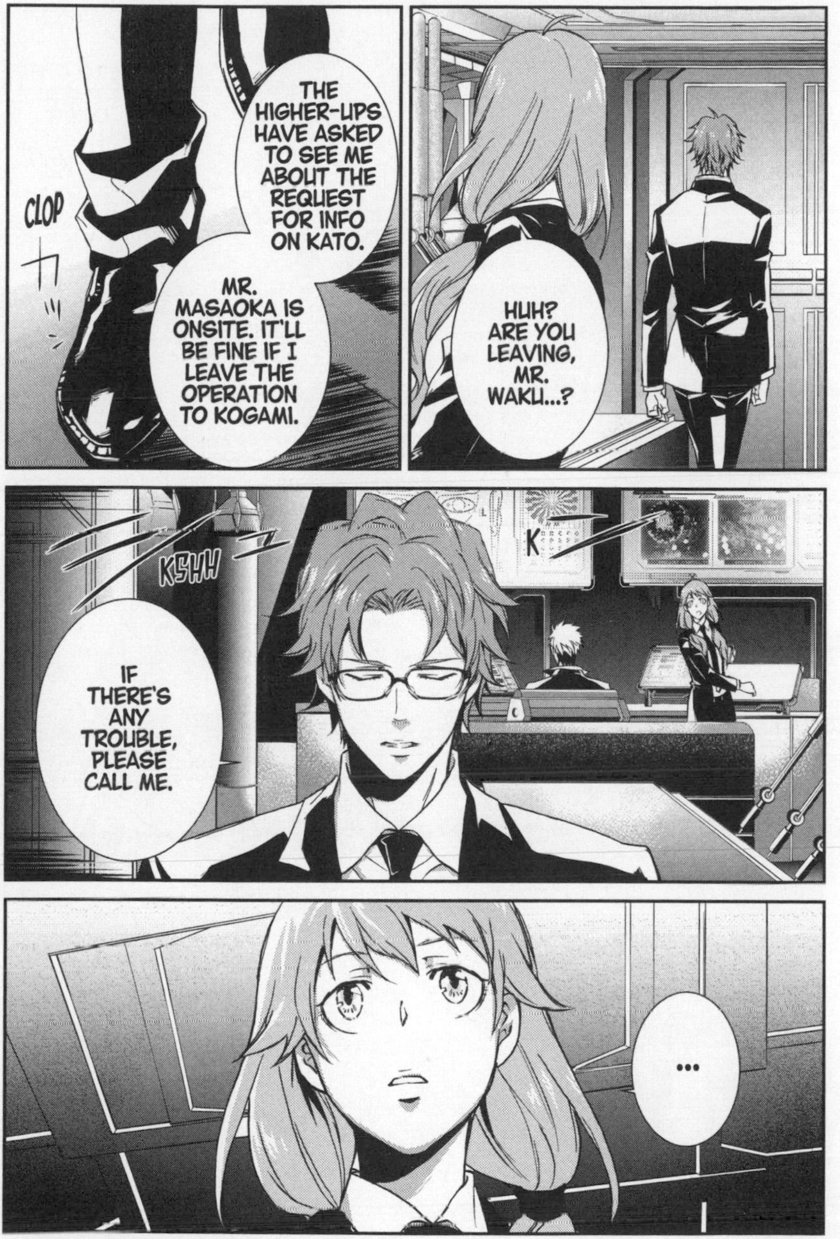
HUH? ARE YOU LEAVING, MR. WAKU...?
THE HIGHER-UPS HAVE ASKED TO SEE ME ABOUT THE REQUEST FOR INFO ON KATO.
MR. MASAOKA IS ONSITE. IT'LL BE FINE IF I LEAVE THE OPERATION TO KOGAMI.
CLOP
K
KSHH
IF THERE'S ANY TROUBLE, PLEASE CALL ME.
...

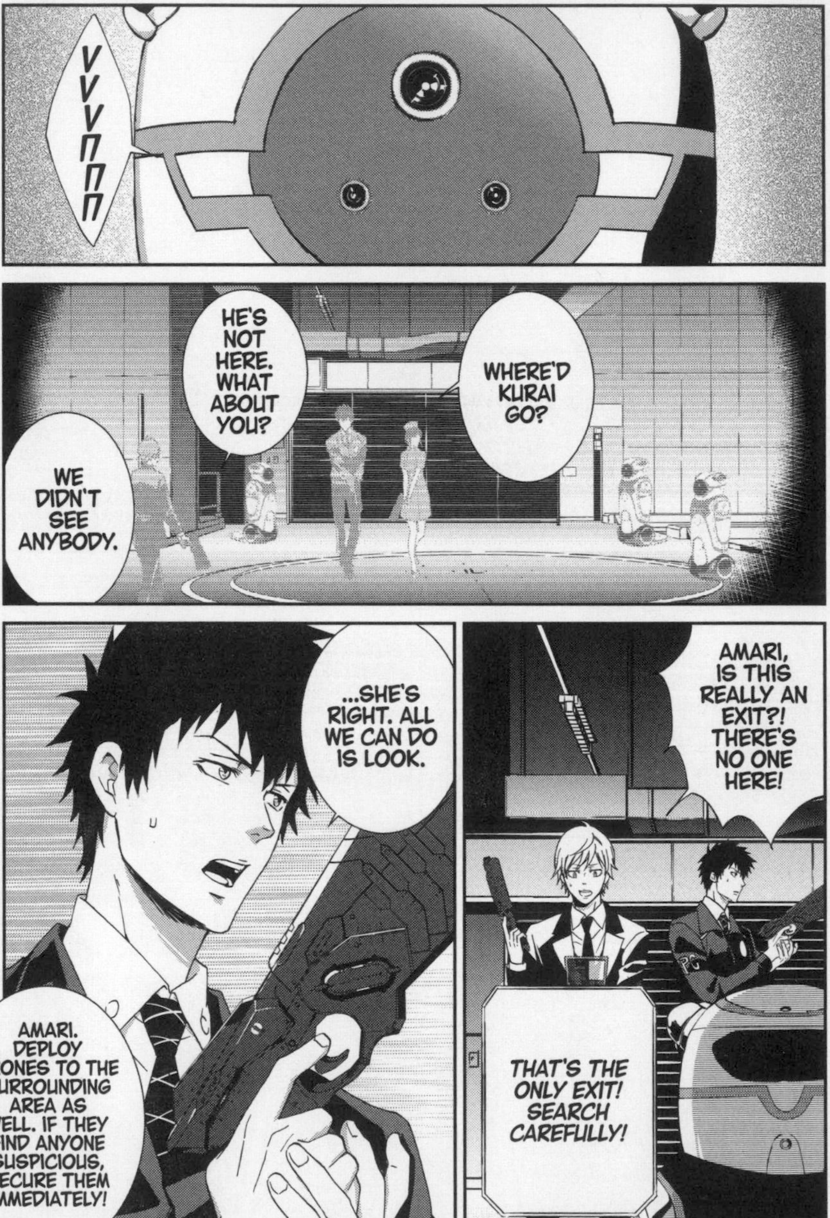
VVVNNN
WHERE'D KURAI GO?
HE'S NOT HERE. WHAT ABOUT YOU?
WE DIDN'T SEE ANYBODY.
AMARI, IS THIS REALLY AN EXIT?! THERE'S NO ONE HERE!
THAT'S THE ONLY EXIT! SEARCH CAREFULLY!
...SHE'S RIGHT. ALL WE CAN DO IS LOOK.
AMARI. DEPLOY DRONES TO THE SURROUNDING AREA AS WELL. IF THEY FIND ANYONE SUSPICIOUS, SECURE THEM IMMEDIATELY!

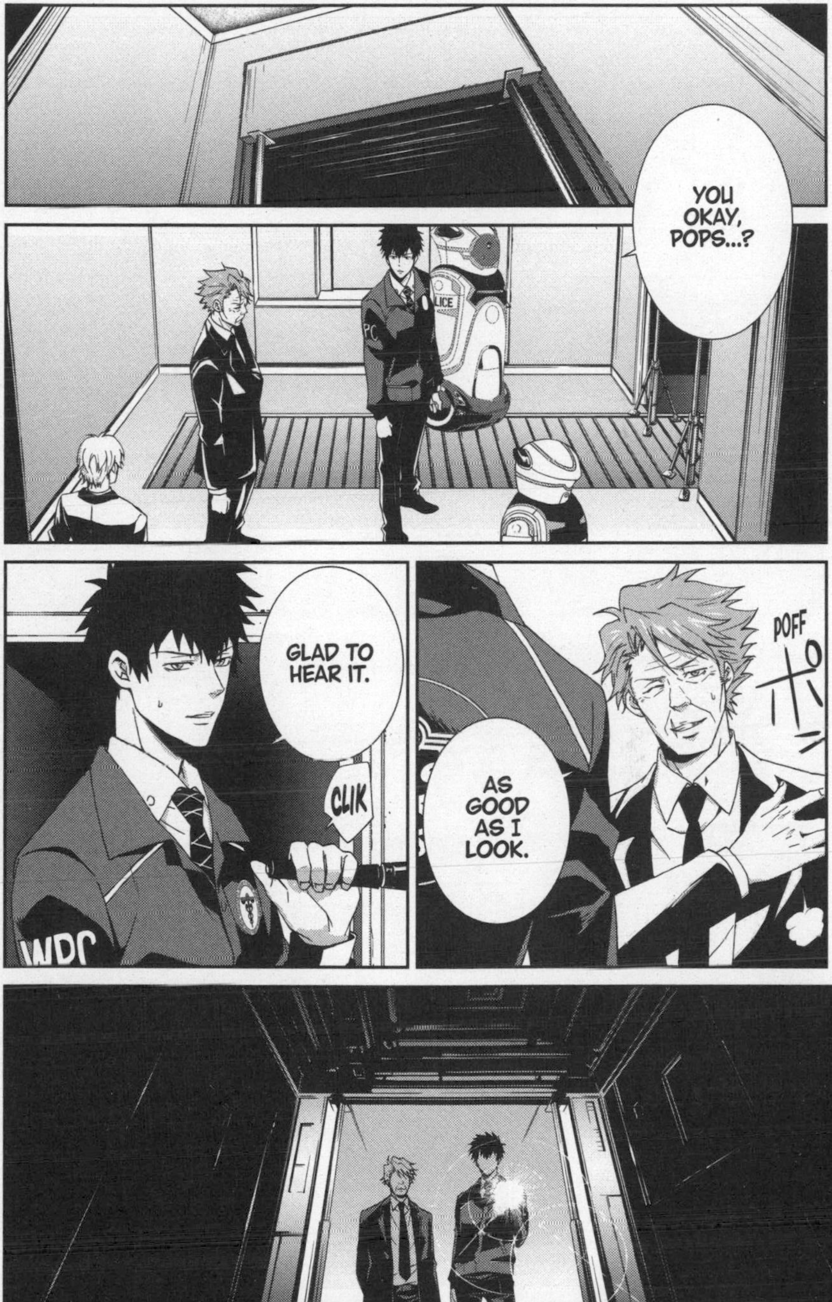
YOU OKAY, POPS...?
POFF
AS GOOD AS I LOOK.
GLAD TO HEAR IT.
CLIK

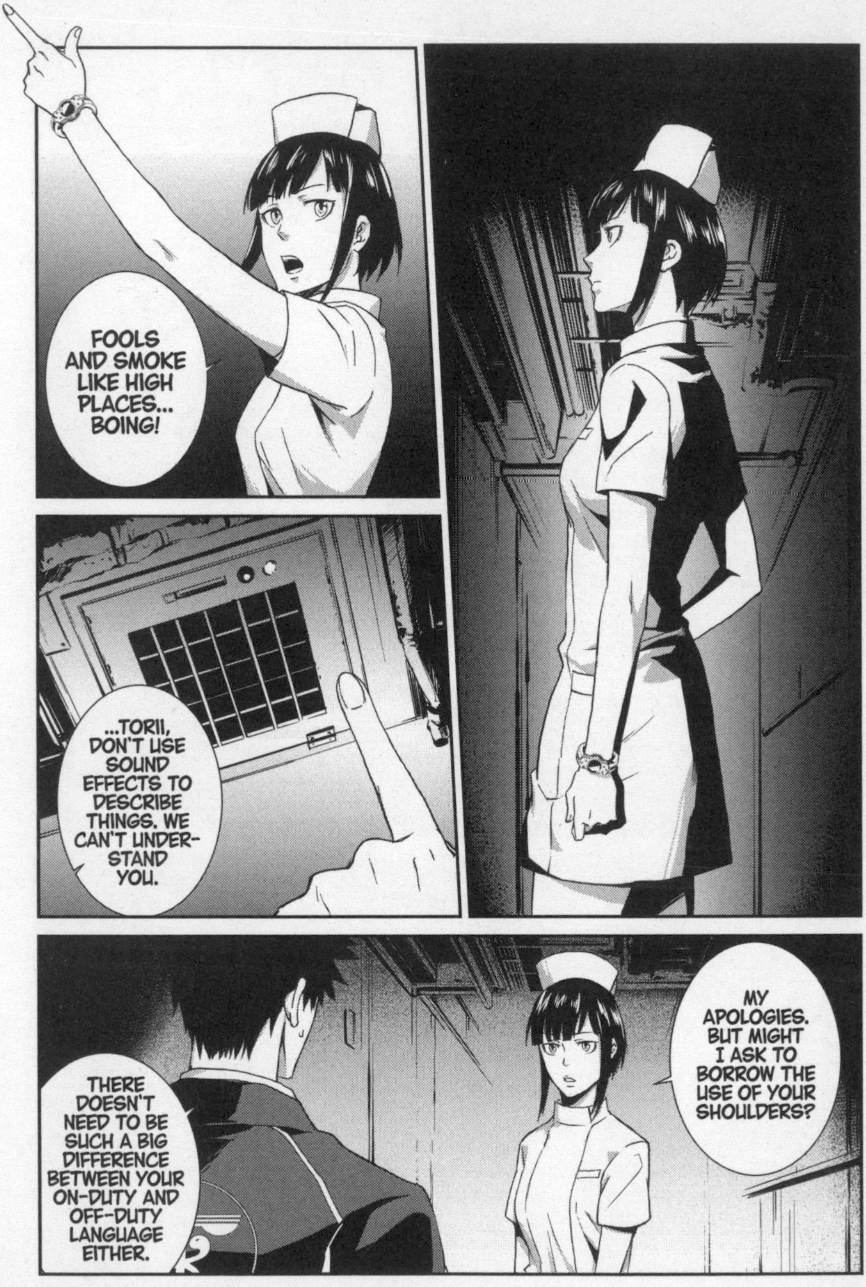
FOOLS AND SMOKE LIKE HIGH PLACES... BOING!
...TORII, DON'T USE SOUND EFFECTS TO DESCRIBE THINGS. WE CAN'T UNDER-STAND YOU.
MY APOLOGIES. BUT MIGHT I ASK TO BORROW THE USE OF YOUR SHOULDERS?
THERE DOESN'T NEED TO BE SUCH A BIG DIFFERENCE BETWEEN YOUR ON-DUTY AND OFF-DUTY LANGUAGE EITHER.

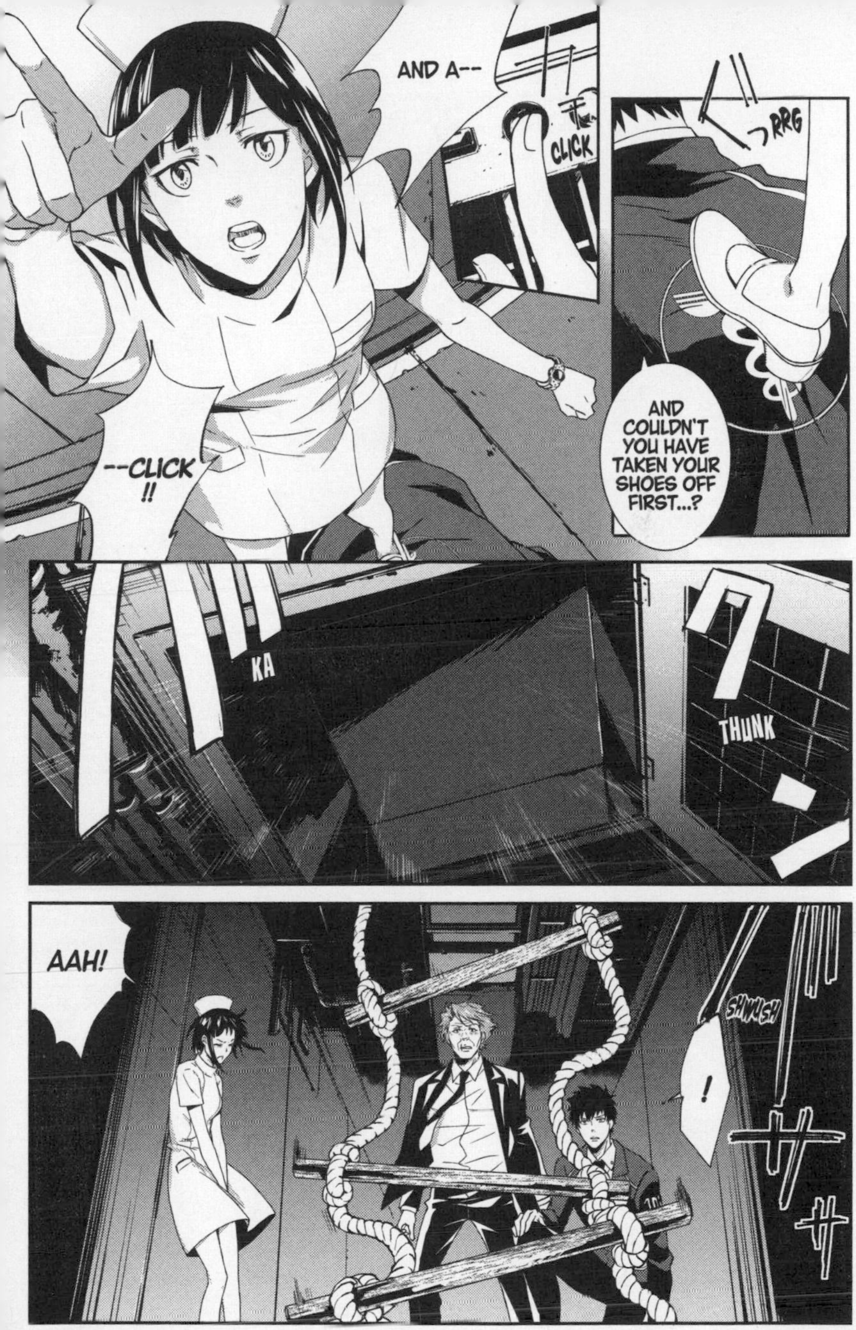
RRG
AND COULDN'T YOU HAVE TAKEN YOUR SHOES OFF FIRST...?
AND A--
CLICK
--CLICK !!
THUNK
KA
SHWUSH
!
AAH!

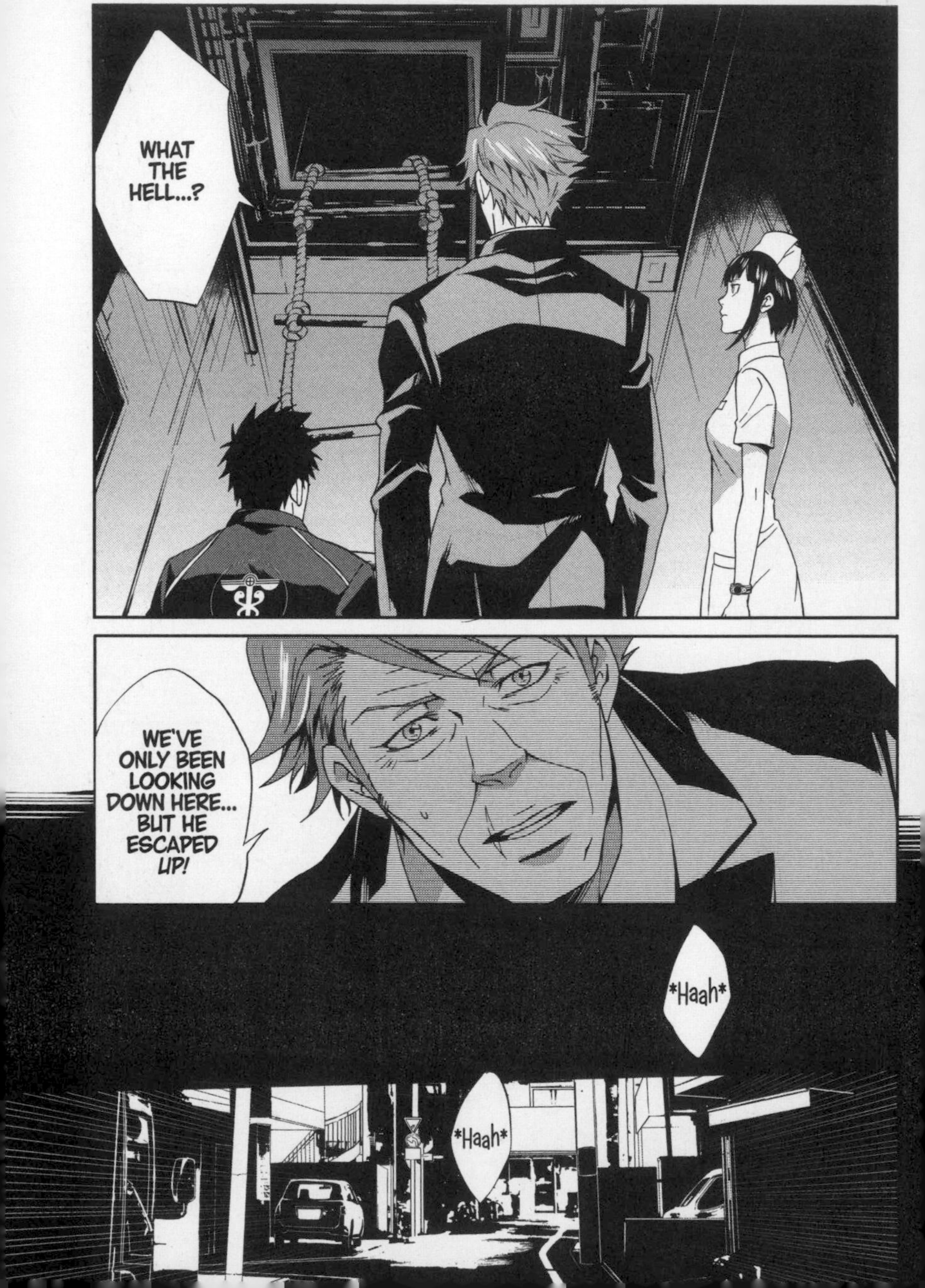
WHAT THE HELL...?
WE'VE ONLY BEEN LOOKING DOWN HERE... BUT HE ESCAPED UP!
Haah
Haah

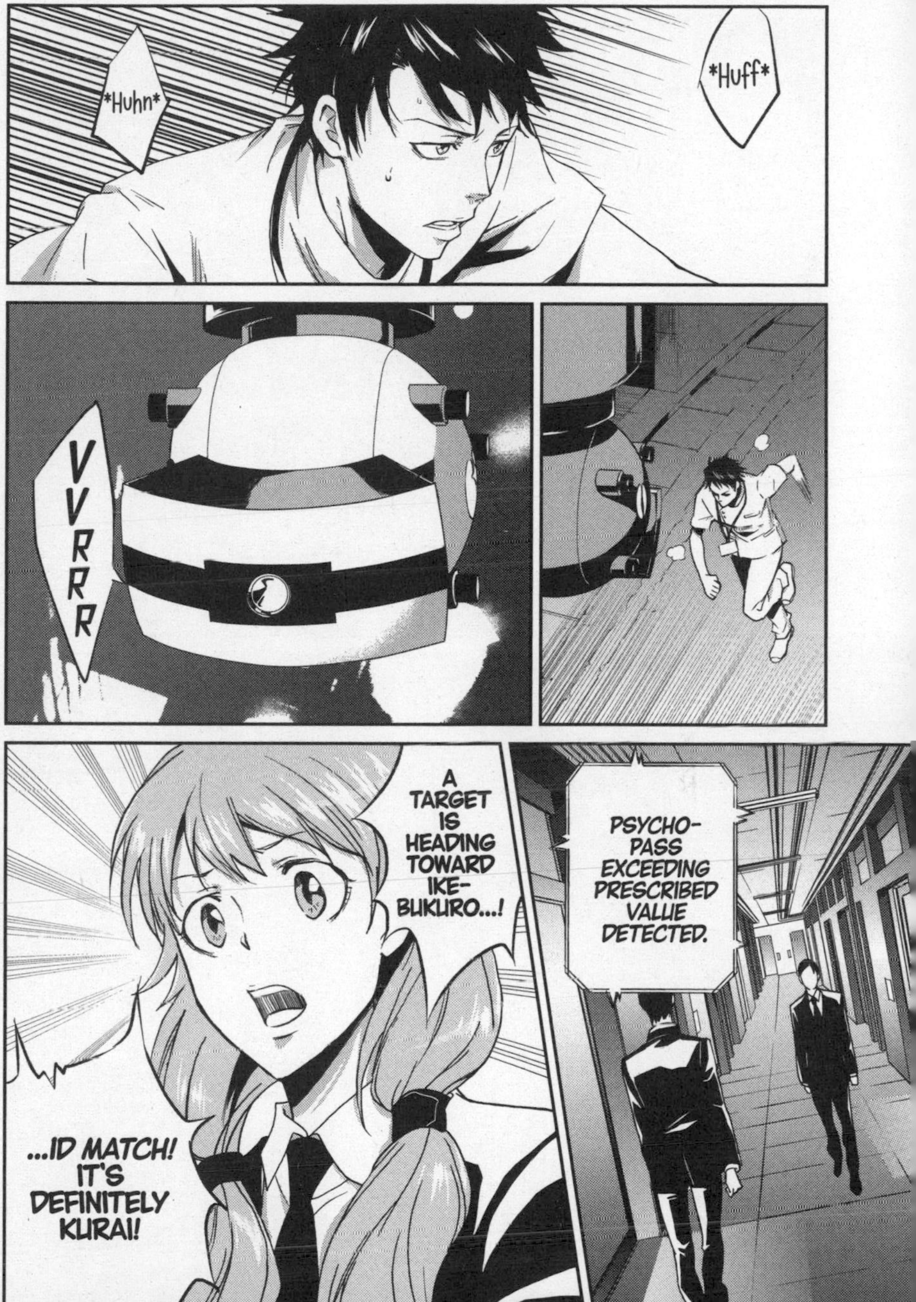
Huff
Huhn
VVRRR
PSYCHO-PASS EXCEEDING PRESCRIBED VALUE DETECTED.
A TARGET IS HEADING TOWARD IKE-BUKURO...!
...ID MATCH! IT'S DEFINITELY KURAI!

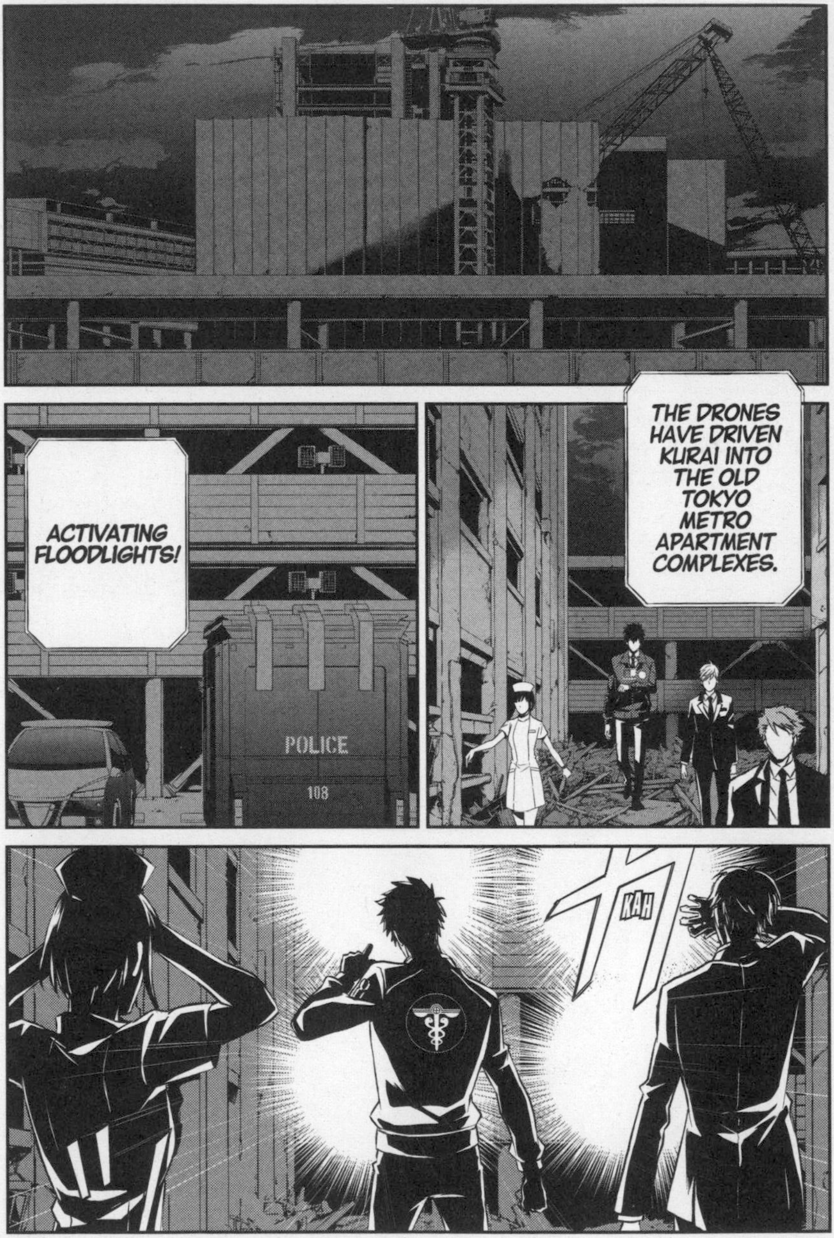
THE DRONES HAVE DRIVEN KURAI INTO THE OLD TOKYO METRO APARTMENT COMPLEXES.
ACTIVATING FLOODLIGHTS!
POLICE
108
KAH

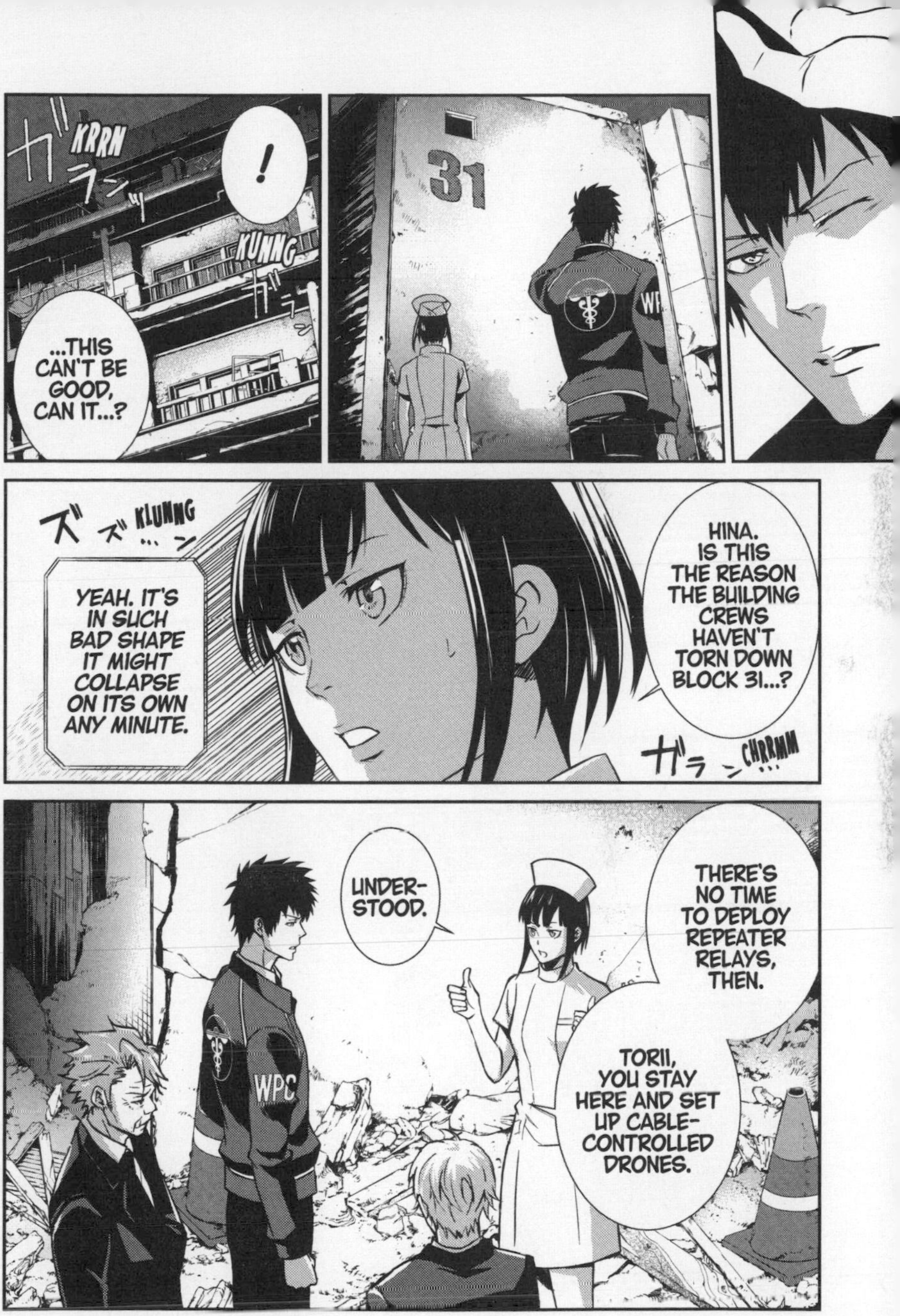

KRRN
!
KUNNG
...THIS CAN'T BE GOOD, CAN IT...?
HINA. IS THIS THE REASON THE BUILDING CREWS HAVEN'T TORN DOWN BLOCK 31...?
KLUNNG
YEAH. IT'S IN SUCH BAD SHAPE IT MIGHT COLLAPSE ON ITS OWN ANY MINUTE.
CHRRMM
31
WPC
THERE'S NO TIME TO DEPLOY REPEATER RELAYS, THEN.
UNDER-STOOD.
TORII, YOU STAY HERE AND SET UP CABLE-CONTROLLED DRONES.

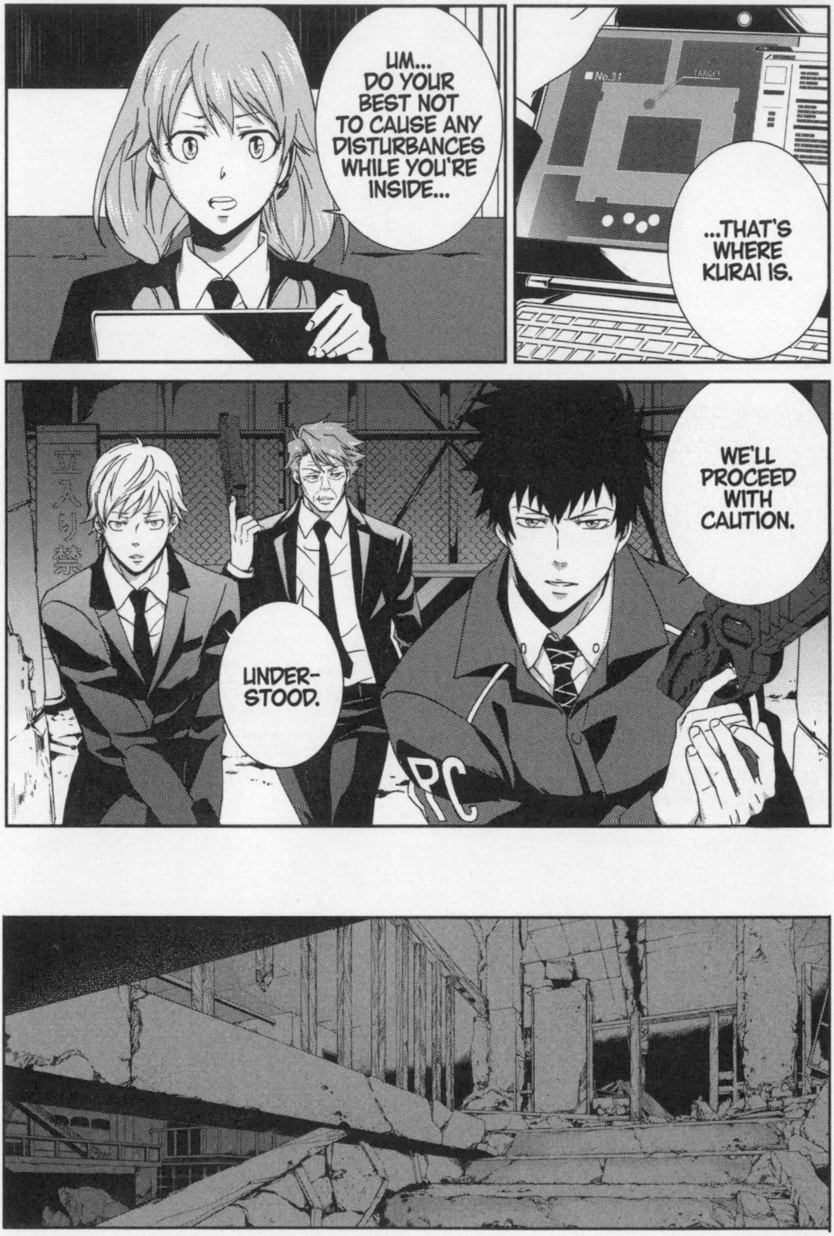
No.31
TARGET
...THAT'S WHERE KURAI IS.
UM... DO YOUR BEST NOT TO CAUSE ANY DISTURBANCES WHILE YOU'RE INSIDE...
WE'LL PROCEED WITH CAUTION.
UNDER-STOOD.

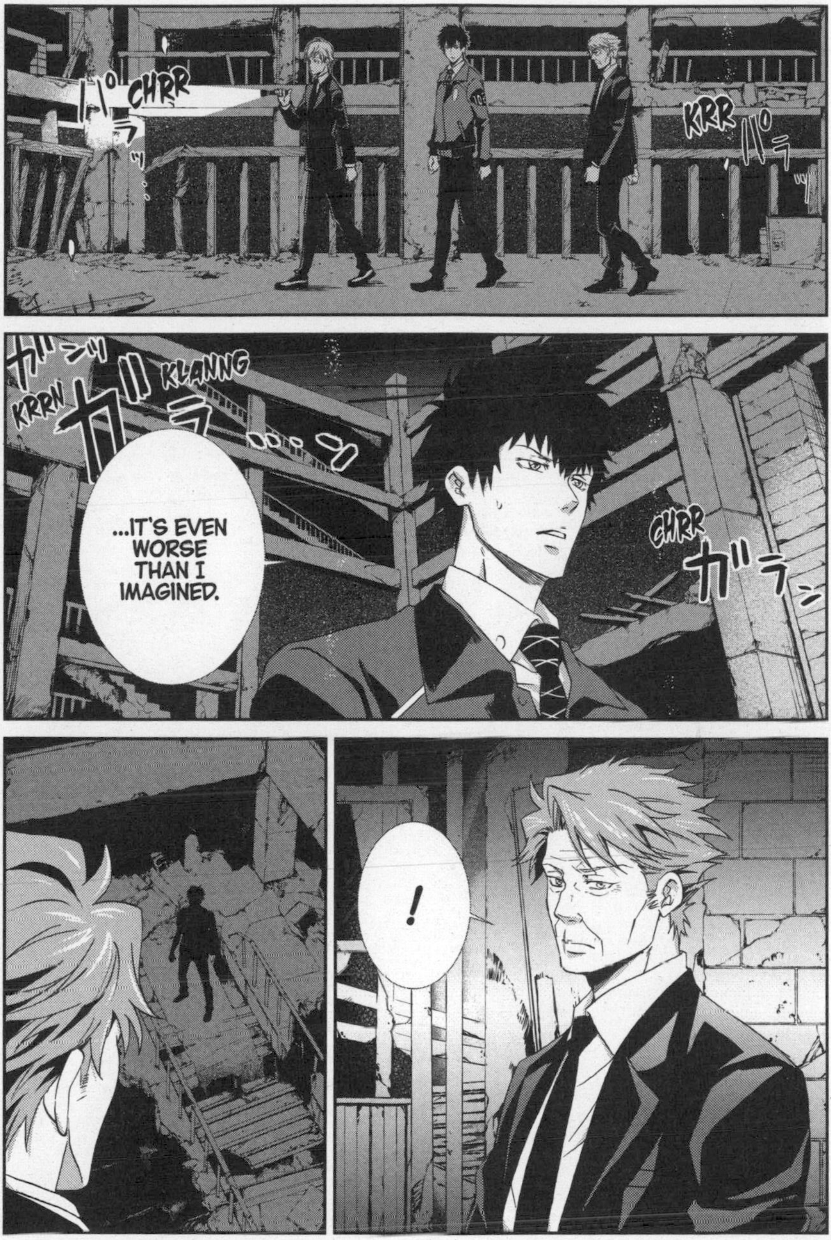
KRR
CHRR
KLANNG
KRRN
CHRR
...IT'S EVEN WORSE THAN I IMAGINED.
!

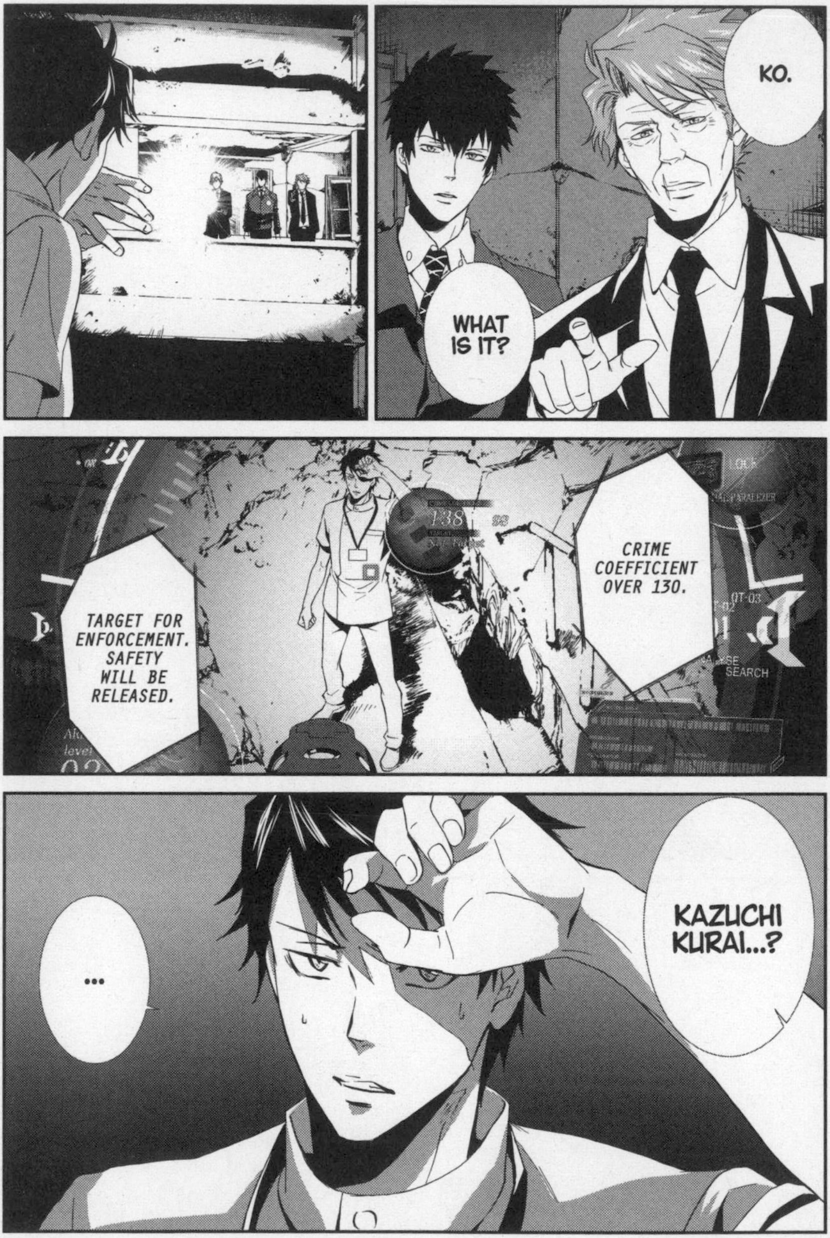
KO.
WHAT IS IT?
CRIME COEFFICIENT OVER 130.
TARGET FOR ENFORCEMENT. SAFETY WILL BE RELEASED.
KAZUCHI KURAI...?
...

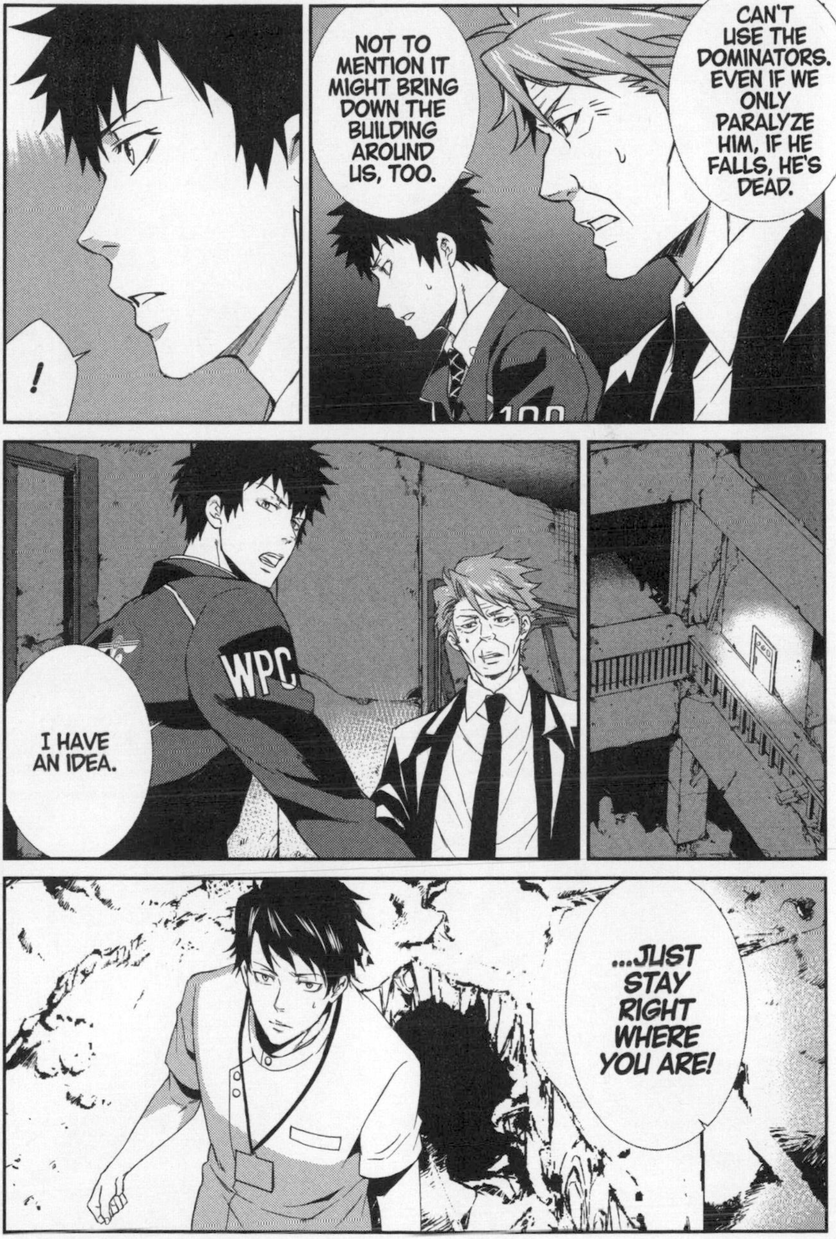
CAN'T USE THE DOMINATORS. EVEN IF WE ONLY PARALYZE HIM, IF HE FALLS, HE'S DEAD.
NOT TO MENTION IT MIGHT BRING DOWN THE BUILDING AROUND US, TOO.
!
I HAVE AN IDEA.
...JUST STAY RIGHT WHERE YOU ARE!

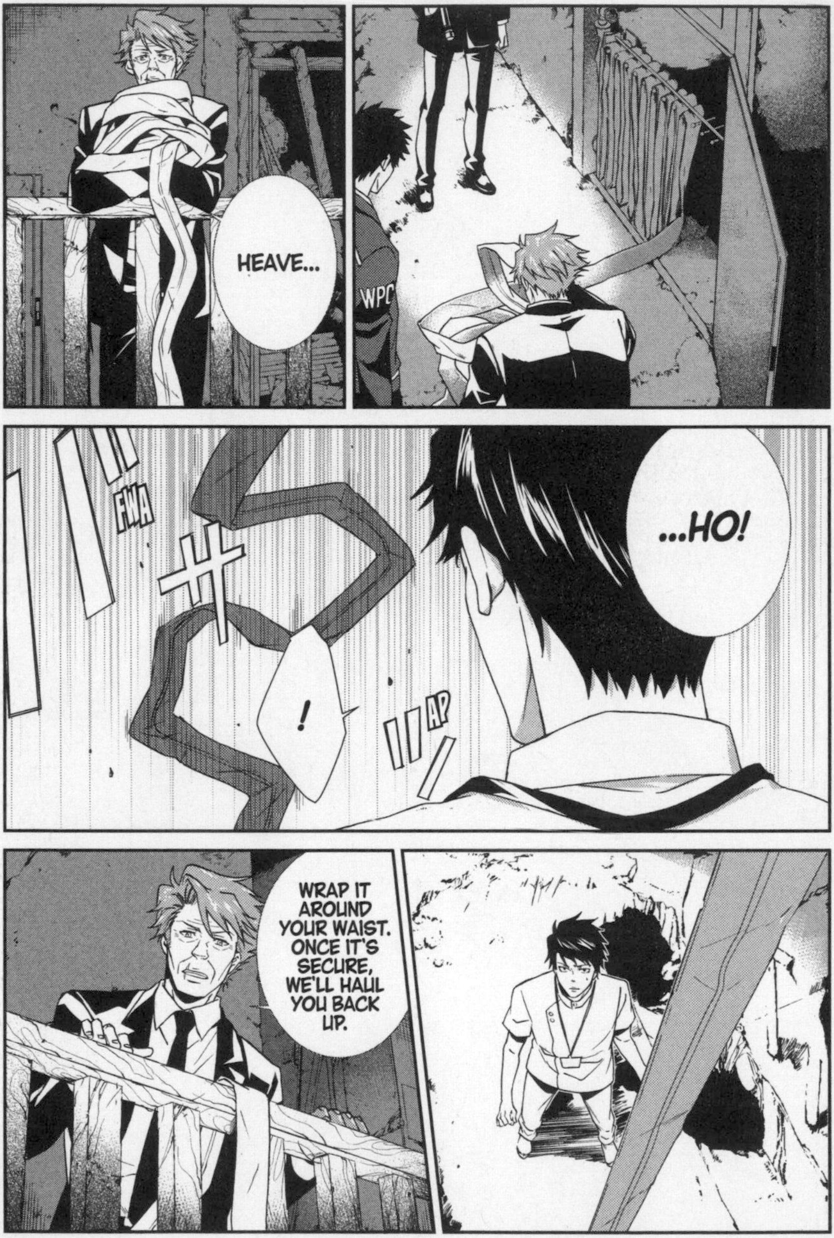
WPC
HEAVE...
...HO!
AP
!
FWA
WRAP IT AROUND YOUR WAIST. ONCE IT'S SECURE, WE'LL HAUL YOU BACK UP.

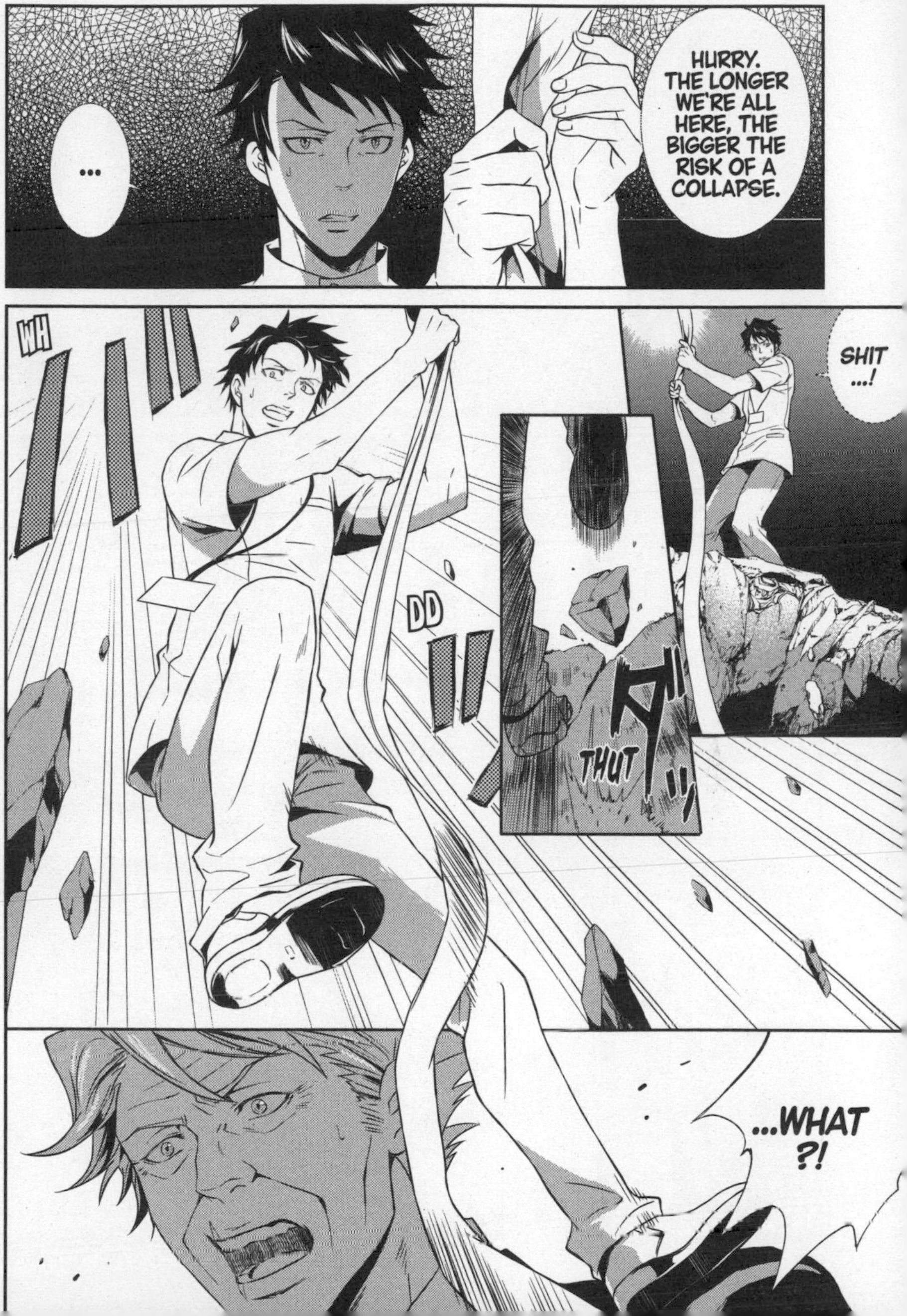
HURRY. THE LONGER WE'RE ALL HERE, THE BIGGER THE RISK OF A COLLAPSE.
...
SHIT ...!
THUT
WH
DD
...WHAT ?!

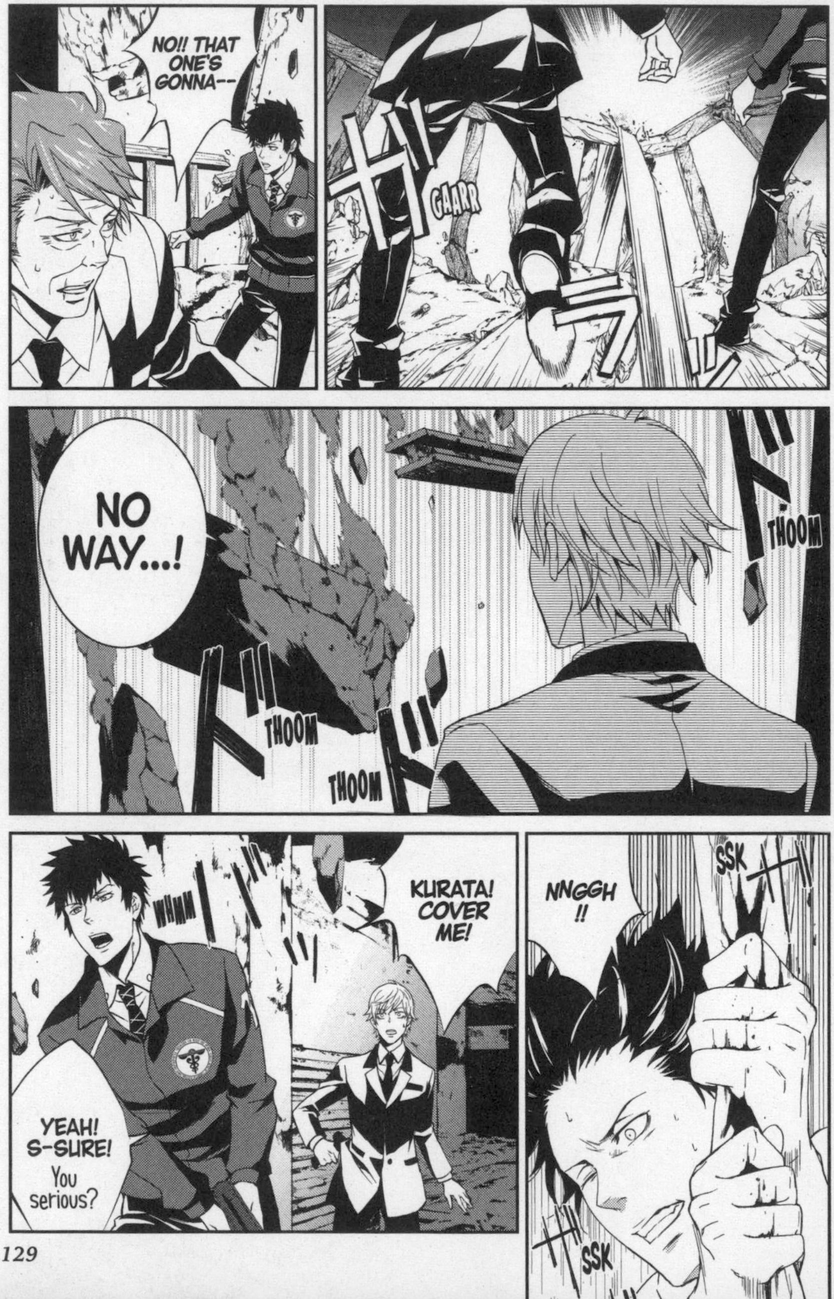
GAARR
NO!! THAT ONE'S GONNA--
THOOM
NO WAY...!
THOOM
THOOM
SSK
NNGGH !!
SSK
KURATA! COVER ME!
WHMM
YEAH! S-SURE!
You serious?

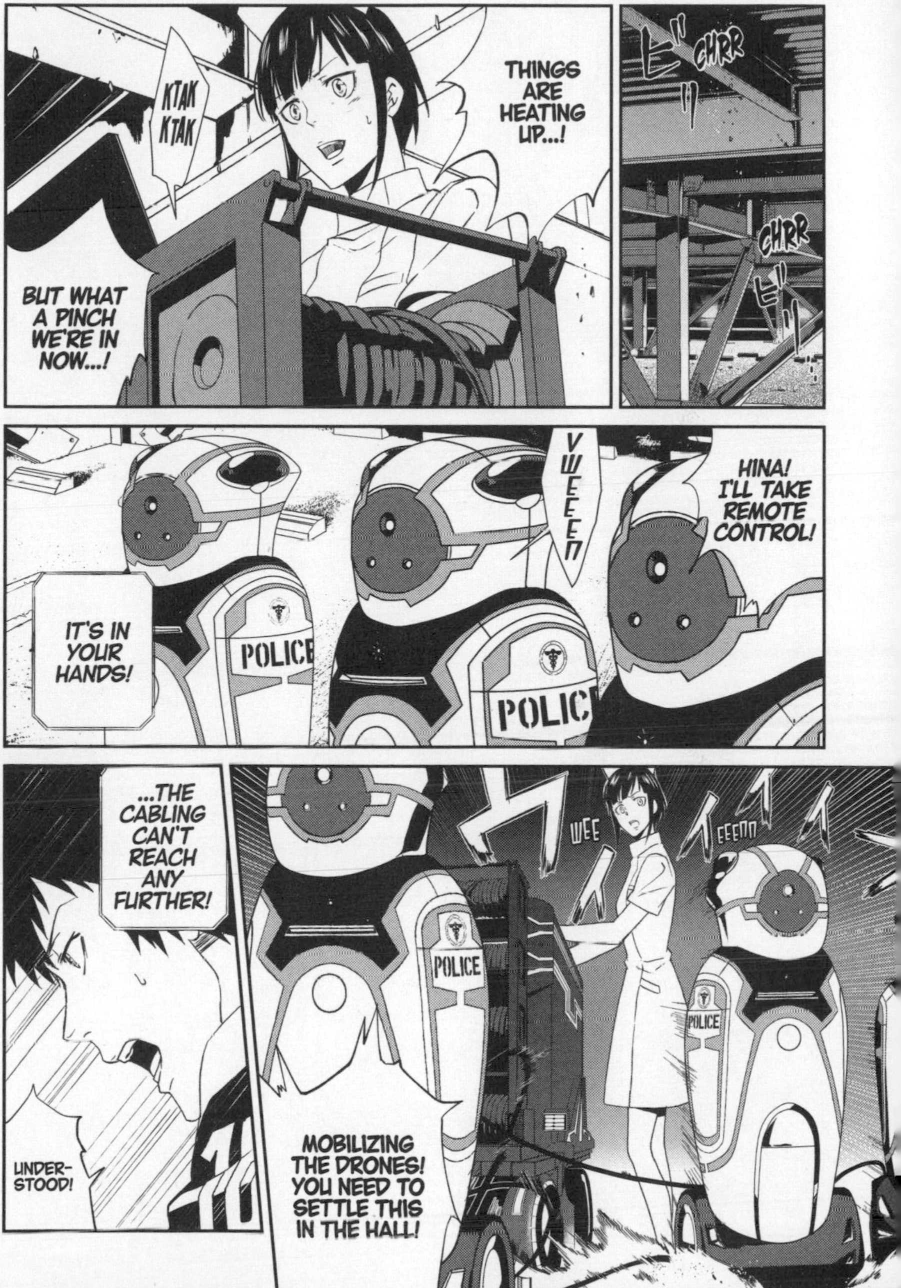
CHRR
CHRR
THINGS ARE HEATING UP...!
KTAK KTAK
BUT WHAT A PINCH WE'RE IN NOW...!
HINA! I'LL TAKE REMOTE CONTROL!
VWEEEEN
POLICE
POLICE
IT'S IN YOUR HANDS!
WEE
EEENN
POLICE
POLICE
MOBILIZING THE DRONES! YOU NEED TO SETTLE THIS IN THE HALL!
...THE CABLING CAN'T REACH ANY FURTHER!
UNDER-STOOD!

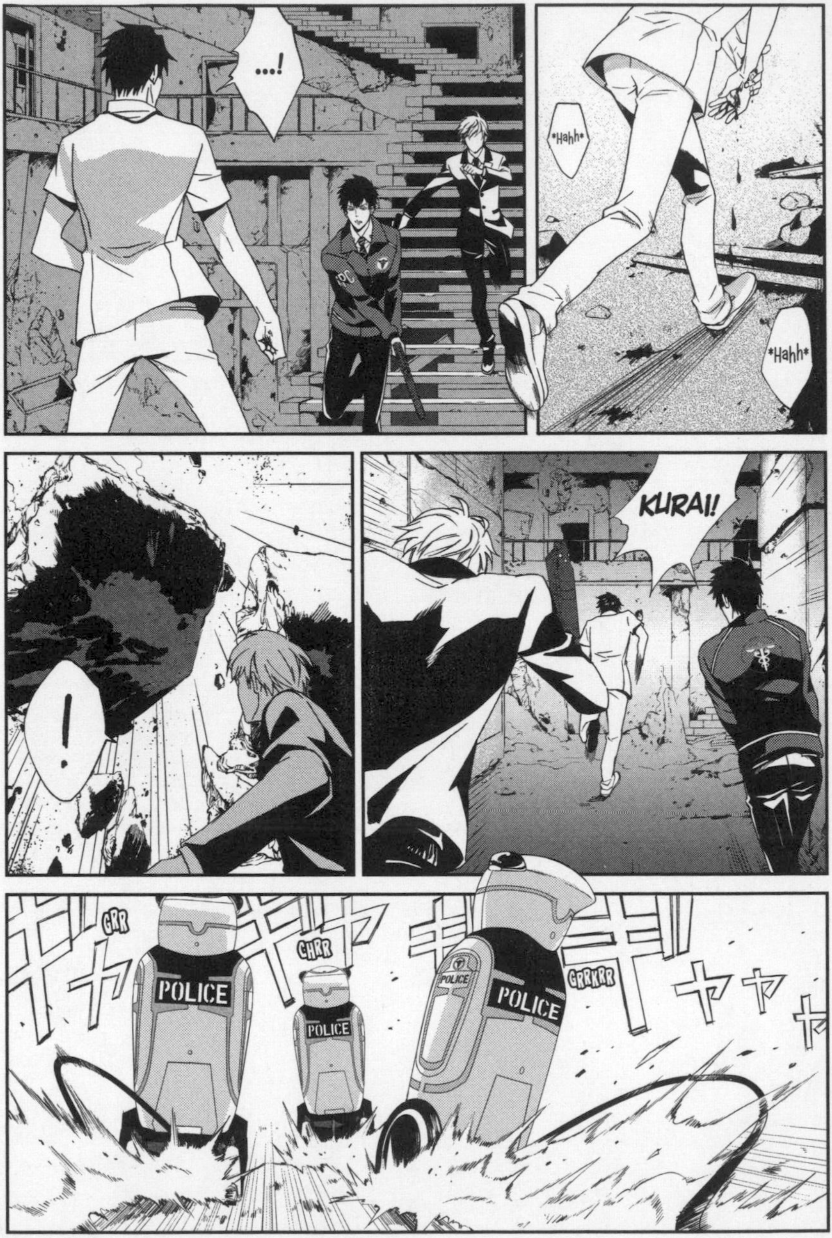
Hahh
Hahh
...!
KURAI!
!
GRRKRR
POLICE
POLICE
CHRR
POLICE
POLICE
GRR

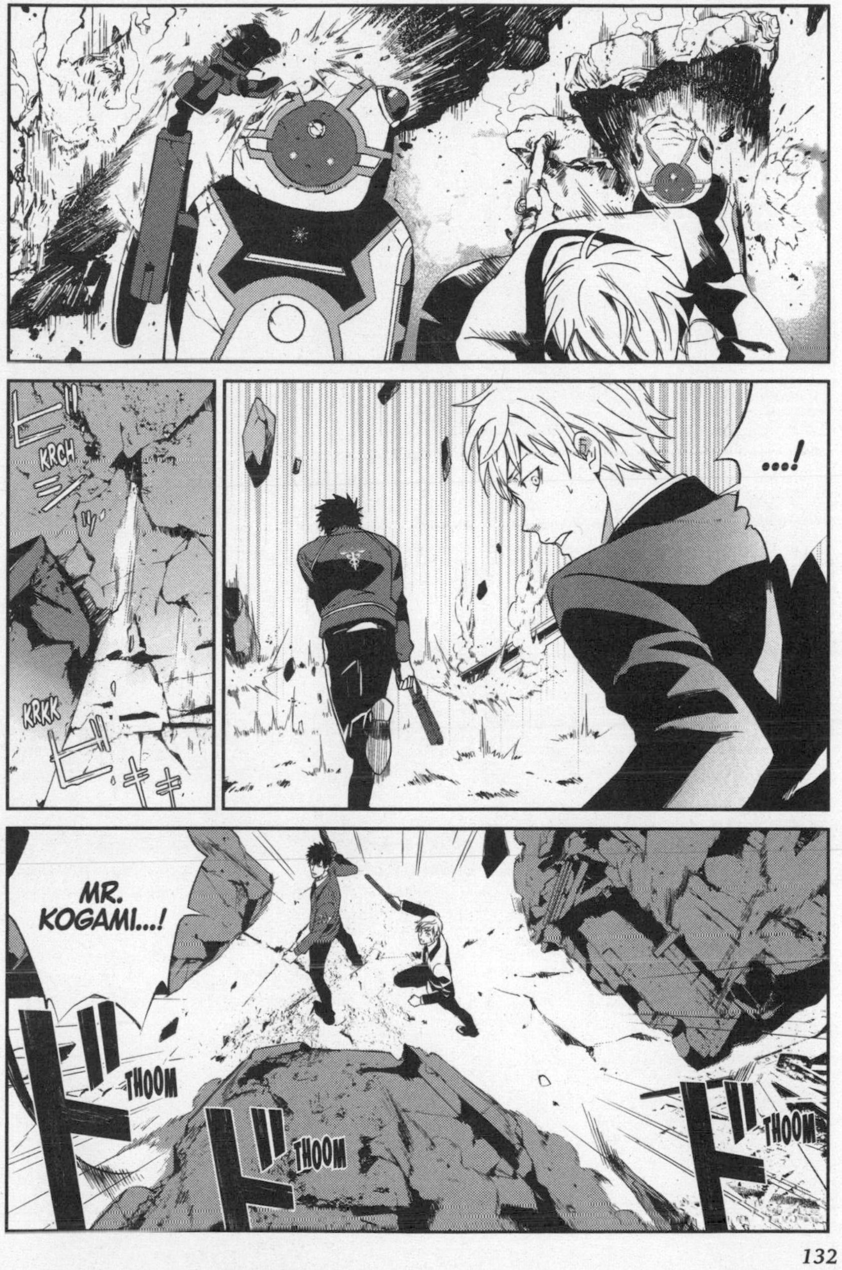
...!
KRCH
KRKK
MR. KOGAMI...!
THOOM
THOOM
THOOM

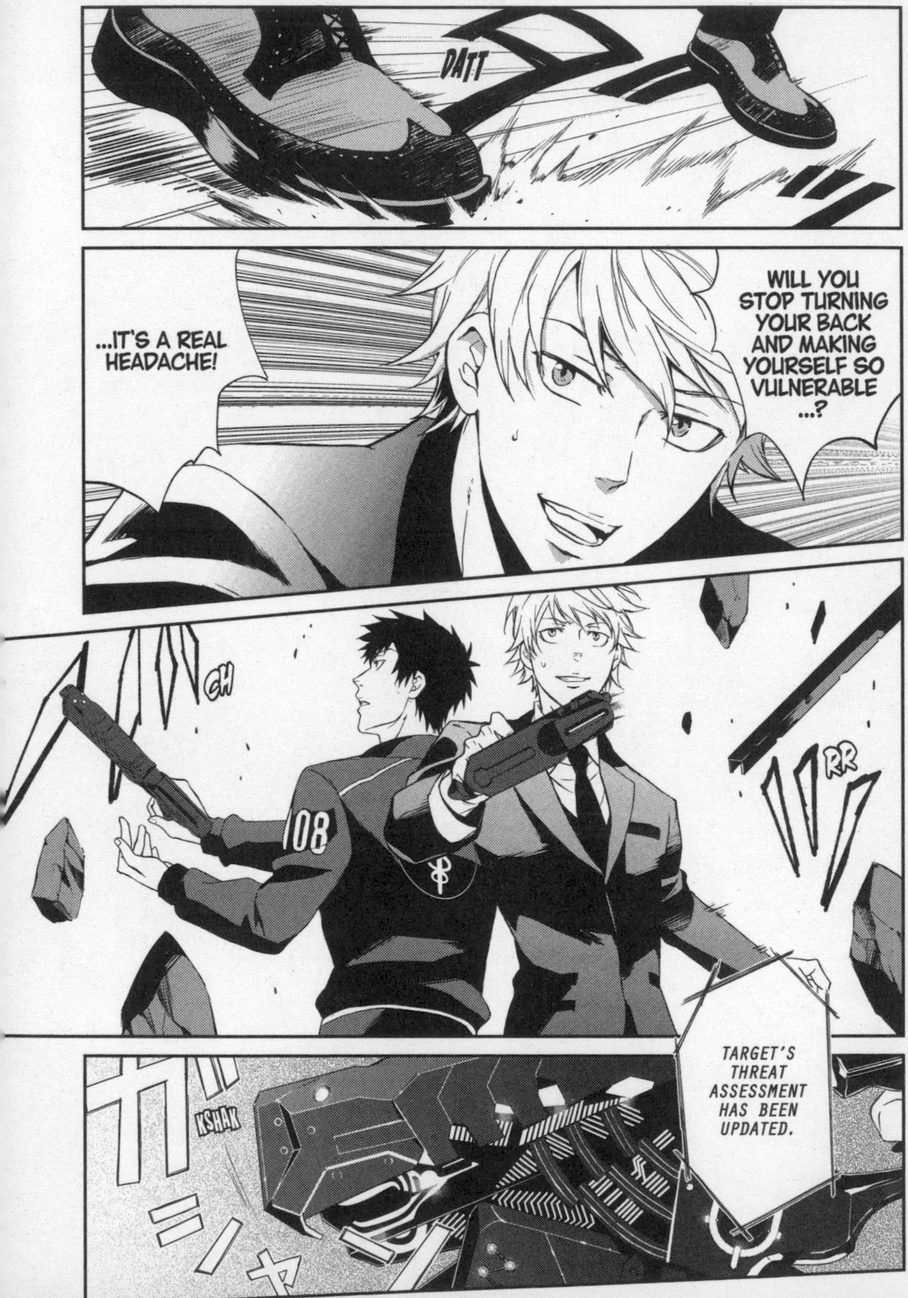
DATT
WILL YOU STOP TURNING YOUR BACK AND MAKING YOURSELF SO VULNERABLE ...?
...IT'S A REAL HEADACHE!
RR
CH
TARGET'S THREAT ASSESSMENT HAS BEEN UPDATED.
KSHAK

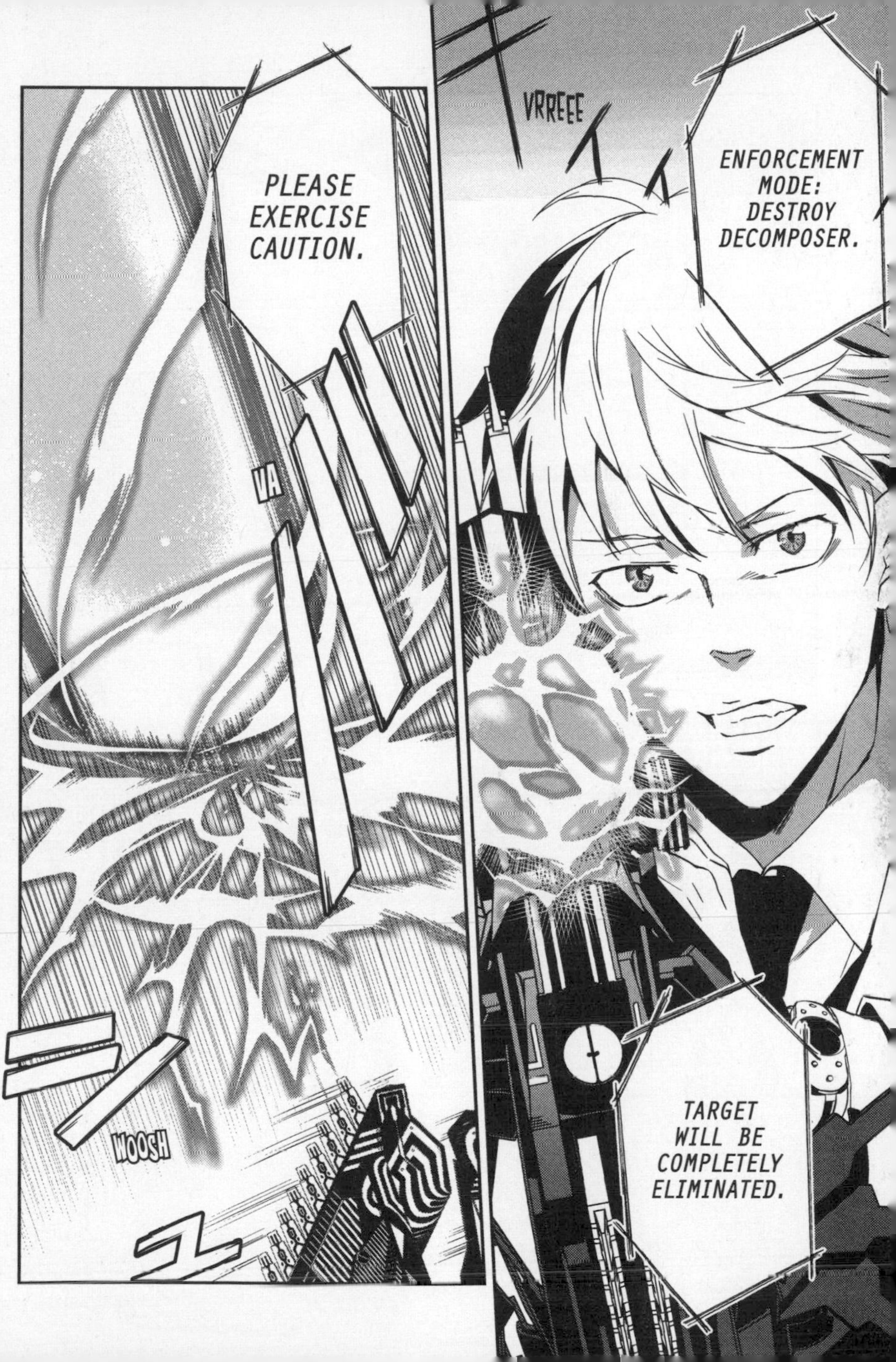
VRREEE
ENFORCEMENT MODE: DESTROY DECOMPOSER.
TARGET WILL BE COMPLETELY ELIMINATED.
PLEASE EXERCISE CAUTION.
VA
WOOSH

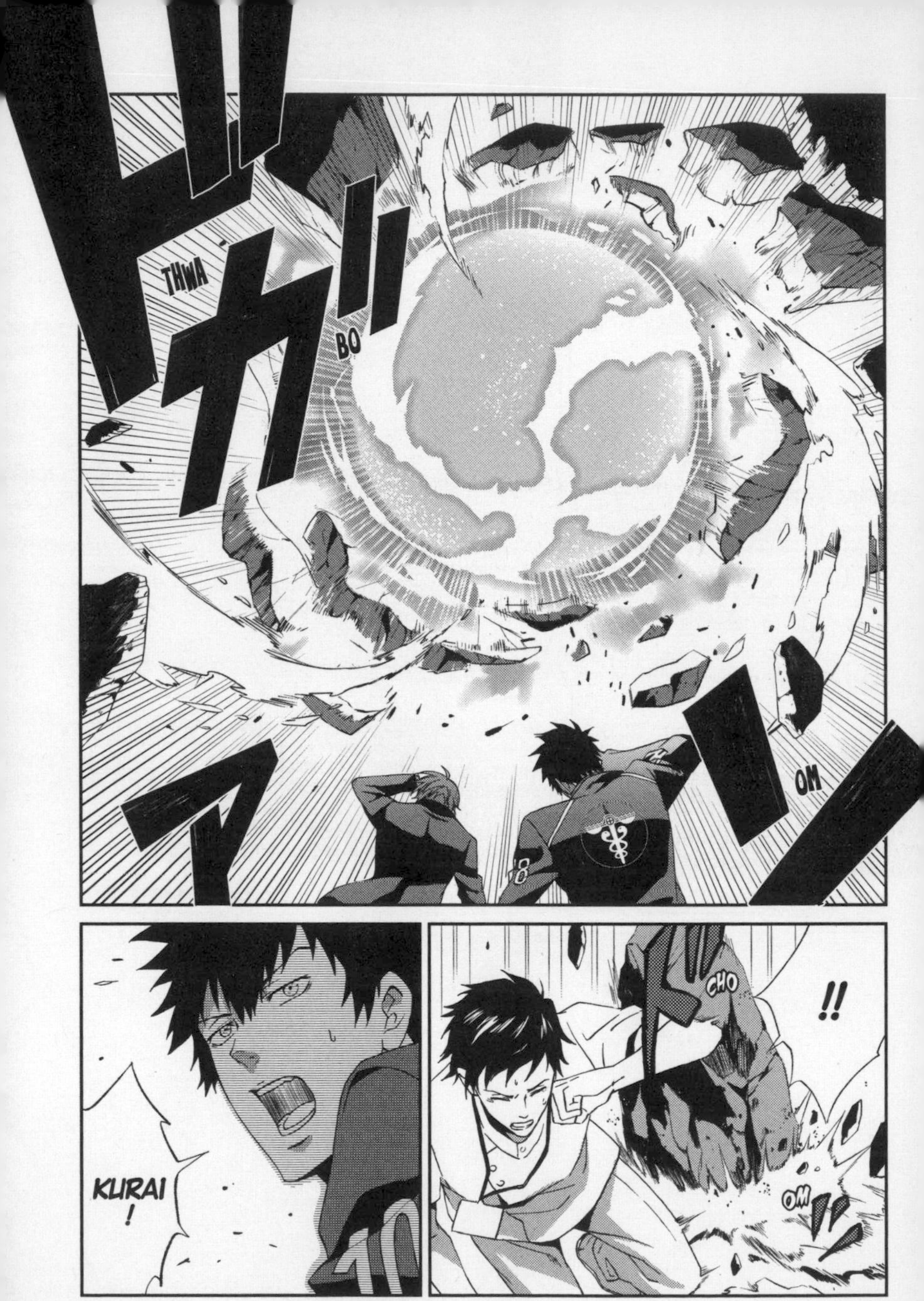
THWA
BO
OM
CHO
OM
!!
KURAI
!

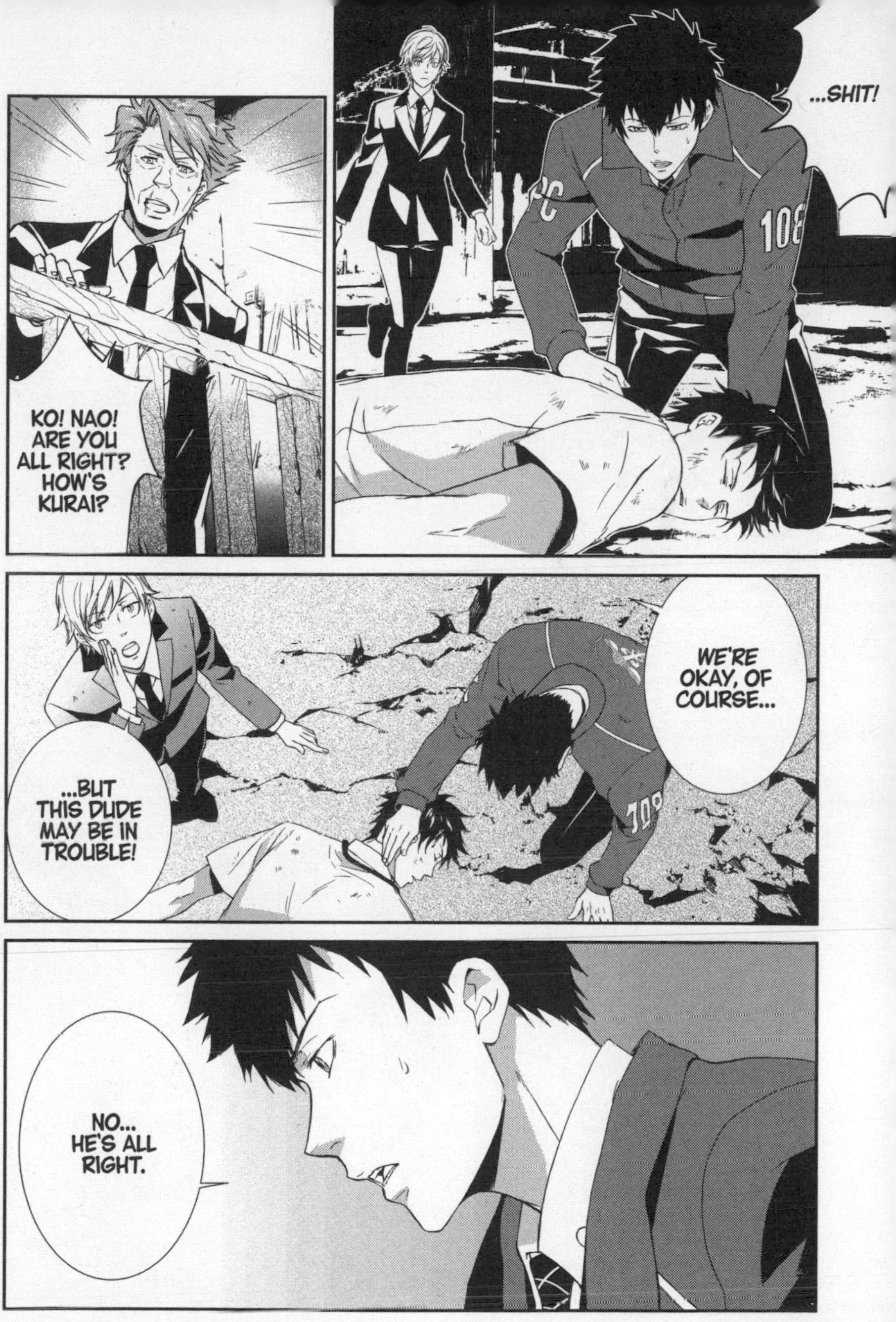
...SHIT!
KO! NAO! ARE YOU ALL RIGHT? HOW'S KURAI?
WE'RE OKAY, OF COURSE...
...BUT THIS DUDE MAY BE IN TROUBLE!
NO... HE'S ALL RIGHT.

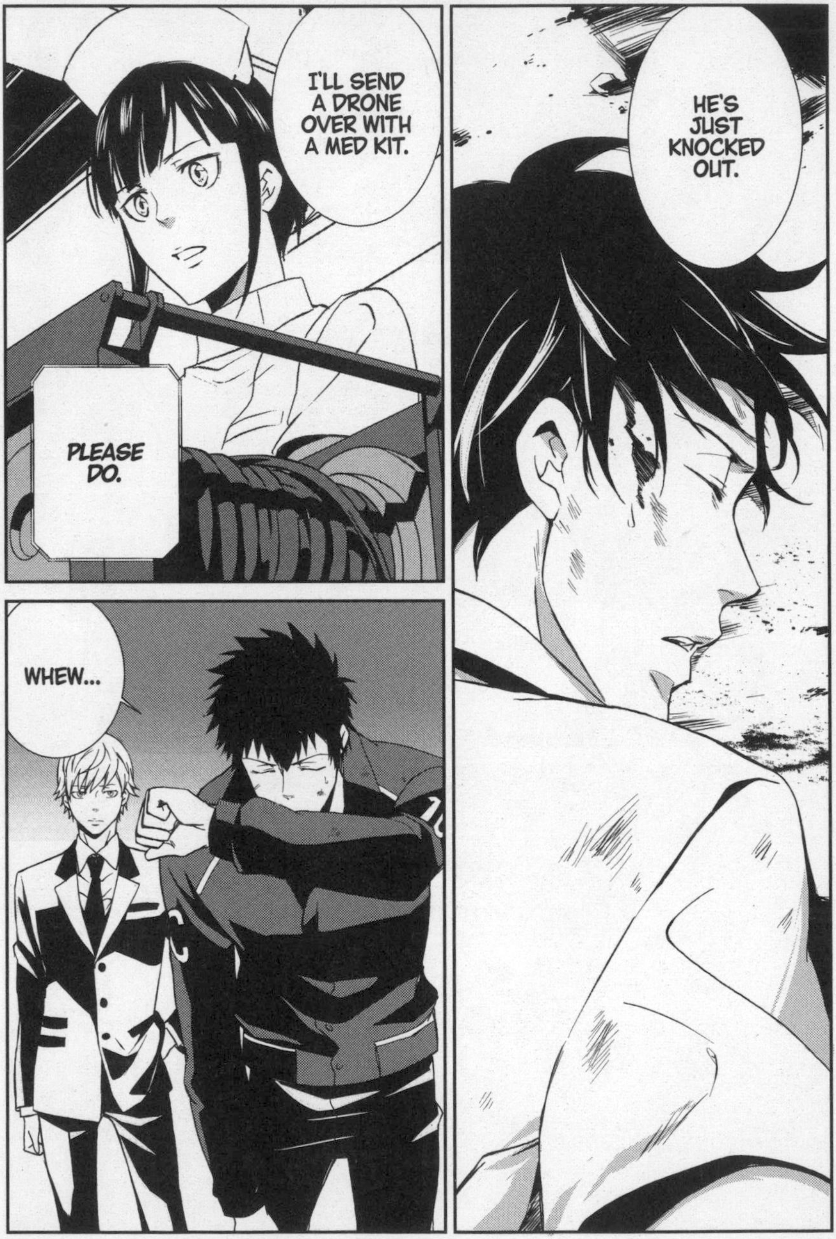
HE'S JUST KNOCKED OUT.
I'LL SEND A DRONE OVER WITH A MED KIT.
PLEASE DO.
WHEW...

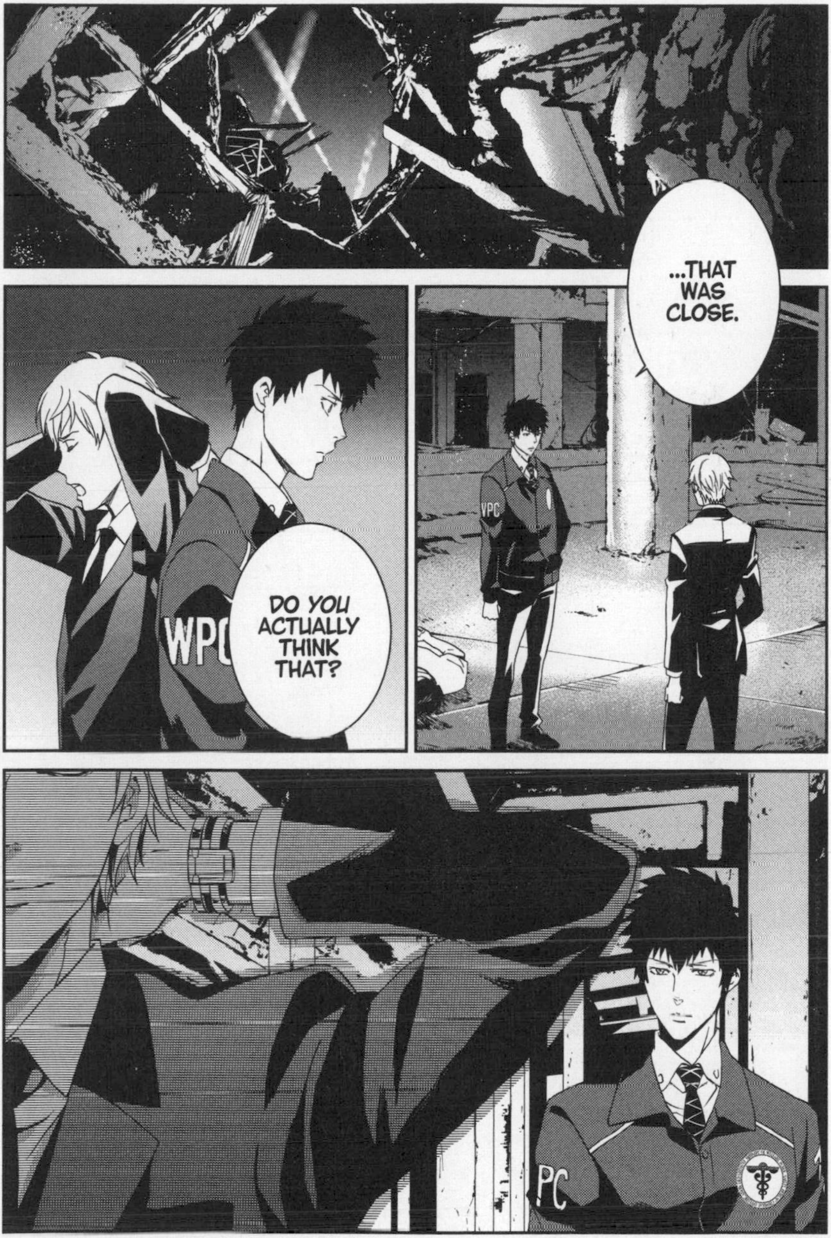
...THAT WAS CLOSE.
DO YOU ACTUALLY THINK THAT?

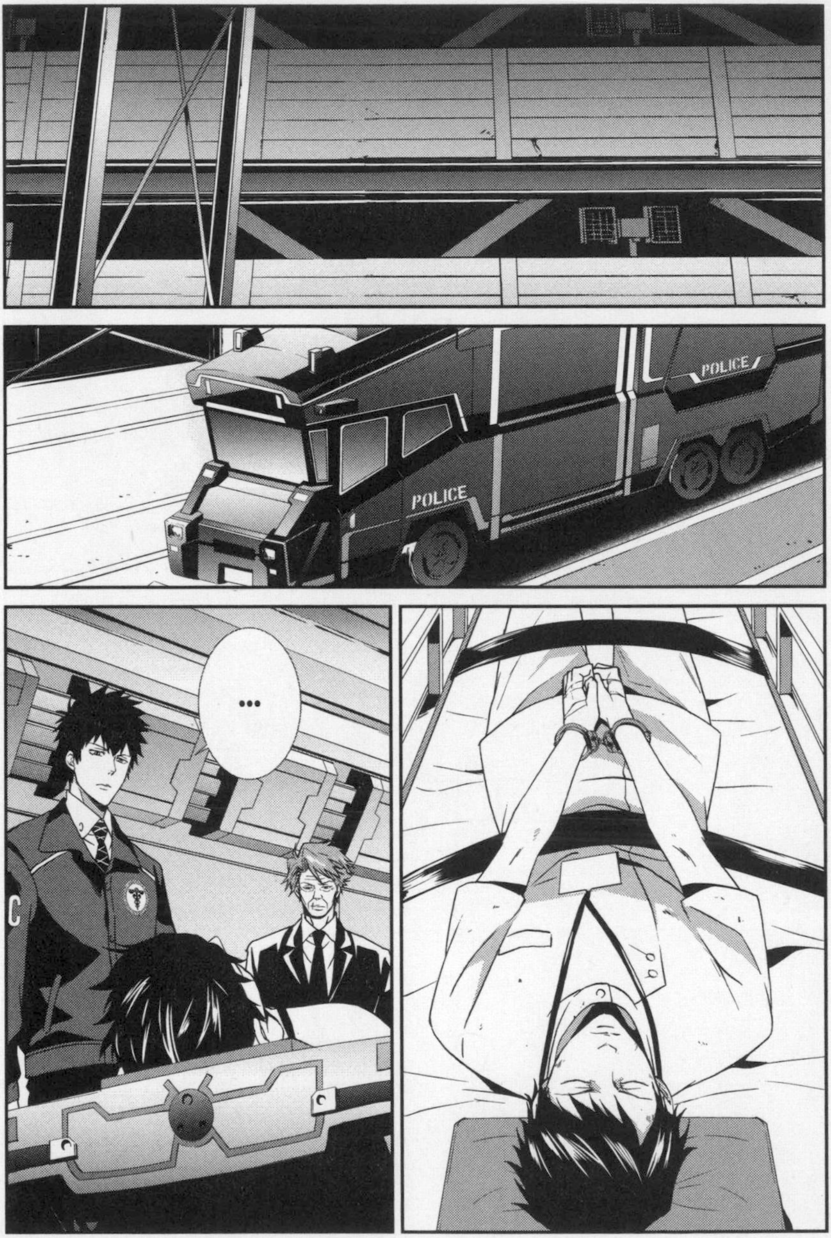
POLICE
POLICE
...

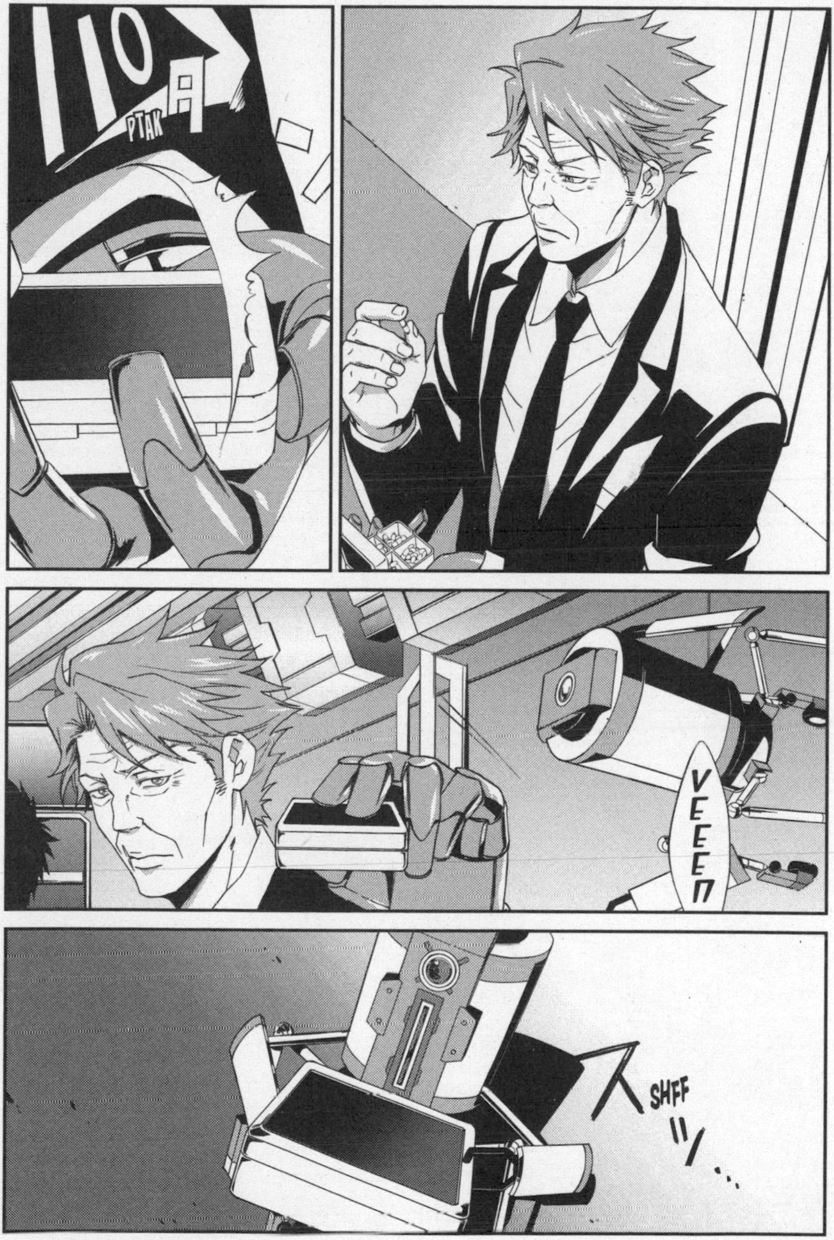
PTAK
VEEEN
SHFF

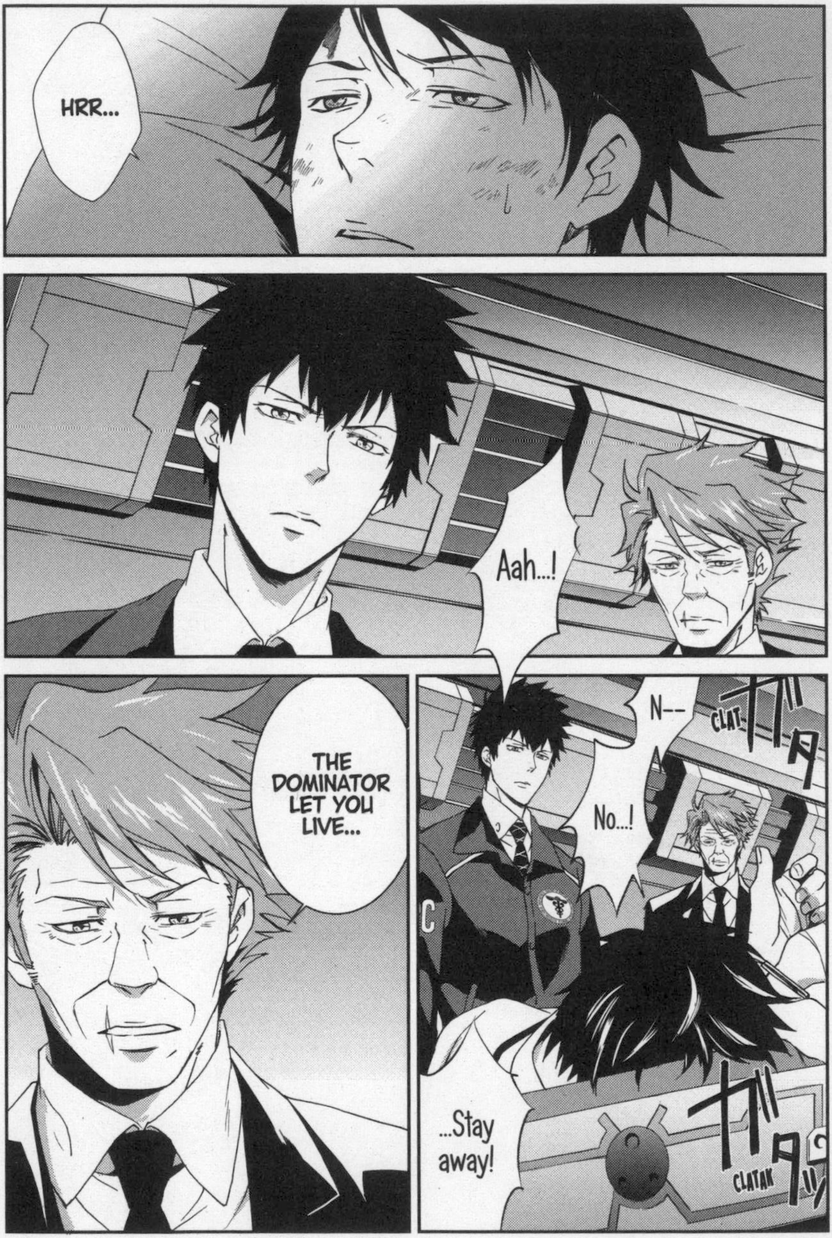
HRR...
Aah...!
N--
CLAT
No...!
...Stay away!
CLATAK
THE DOMINATOR LET YOU LIVE...

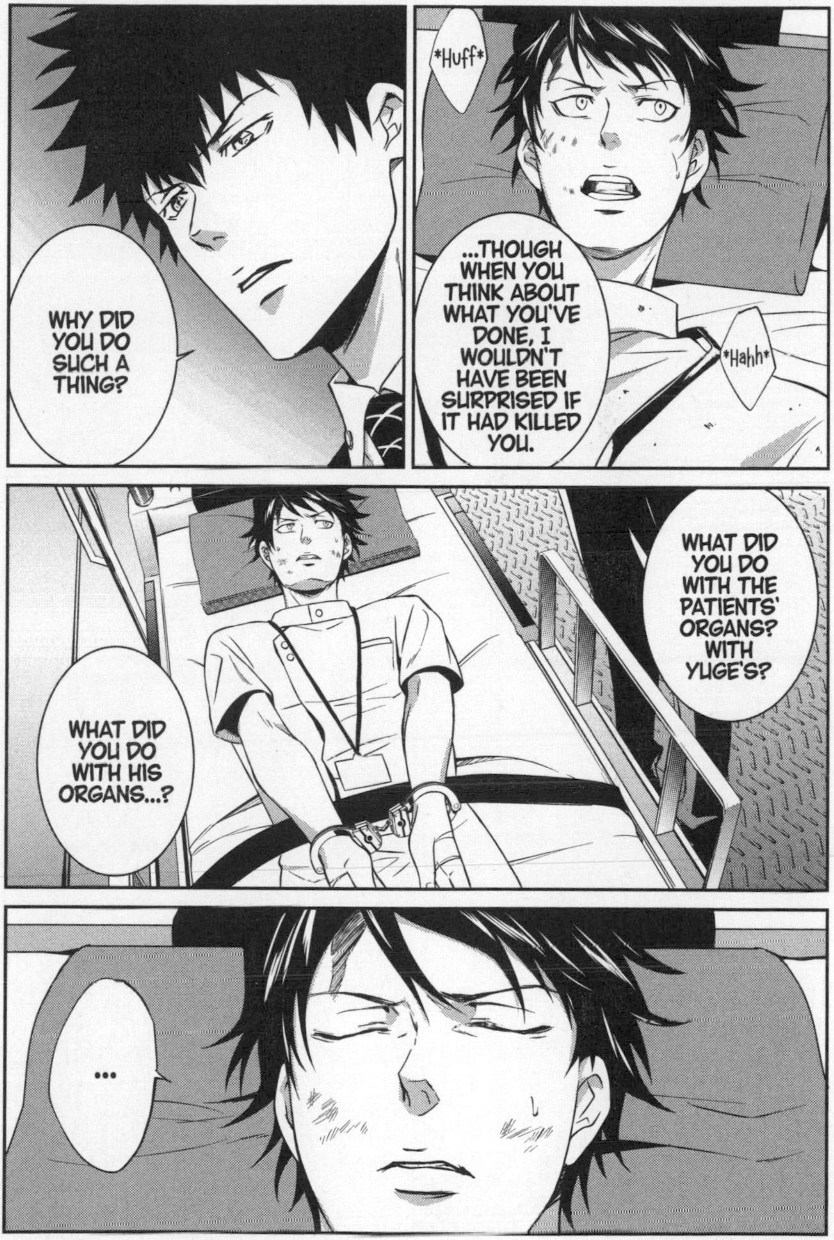
Huff
...THOUGH WHEN YOU THINK ABOUT WHAT YOU'VE DONE, I WOULDN'T HAVE BEEN SURPRISED IF IT HAD KILLED YOU.
Hahh
WHY DID YOU DO SUCH A THING?
WHAT DID YOU DO WITH THE PATIENTS' ORGANS? WITH YUGE'S?
WHAT DID YOU DO WITH HIS ORGANS...?
...

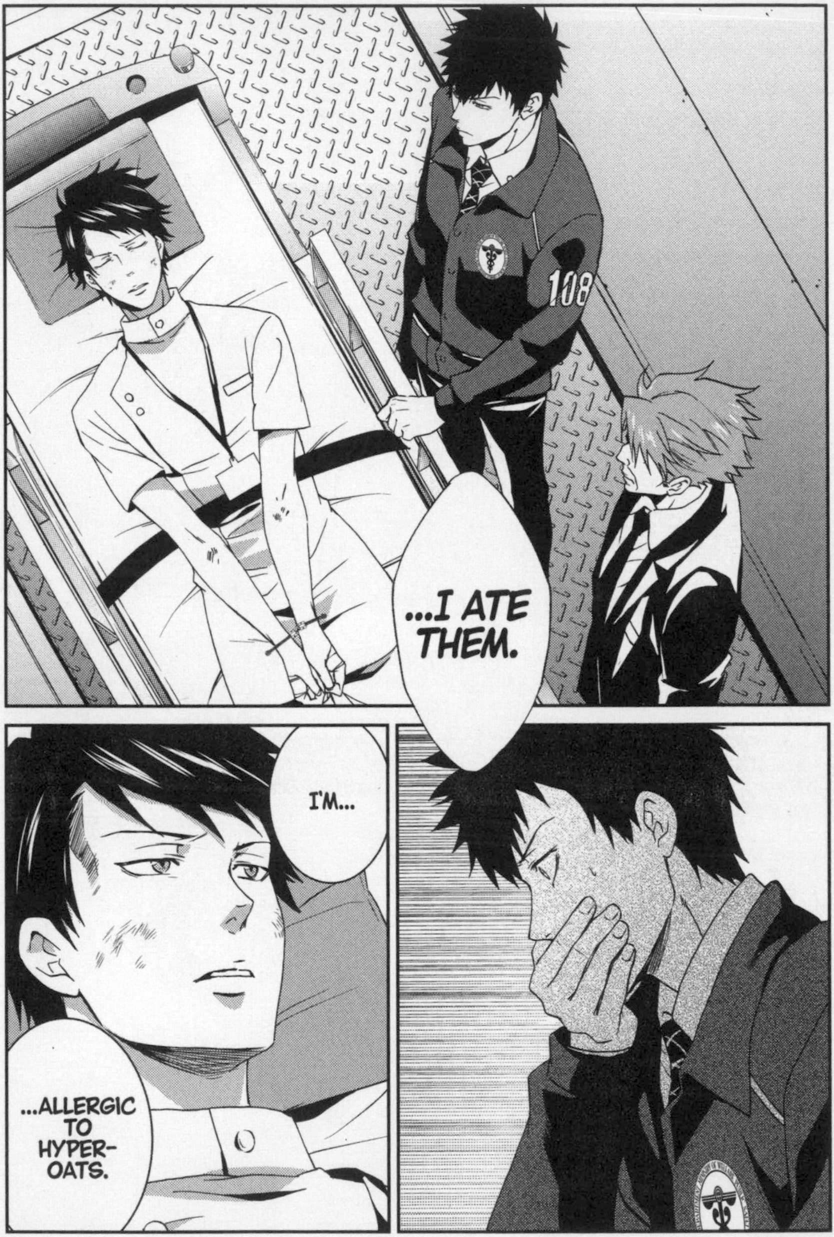
...I ATE THEM.
I'M...
...ALLERGIC TO HYPER-OATS.

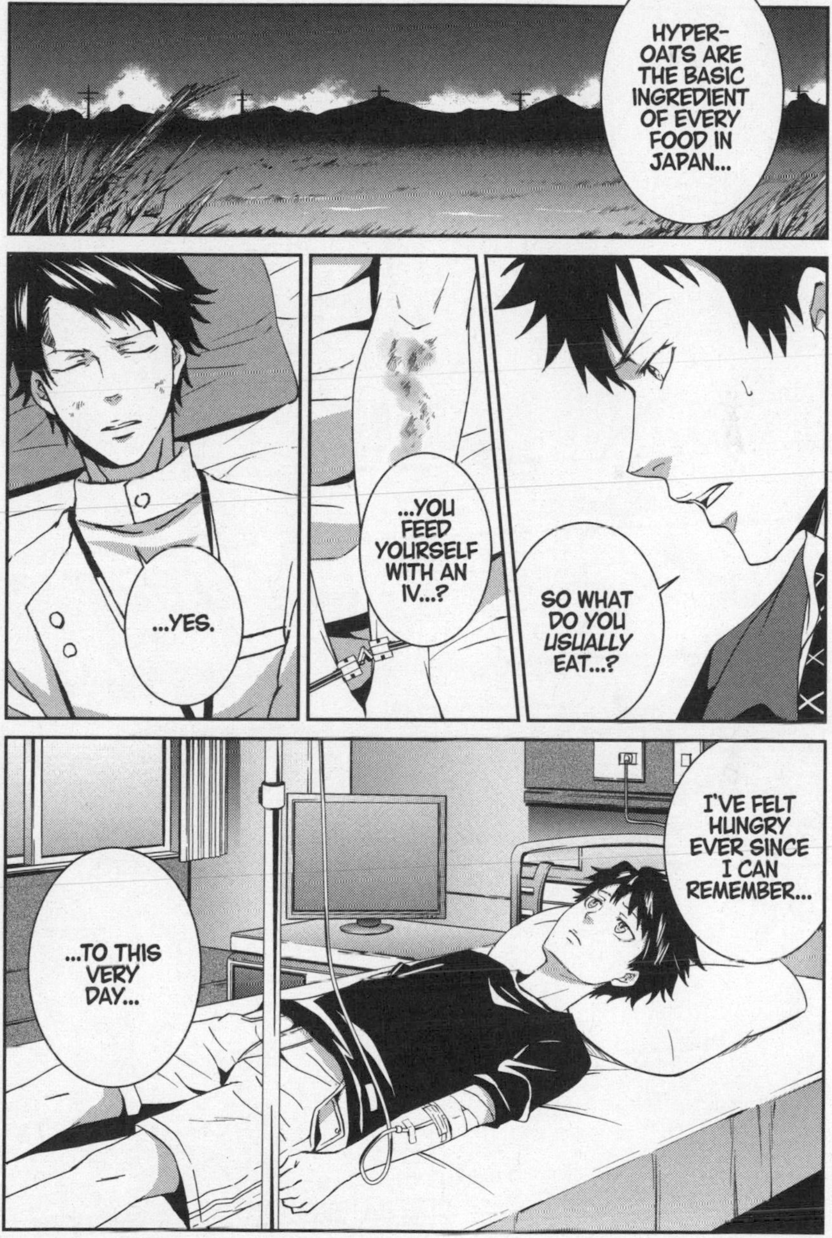
HYPER-OATS ARE THE BASIC INGREDIENT OF EVERY FOOD IN JAPAN...
SO WHAT DO YOU USUALLY EAT...?
...YOU FEED YOURSELF WITH AN IV...?
...YES.
I'VE FELT HUNGRY EVER SINCE I CAN REMEMBER...
...TO THIS VERY DAY...

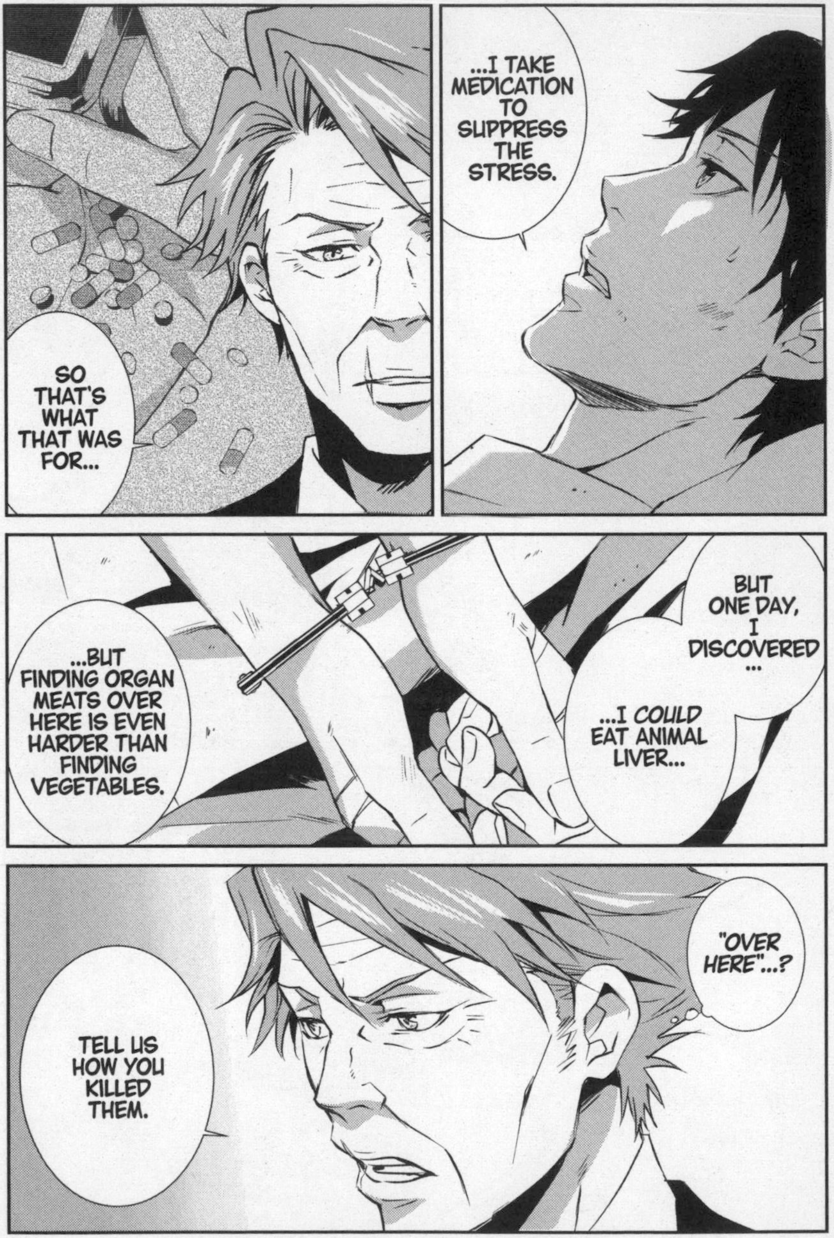
...I TAKE MEDICATION TO SUPPRESS THE STRESS.
SO THAT'S WHAT THAT WAS FOR...
BUT ONE DAY, I DISCOVERED ...
...I COULD EAT ANIMAL LIVER...
...BUT FINDING ORGAN MEATS OVER HERE IS EVEN HARDER THAN FINDING VEGETABLES.
"OVER HERE"...?
TELL US HOW YOU KILLED THEM.

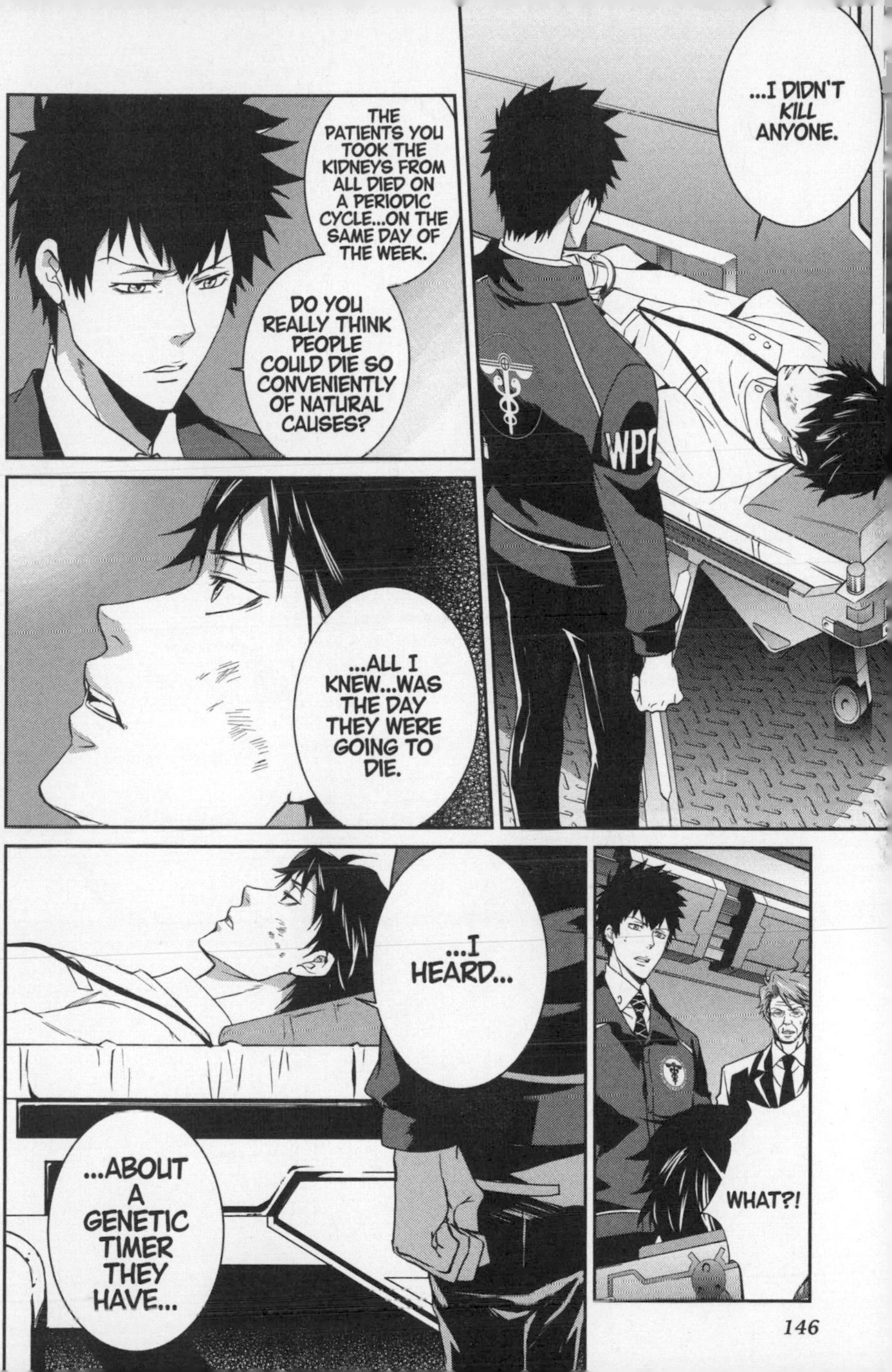
...I DIDN'T KILL ANYONE.
THE PATIENTS YOU TOOK THE KIDNEYS FROM ALL DIED ON A PERIODIC CYCLE...ON THE SAME DAY OF THE WEEK.
DO YOU REALLY THINK PEOPLE COULD DIE SO CONVENIENTLY OF NATURAL CAUSES?
WPC
...ALL I KNEW...WAS THE DAY THEY WERE GOING TO DIE.
WHAT?!
...I HEARD...
...ABOUT A GENETIC TIMER THEY HAVE...

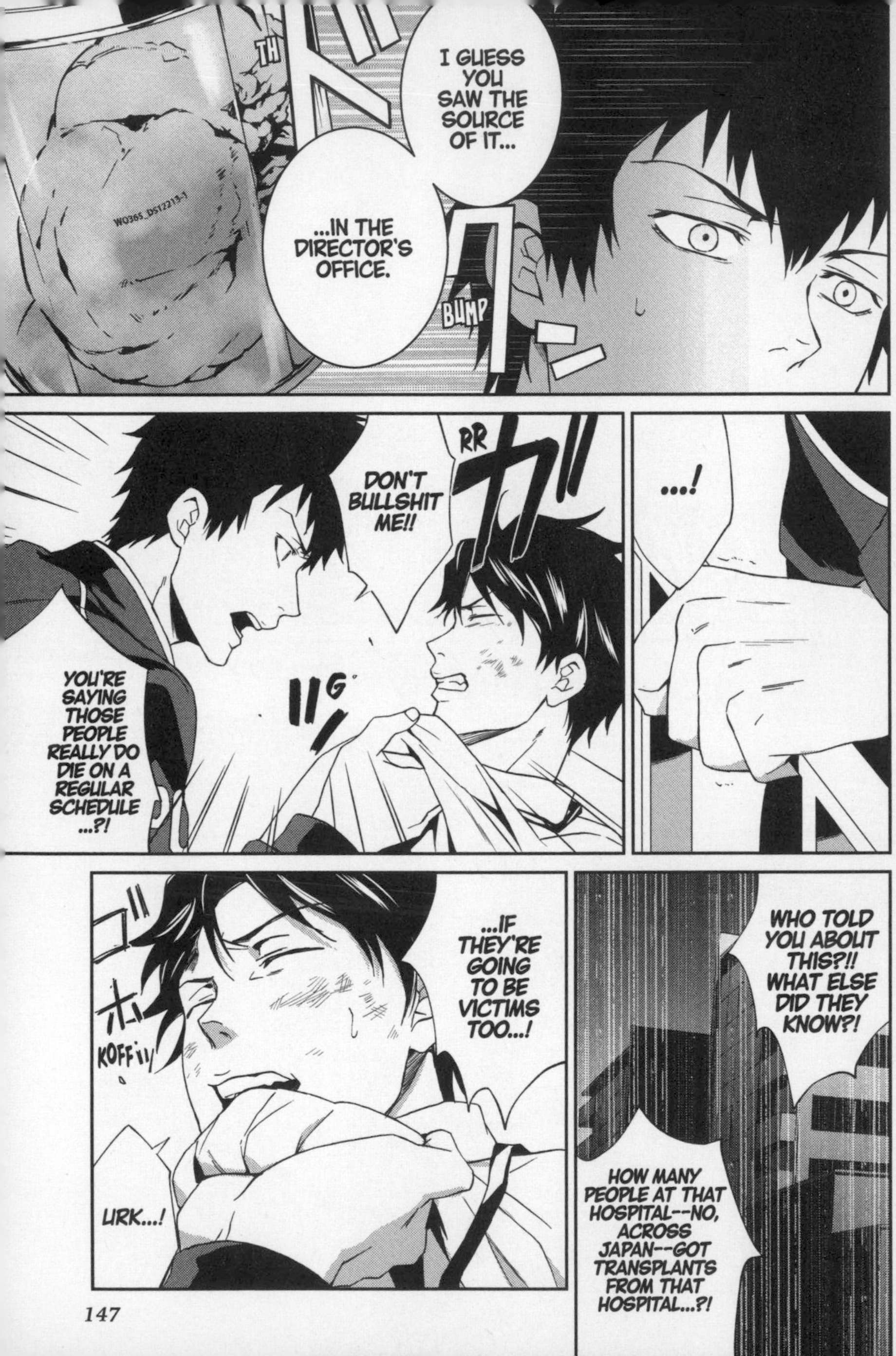
TH
I GUESS YOU SAW THE SOURCE OF IT...
...IN THE DIRECTOR'S OFFICE.
BUMP
...!
RR
DON'T BULLSHIT ME!!
YOU'RE SAYING THOSE PEOPLE REALLY DO DIE ON A REGULAR SCHEDULE ...?!
G
WHO TOLD YOU ABOUT THIS?!! WHAT ELSE DID THEY KNOW?!
HOW MANY PEOPLE AT THAT HOSPITAL--NO, ACROSS JAPAN--GOT TRANSPLANTS FROM THAT HOSPITAL...?!
...IF THEY'RE GOING TO BE VICTIMS TOO...!
KOFF
URK...!

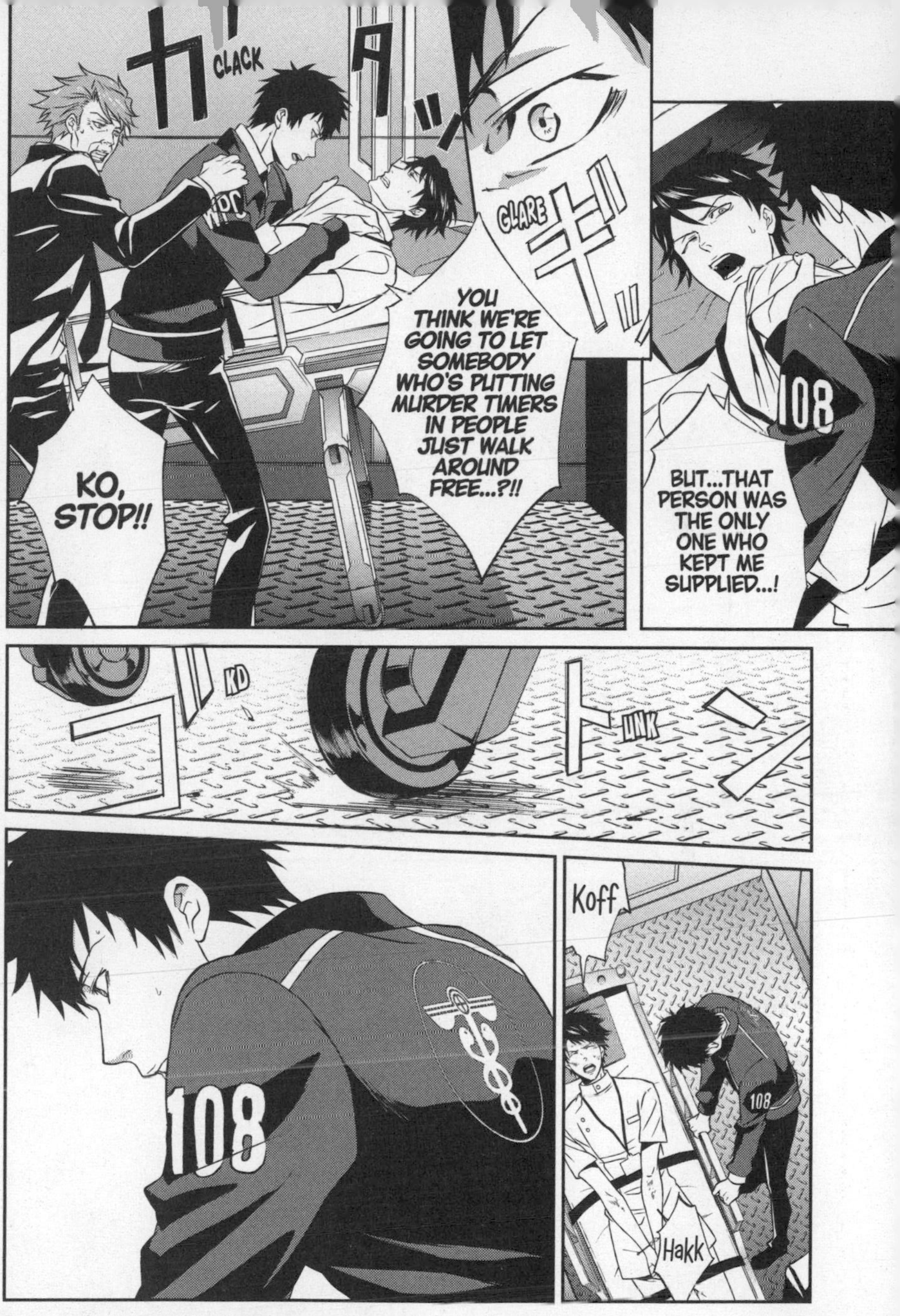
CLACK
KO, STOP!!
GLARE
YOU THINK WE'RE GOING TO LET SOMEBODY WHO'S PUTTING MURDER TIMERS IN PEOPLE JUST WALK AROUND FREE...?!!
BUT...THAT PERSON WAS THE ONLY ONE WHO KEPT ME SUPPLIED...!
UNK
KD
Koff
Hakk

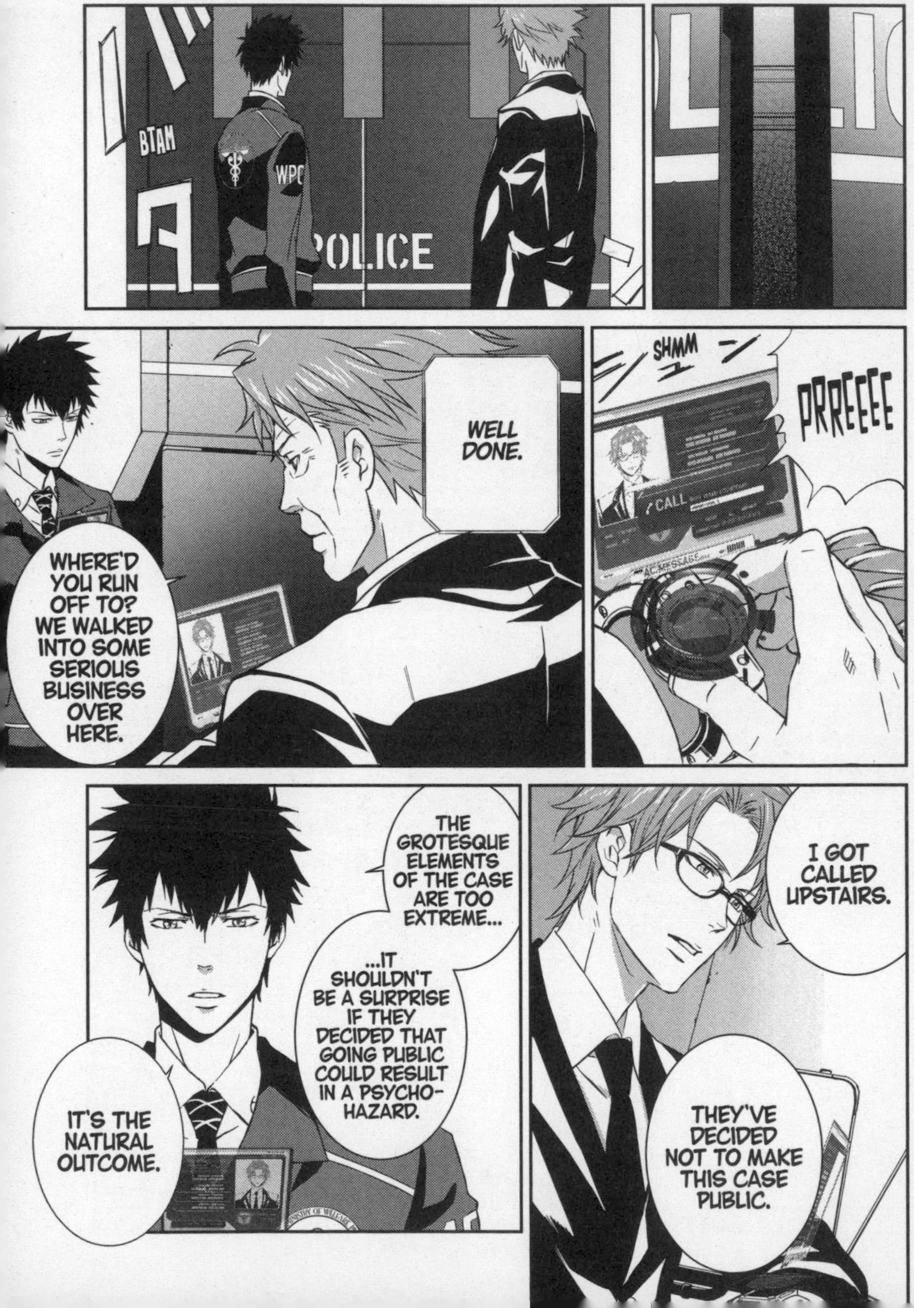
BTAM
WPC
POLICE
SHMM
PRREEEE
CALL
WELL DONE.
WHERE'D YOU RUN OFF TO? WE WALKED INTO SOME SERIOUS BUSINESS OVER HERE.
I GOT CALLED UPSTAIRS.
THEY'VE DECIDED NOT TO MAKE THIS CASE PUBLIC.
THE GROTESQUE ELEMENTS OF THE CASE ARE TOO EXTREME...
...IT SHOULDN'T BE A SURPRISE IF THEY DECIDED THAT GOING PUBLIC COULD RESULT IN A PSYCHO-HAZARD.
IT'S THE NATURAL OUTCOME.

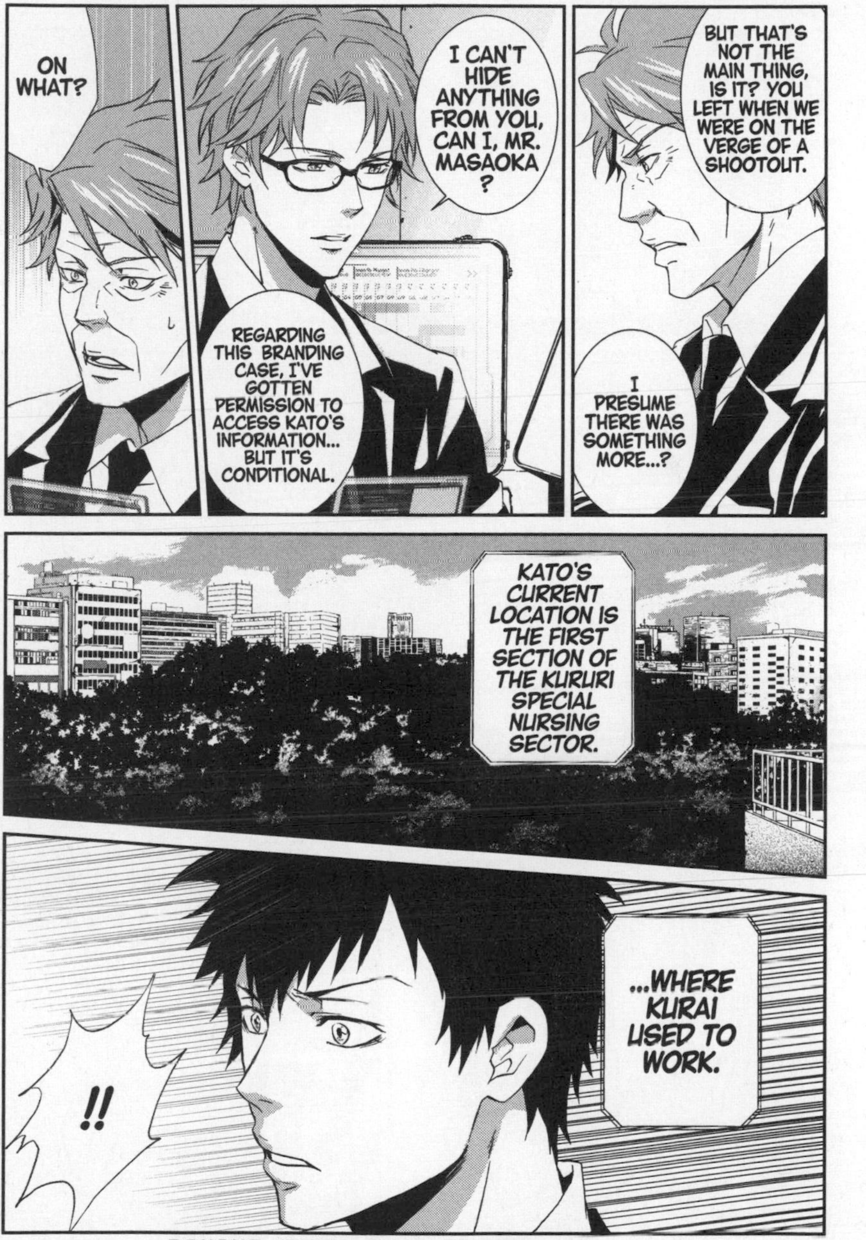
BUT THAT'S NOT THE MAIN THING, IS IT? YOU LEFT WHEN WE WERE ON THE VERGE OF A SHOOTOUT.
I PRESUME THERE WAS SOMETHING MORE...?
I CAN'T HIDE ANYTHING FROM YOU, CAN I, MR. MASAOKA?
REGARDING THIS BRANDING CASE, I'VE GOTTEN PERMISSION TO ACCESS KATO'S INFORMATION... BUT IT'S CONDITIONAL.
ON WHAT?
KATO'S CURRENT LOCATION IS THE FIRST SECTION OF THE KURURI SPECIAL NURSING SECTOR.
...WHERE KURAI USED TO WORK.
!!

PSYCHO-PASS サイコパス 監視官 狡噛慎也 1 END

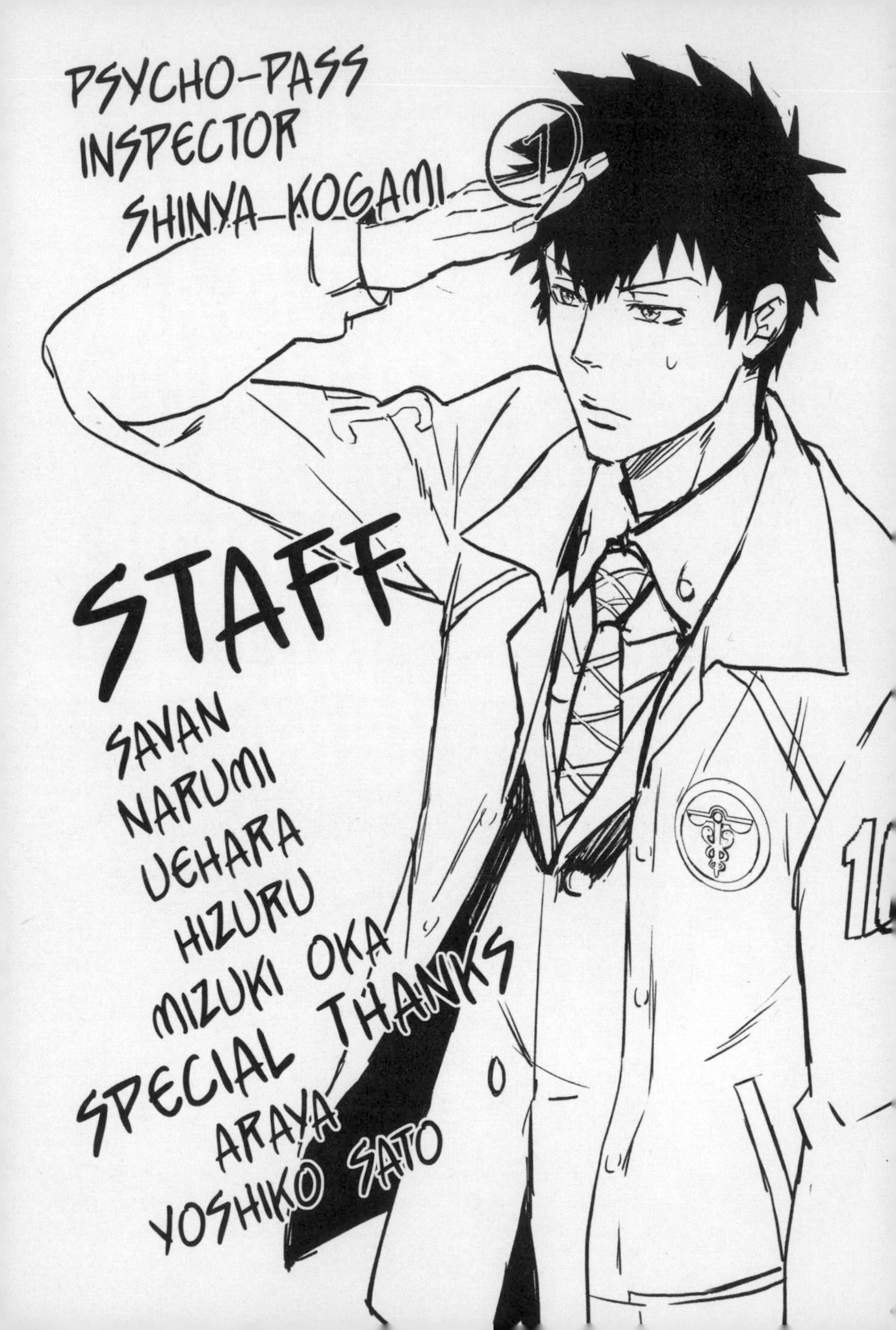

PSYCHO-PASS
INSPECTOR
SHINYA KOGAMI
STAFF
SAVAN
NARUMI
UEHARA
HIZURU
MIZUKI OKA
SPECIAL THANKS
ARAYA
YOSHIKO SATO

KOGAMI AND THE OTHERS HAVE SECURED THE PERPETRATOR, KURAI, BUT HE INSISTS SOMEONE ELSE CARRIED OUT THE MURDERS! DIVISION 3 CONCLUDES THAT THE KEY TO SOLVING THE CASE IS IN THE "SPECIAL NURSING SECTOR," BUT...

WHEN ALL THE PIECES ARE COLLECTED... WHAT ANSWERS WILL BE REVEALED...

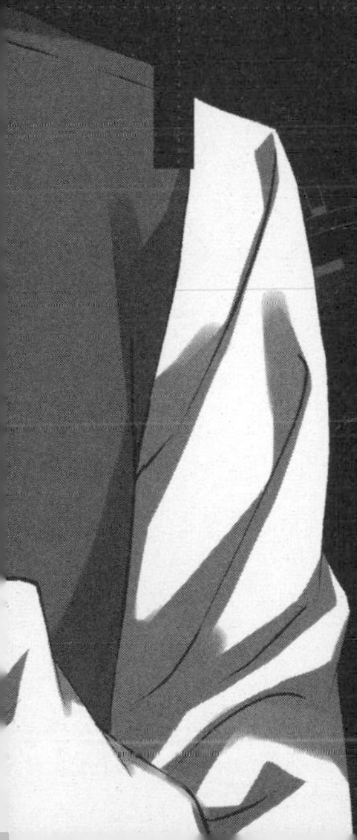

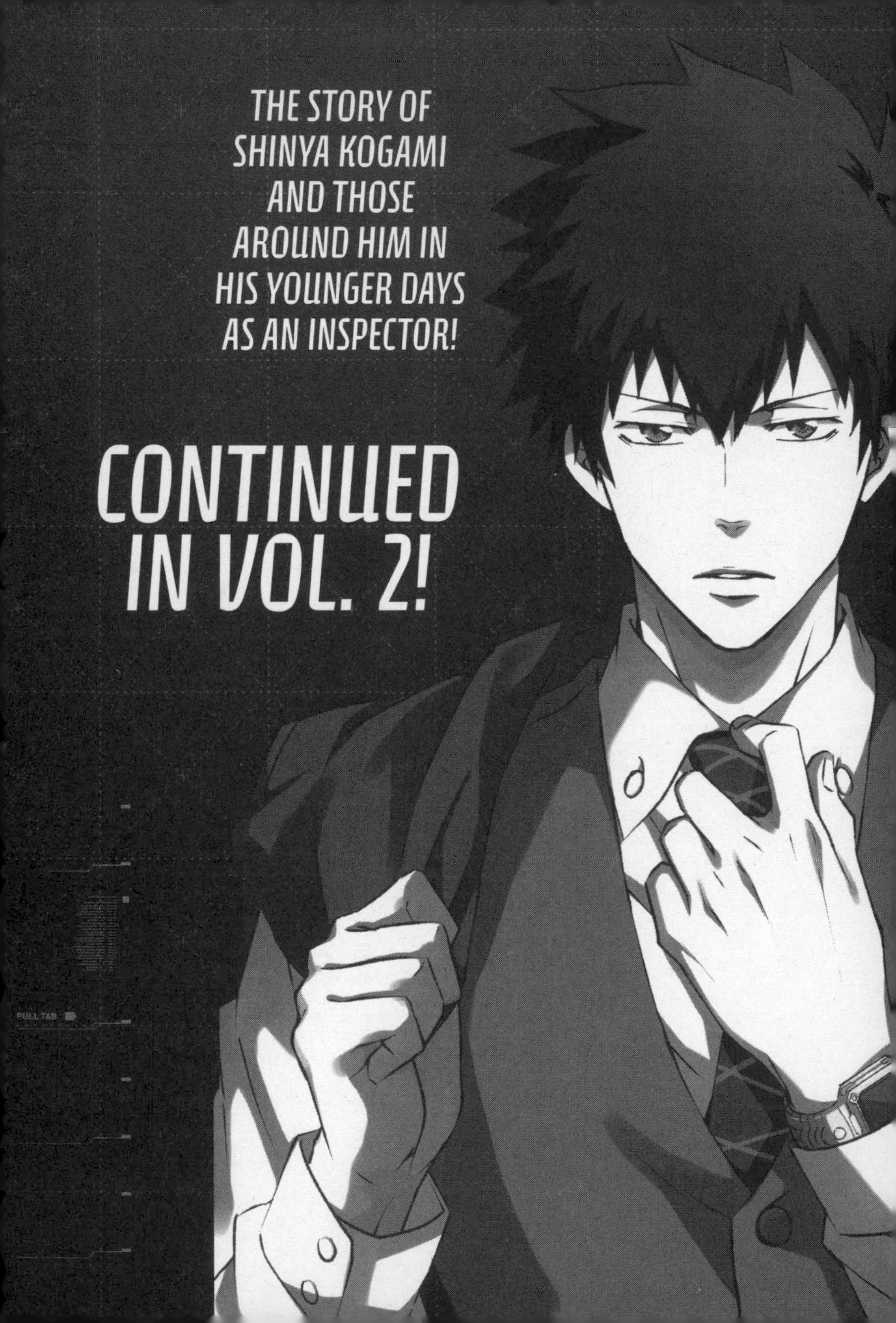
THE STORY OF SHINYA KOGAMI AND THOSE AROUND HIM IN HIS YOUNGER DAYS AS AN INSPECTOR!
CONTINUED IN VOL. 2!
PULL TAB

PRESIDENT AND PUBLISHER
MIKE RICHARDSON

DESIGNER
SANDY TANAKA

DIGITAL ART TECHNICIAN
CHRISTINA McKENZIE

English-language version produced by Dark Horse Comics

PSYCHO-PASS: INSPECTOR SHINYA KOGAMI VOLUME 1

Published by
Dark Horse Manga
A division of Dark Horse Comics, Inc.
10956 SE Main Street
Milwaukie, OR 97222

DarkHorse.com

To find a comics shop in your area, call the Comic Shop Locator Service toll-free
at 1-888-266-4226

First edition: November 2016
ISBN 978-1-50670-120-2

1 3 5 7 9 10 8 6 4 2
Printed in the United States of America

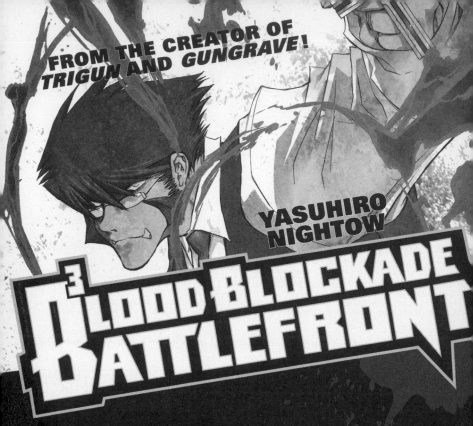

FROM THE CREATOR OF *TRIGUN* AND *GUNGRAVE*!

YASUHIRO NIGHTOW

BLOOD BLOCKADE BATTLEFRONT

Three years ago, a gateway between Earth and the Beyond opened over New York City. In one terrible night, New York was destroyed and rebuilt, trapping New Yorkers and extradimensional creatures alike in an impenetrable bubble. New York is now Jerusalem's Lot, a paranormal melting pot where magic and madness dwell alongside the mundane, where human vermin gather to exploit otherworldly assets for earthly profit. Now someone is threatening to breach the bubble and release New Jerusalem's horrors, but the mysterious superagents of Libra fight to prevent the unthinkable.

Trigun creator Yasuhiro Nightow returns with *Blood Blockade Battlefront*, an action-packed supernatural science-fiction steamroller as only Nightow can conjure.

VOLUME ONE
ISBN 978-1-59582-718-0 | $10.99

VOLUME TWO
ISBN 978-1-59582-912-2 | $10.99

VOLUME THREE
ISBN 978-1-59582-913-9 | $10.99

VOLUME FOUR
ISBN 978-1-61655-223-7 | $12.99

VOLUME FIVE
ISBN 978-1-61655-224-4 | $12.99

VOLUME SIX
ISBN 978-1-61655-557-3 | $12.99

VOLUME SEVEN
ISBN 978-1-61655-568-9 | $12.99

AVAILABLE AT YOUR LOCAL COMICS SHOP OR BOOKSTORE To find a comics shop in your area, call 1-888-266-4226 For more information or to order direct: • On the web: DarkHorse.com
E-mail: mailorder@darkhorse.com • Phone: 1-800-862-0052 Mon.–Fri. 9 AM to 5 PM Pacific Time.

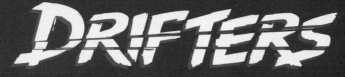

DRIFTERS

KOHTA HIRANO

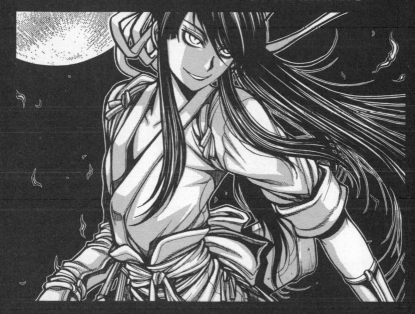

Heroes from Earth's history are deposited in an enchanted land where humans subjugate the nonhuman races. This wild, action-packed series features historical characters such as Joan of Arc, Hannibal, and Rasputin being used as chess pieces in a bloody, endless battle!

From Kohta Hirano, creator of the smash-hit *Hellsing*, *Drifters* is an all-out fantasy slugfest of epic proportion!

VOLUME ONE
978-1-59582-769-2

VOLUME TWO
978-1-59582-933-7

VOLUME THREE
978-1-61655-339-5

$12.99 each

Ten years ago, he was abducted and confined to a private prison. He was never told why he was there, or who put him there. Suddenly his incarceration has ended, again without explanation. He is sedated, stuffed inside a trunk, and dumped in a park. When he awakes, he is free to reclaim what's left of his life . . . and what's left is revenge.

This series is the inspiration of the *Oldboy* film directed by Chan-wook Park, which was awarded the Grand Jury prize at the 2004 Cannes Film Festival!

Winner of the 2007 Eisner Award for Best U.S. Edition of International Material—Japan!

GARON TSUCHIYA AND NOBUAKI MINEGISHI'S

OLDBOY

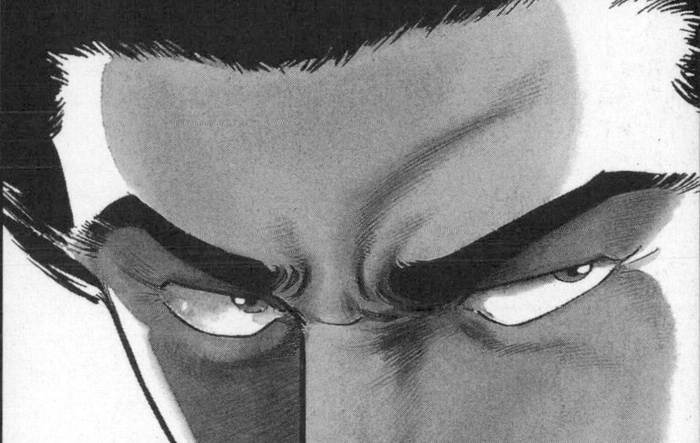

VOLUME 1:
ISBN 978-1-59307-568-2

VOLUME 2:
ISBN 978-1-59307-569-9

VOLUME 3:
ISBN 978-1-59307-570-5

VOLUME 4:
ISBN 978-1-59307-703-7

VOLUME 5:
ISBN 978-1-59307-714-3

VOLUME 6:
ISBN 978-1-59307-720-4

VOLUME 7:
ISBN 978-1-59307-721-1

VOLUME 8:
ISBN 978-1-59307-722-8

$13.99 EACH!

DARK HORSE MANGA

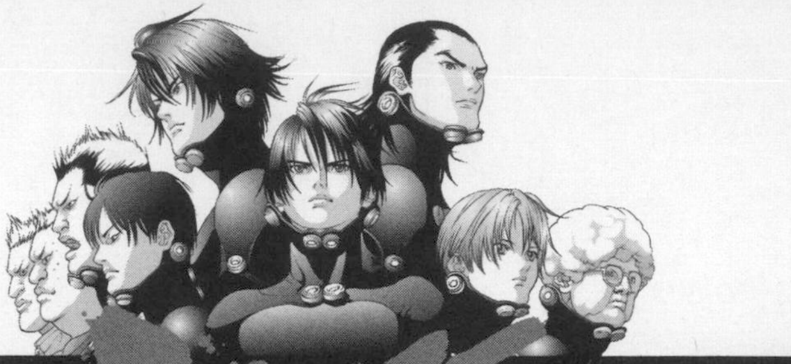

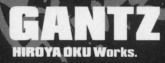

GANTZ

HIROYA OKU Works.

The last thing Kei and Masaru remember was being struck dead by a subway train while saving the life of a drunken bum. What a waste! And yet somehow they're still alive. Or semi-alive? Maybe reanimated . . . by some kind of mysterious orb! And this orb called "Gantz" intends to make them play games of death, hunting all kinds of odd aliens, along with a bunch of other ordinary citizens who've recently met a tragic semi-end. The missions they embark upon are often dangerous. Many die—and die again. This dark and action-packed manga deals with the moral conflicts of violence, teenage sexual confusion and angst, and our fascination with death.

Dark Horse is proud to deliver one of the most requested manga ever to be released. Hang on to your gear and keep playing the game, whatever you do; *Gantz* is unrelenting!

VOLUME ONE
ISBN 978-1-59307-949-9

VOLUME TWO
ISBN 978-1-59582-188-1

VOLUME THREE
ISBN 978-1-59582-232-1

VOLUME FOUR
ISBN 978-1-59582-250-5

VOLUME FIVE
ISBN 978-1-59582-301-4

VOLUME SIX
ISBN 978-1-59582-320-5

VOLUME SEVEN
ISBN 978-1-59582-373-1

VOLUME EIGHT
ISBN 978-1-59582-383-0

VOLUME NINE
ISBN 978-1-59582-452-3

VOLUME TEN
ISBN 978-1-59582-459-2

VOLUME ELEVEN
ISBN 978-1-59582-518-6

VOLUME TWELVE
ISBN 978-1-59582-526-1

VOLUME THIRTEEN
ISBN 978-1-59582-587-2

VOLUME FOURTEEN
ISBN 978-1-59582-598-8

VOLUME FIFTEEN
ISBN 978-1-59582-662-6

VOLUME SIXTEEN
ISBN 978-1-59582-663-3

VOLUME SEVENTEEN
ISBN 978-1-59582-664-0

VOLUME EIGHTEEN
ISBN 978-1-59582-776-0

VOLUME NINETEEN
ISBN 978-1-59582-813-2

VOLUME TWENTY
ISBN 978-1-59582-846-0

VOLUME TWENTY-ONE
ISBN 978-1-59582-847-7

VOLUME TWENTY-TWO
ISBN 978-1-59582-848-4

VOLUME TWENTY-THREE
ISBN 978-1-59582-849-1

VOLUME TWENTY-FOUR
ISBN 978-1-59582-907-8

VOLUME TWENTY-FIVE
ISBN 978-1-59582-908-5

$12.99 EACH

VOLUME TWENTY-SIX
ISBN 978-1-61655-048-6

VOLUME TWENTY-SEVEN
ISBN 978-1-61655-049-3

VOLUME TWENTY-EIGHT
ISBN 978-1-61655-050-9

VOLUME TWENTY-NINE
ISBN 978-1-61655-150-6

VOLUME THIRTY
ISBN 978-1-61655-151-3

VOLUME THIRTY-ONE
ISBN 978-1-61655-152-0

VOLUME THIRTY-TWO
ISBN 978-1-61655-428-6

VOLUME THIRTY-THREE
ISBN 978-1-61655-429-3

VOLUME THIRTY-FOUR
ISBN 978-1-61655-573-3

VOLUME THIRTY-FIVE
ISBN 978-1-61655-586-3

VOLUME THIRTY-SIX
ISBN 978-1-61655-587-0

VOLUME THIRTY-SEVEN
ISBN 978-1-61655-588-7

$13.99 EACH

DARK HORSE MANGA

AVAILABLE AT YOUR LOCAL COMICS SHOP OR BOOKSTORE
TO FIND A COMICS SHOP IN YOUR AREA, CALL 1-888-266-4226

For more information or to order direct: On the web: darkhorse.com E-mail: mailorder@darkhorse.com
Phone. 1-800-862-0052 Mon.–Fri. 9 A.M. to 5 P.M Pacific Time.

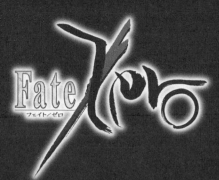

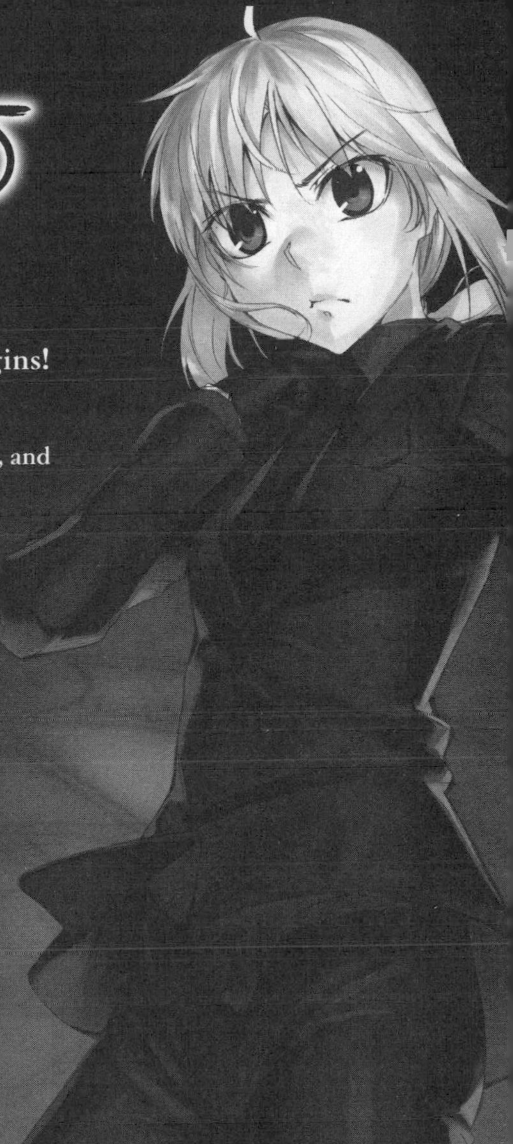

VAMPIRE HUNTER D

HIDEYUKI KIKUCHI | ILLUSTRATIONS BY YOSHITAKA AMANO

12,090 A.D. It is a dark time for the world. Humanity is just emerging from three hundred years of domination by the race of vampires known as the Nobility. The war against the vampires has taken its toll; cities lie in ruin, the countryside is fragmented into small villages and fiefdoms that still struggle against nightly raids by the fallen vampires–and the remnants of their genetically manufactured demons and werewolves.

Every village wants a Hunter–one of the warriors who have pledged their laser guns and their swords to the eradication of the Nobility. But some Hunters are better than others, and some bring their own kind of danger with them . . .

From creator Hideyuki Kikuchi, one of Japan's leading horror authors, with illustrations by renowned Japanese artist Yoshitaka Amano, this series is here printed in an English translation for the first time anywhere!

Volume 1
ISBN 978-1-59582-012-9 | $8.99

Volume 2:
RAISER OF GALES
ISBN 978-1-59582-014-3 | $8.99

Volume 3:
DEMON DEATHCHASE
ISBN 978-1-59582-031-0 | $8.99

Volume 4:
TALE OF THE DEAD TOWN
ISBN 978-1-59582-093-8 | $9.99

Volume 5:
THE STUFF OF DREAMS
ISBN 978-1-59582-094-5 | $8.99

Volume 6:
PILGRIMAGE OF THE SACRED
AND THE PROFANE
ISBN 978-1-59582-106-5 | $8.99

Volume 7:
MYSTERIOUS JOURNEY TO
THE NORTH SEA PART ONE
ISBN 978-1-59582-107-2 | $8.99

Volume 8:
MYSTERIOUS JOURNEY TO
THE NORTH SEA PART TWO
ISBN 978-1-59582-108-9 | $8.99

Volume 9:
THE ROSE PRINCESS
ISBN 978-1-59582-109-6 | $8.99

Volume 10:
DARK NOCTURNE
ISBN 978-1-59582-132-4 | $8.99

Volume 11:
PALE FALLEN ANGEL
PARTS ONE AND TWO
ISBN 978-1-59582-130-0 | $14.99

Volume 12:
PALE FALLEN ANGEL
PARTS THREE AND FOUR
ISBN 978-1-59582-131-7 | $14.99

Volume 13:
TWIN-SHADOWED KNIGHT
PARTS ONE AND TWO
ISBN 978-1-59307-930-7 | $14.99

Volume 14:
DARK ROAD PARTS ONE
AND TWO
ISBN 978-1-59582-440-0 | $14.99

Volume 15:
DARK ROAD PART THREE
ISBN 978-1-59582-500-1 | $9.99

Volume 16:
TYRANT'S STARS
PARTS ONE AND TWO
ISBN 978-1-59582-572-8 | $14.99

Volume 17:
TYRANT'S STARS PARTS
THREE AND FOUR
ISBN 978-1-59582-820-0 | $14.99

Volume 18:
FORTRESS OF
THE ELDER GOD
ISBN 978-1-59582-976-4 | $10.99

Volume 19:
MERCENARY ROAD
ISBN 978-1-61655-073-8 | $11.99

Volume 20:
SCENES FROM
AN UNHOLY WAR
ISBN 978-1-61655-255-8 | $11.99

Volume 21:
RECORD OF
THE BLOOD BATTLE
ISBN 978-1-61655-437-8 | $11.99

Volume 22:
WHITE DEVIL MOUNTAIN
PARTS ONE AND TWO
ISBN 978-1-61655-509-2 | $11.99

Volume 23:
IRIYA THE BERSERKER
ISBN 978-1-61655-706-5 | $11.99

Volume 24:
THRONG OF HERETICS
ISBN 978-1-61655-789-8 | $11.99

AVAILABLE AT YOUR LOCAL COMICS SHOP OR BOOKSTORE

To find a comics shop in your area, call 1-888-266-4226 · For more information or to order direct: On the web: DarkHorse.com · E-mail: mailorder@DarkHorse.com · Phone: 1-800-862-0052 Mon.–Fri. 9 AM to 5 PM Pacific Time.

DARK HORSE BOOKS
DarkHorse.com

WE CAN STILL TU

This manga is published in the
drawn and printed in Japan, re
actually the last page, rather th
the direction in whi

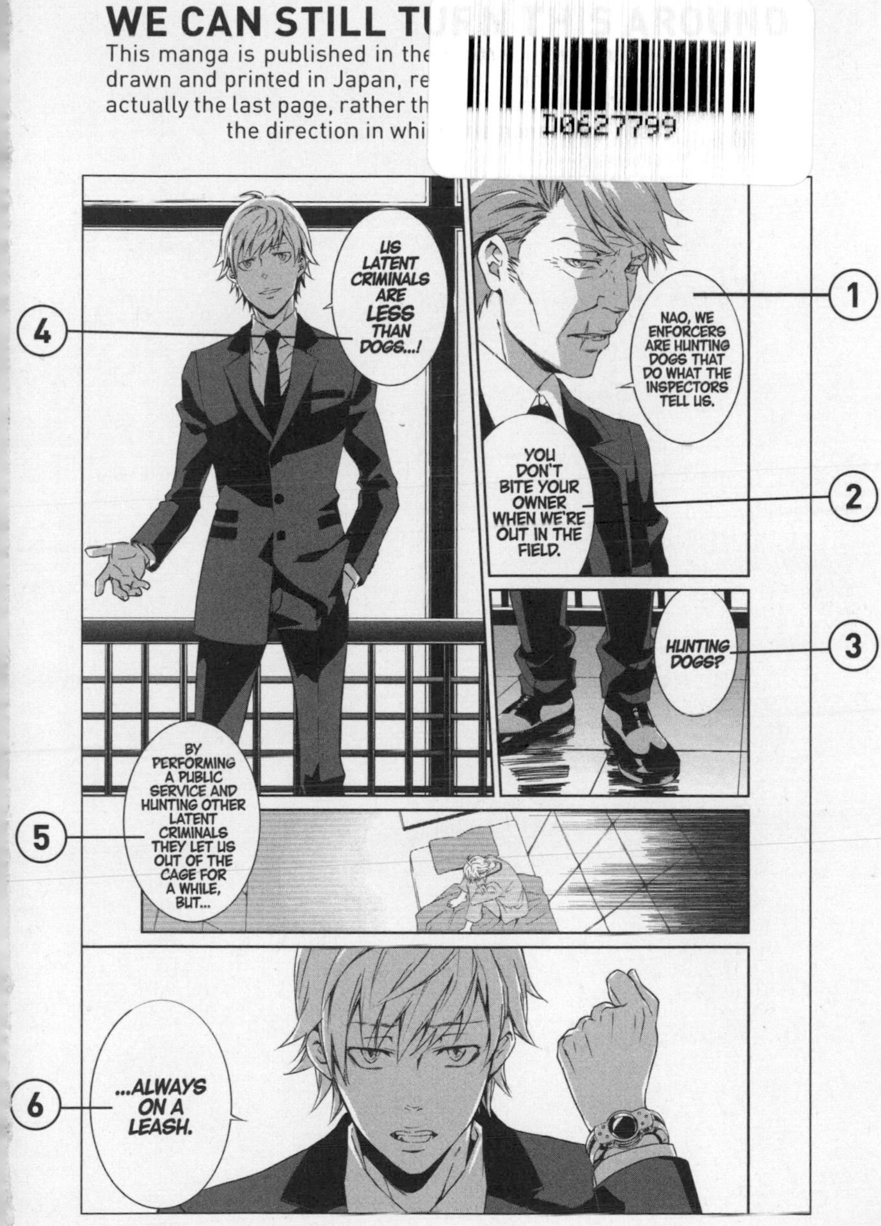
1
NAO, WE ENFORCERS ARE HUNTING DOGS THAT DO WHAT THE INSPECTORS TELL US.
2
YOU DON'T BITE YOUR OWNER WHEN WE'RE OUT IN THE FIELD.
3
HUNTING DOGS?
4
US LATENT CRIMINALS ARE LESS THAN DOGS...!
5
BY PERFORMING A PUBLIC SERVICE AND HUNTING OTHER LATENT CRIMINALS THEY LET US OUT OF THE CAGE FOR A WHILE, BUT...
6
...ALWAYS ON A LEASH.